T0317568

ADDITIONAL PRAISE FOR THE COMPLETE DIRECT INVESTING HANDBOOK

Dr. Kirby Rosplock has created an indispensable resource for family offices seeking to invest in private equity. She explains how to analyze winners and avoid the pitfalls, and discusses the extensive due diligence required even after initial investment. This is the conclusive guide to direct investing, which provides investors with the information necessary to ascertain how to proceed. Rosplock has written the essential manual for what will be a major investment trend for family offices in the years to come.

Howard Cooper, CEO, Cooper Family Office

Once again Dr. Rosplock gets it right! In my experience, few have the insider's knowledge that comes shining through in this book. Not only was it helpful, it was a pleasure to read.

Wendy L Craft, COO, Favara, LLC (SFO), New York, NYC

Kirby Rosplock's *The Complete Direct Investing Handbook* is a must read for *anyone* interested in direct investing. With key insights reinforced by practical case studies from noted experts in the field, this is an essential guide for current and potential direct investors.

*Joanne Pace, Former Managing Director and Chief Operating Officer,
Morgan Stanley Investment Management*

The world's best and brightest family offices are devoting ever more capital to direct investing. Now is the critical time for advisors, CIOs, and family members to share a common understanding on how to source, screen, diligence, structure, monitor, and harvest direct investments. Dr. Rosplock's handbook provides the roadmap.

Brian Smiga, Partner & Co-founder, Alpha Venture Partners

THE COMPLETE DIRECT INVESTING HANDBOOK

The Bloomberg Financial Series provides both core reference knowledge and actionable information for financial professionals. The books are written by experts familiar with the work flows, challenges, and demands of investment professionals who trade the markets, manage money, and analyze investments in their capacity of growing and protecting wealth, hedging risk, and generating revenue.

Since 1996, Bloomberg Press has published books for financial professionals on investing, economics, and policy affecting investors. Titles are written by leading practitioners and authorities, and have been translated into more than 20 languages.

For a list of available titles, please visit our Web site at www.wiley.com/go/bloombergpress.

THE COMPLETE DIRECT INVESTING HANDBOOK

A Guide for Family Offices, Qualified Purchasers, and Accredited Investors

Kirby Rosplock, PhD

WILEY

Copyright © 2017 by Kirby Rosplock. All rights reserved.

Published by John Wiley & Sons, Inc., Hoboken, New Jersey.
Published simultaneously in Canada.

No part of this publication may be reproduced, stored in a retrieval system, or transmitted in any form or by any means, electronic, mechanical, photocopying, recording, scanning, or otherwise, except as permitted under Section 107 or 108 of the 1976 United States Copyright Act, without either the prior written permission of the Publisher, or authorization through payment of the appropriate per-copy fee to the Copyright Clearance Center, Inc., 222 Rosewood Drive, Danvers, MA 01923, (978) 750–8400, fax (978) 646–8600, or on the Web at www.copyright.com. Requests to the Publisher for permission should be addressed to the Permissions Department, John Wiley & Sons, Inc., 111 River Street, Hoboken, NJ 07030, (201) 748–6011, fax (201) 748–6008, or online at http://www.wiley.com/go/permissions.

Limit of Liability/Disclaimer of Warranty: While the publisher and author have used their best efforts in preparing this book, they make no representations or warranties with respect to the accuracy or completeness of the contents of this book and specifically disclaim any implied warranties of merchantability or fitness for a particular purpose. No warranty may be created or extended by sales representatives or written sales materials. The advice and strategies contained herein may not be suitable for your situation. You should consult with a professional where appropriate. Neither the publisher nor author shall be liable for any loss of profit or any other commercial damages, including but not limited to special, incidental, consequential, or other damages.

For general information on our other products and services or for technical support, please contact our Customer Care Department within the United States at (800) 762–2974, outside the United States at (317) 572–3993 or fax (317) 572–4002.

Wiley publishes in a variety of print and electronic formats and by print-on-demand. Some material included with standard print versions of this book may not be included in e-books or in print-on-demand. If this book refers to media such as a CD or DVD that is not included in the version you purchased, you may download this material at http://booksupport.wiley.com. For more information about Wiley products, visit www.wiley.com.

Library of Congress Cataloging-in-Publication Data is Available:

ISBN 9781119094715 (Hardcover)
ISBN 9781119094739 (ePDF)
ISBN 9781119094722 (ePub)

Cover Design: Wiley
Cover Image: ©Westend61/Getty
         Images, Inc.

Printed in the United States of America

10 9 8 7 6 5 4 3 2 1

This book is dedicated to the memory of my father, Thomas L. Harbeck, who inspired me to dream big and to lean into new endeavors with a passion to first ask, learn, and seek knowledge before jumping off the deep end. His keen business sensibilities and wise counsel will always be treasured and appear throughout this book.

Contents

CHAPTER 7
Sourcing, Deal Flow, Screening, and Deploying
Direct Investments   141
Contributing Author: Euclid Walker

CHAPTER 8
Direct Investments: Deal Structures, Terms, and
Portfolio Construction   157
Contributing Author: Jolyne Caruso

CHAPTER 9
Investment Monitoring, Exit Strategies, and
Harvesting Returns   177
Contributing Author: Adam Goodfriend

PART III: DIRECT INVESTING PERSPECTIVES

CHAPTER 10

CHAPTER 11

Foreword

Family offices are in the business of exploring the investment landscape for new and creative ways to enhance returns and diversify from traditional models of investing. I have spent the better portion of my career looking at investments through both an institutional as well as a private investor's lens. The array of investment possibilities within the privately held marketplace is vast and growing, affording the burgeoning family office arena significant possibilities for investment. I see this as the new frontier of investing, and where some of the most exciting opportunities will be unearthed.

Dr. Rosplock's book, *The Complete Direct Investing Handbook*, provides a valuable and practical framework for approaching the direct investing landscape that appeal to both the neophyte and the most seasoned investor. It imparts not only her wealth of knowledge, but the insights and experiences of some of the private investment industry's most successful and respected leaders. The book includes valuable case studies, research, and practical tools and metrics to apply to this facet of investing. To date, there have been limited resources beyond the MBA textbooks to delve into this nuanced topic, but finally we have a playbook.

Interest in direct investing over the last decade has caught the attention of accredited investors, angels, and family offices. Yet Dr. Rosplock puts great emphasis on the fact that this specialized type of investing may not be suitable for every family office or accredited investor. She provides sage advice throughout the handbook on the importance of proper sourcing, vetting, due diligence, analysis, and structuring before deploying capital. Investing in private companies carries with it the seeds for outsized returns, but also the corollary risks. It should not be undertaken without a full understanding of the implications of those factors for the total portfolio.

Current research indicates that, despite the enhanced return potential in the private investment arena, the failure rate will still exceed the success rate for all but the most skillful investor. There has no doubt been a sea change in the investment world over the last 40 years, and the pace seems to be accelerating.

As an active investor in both the private and public markets, I have found particular appeal in the nonpublic sector because of the ability to participate in a variety of investment vehicles. The bespoke nature of private investing requires creativity and investment savvy on the part of either the lead investor or the banking firm, and when done well it has the ability to enhance returns while reducing risk in the admittedly risky world of private investing. Investments can be tailored, with carrots and sticks, to provide incentives for management to reach particular milestones. I have found such instruments to have a beneficial impact on both the investor and the company.

Many family offices are uniquely positioned to take advantage of the opportunity of direct investing because they often have the luxury to be patient investors, something that seems to have fallen by the wayside in the larger world of investing, which has adopted a trader's mentality. Focusing on quarterly investment returns defies the concept of true investing, which is long term in nature. Yet it has become the yardstick imposed on the investing public, particularly since the onslaught of hedge funds. The value of making private investments is embedded in the belief that a good investment idea has merit over a period of years, not months. Many family offices are in a position to take advantage of this sound investment concept because, unlike numerous endowments, foundations, pension plans, and private equity firms, they are generally not hostage to the cash flow and exit requirements of these institutions.

The Complete Direct Investing Handbook is the go-to resource for private equity investors and family offices. It compiles insights from leading minds and provides specific examples and recommendations on best practices. Each of its contributors provides a window into an important element of investing in the nonpublic arena. I would recommend that this book be kept nearby for investment decision-makers in the family office world.

Patricia W. Chadwick
President, Ravengate Partners LLC

Preface

If you are reading this book, it is likely that you have a curiosity for, or a pre-existing interest in, direct investing, or are already a seasoned direct investor. Whichever camp you fall into, I hope this book will expand your view on direct investing and provide insights from leading experts, advisors, and consultants within the direct investing space. More than half of the book consists of original chapters from contributing authors who are leaders in the field of direct investing and/or the family office realm; thus, the book provides a wide array of thinking from the best and brightest. Additionally, the book features anonymous case studies and innovative research from multiple institutions as well as proprietary data from a direct investing survey from Tamarind Partners in 2016.

So, what inspired me to write this book? One of my first positions out of college was working in a small brokerage firm in Milwaukee, Wisconsin, as an analyst helping administer a series of private equity partnerships. I was green in my career; however, I admired the passion and interest by accredited investors to back and invest into various direct deals. I quickly learned how these investors found an affinity to invest in this manner that was typically noncorrelated to public markets. Additionally, these investments provided portfolio diversification, the opportunity for outsized returns, and the ability to access niche, specialized investments not typically offered to the public. A few became winners, others barely broke even, and the majority failed. As my career evolved and I became more involved in the family office domain, I quickly realized how important private capital continued to be in closely held businesses. Some family offices continue to have a large segment of capital committed to operating businesses, and for many the source of wealth was a function of one or more of these positions.

Later in my life, I personally deployed capital into direct deals. Some investments succeeded and some failed. Like many of you, I learned the hard way the importance of sourcing, vetting, and due diligence after investing in what I was told would be a "sure homerun" that ultimately failed. My other co-investors were also confident in what we thought had been sufficient due diligence in the investment and adequate preferences and provisions for the investors. We were completely off-base, and my original investment has yet to return my initial capital. As Oscar Wilde put it, "Experience is simply the name we give our mistakes."

I relay this quick reference point to provide context that I, too, am still learning, and that even the best and brightest in the direct investment world likely have a similar war story to tell. I know I am not alone or special. After this experience, I decided to look further into the literature on direct investing, and found that most books are texts or casebooks written for MBA programs or focused mainly on venture capital. There are some excellent reads from top business school professors and academics, but few books focus on the narrow domain of direct investing, and none to my knowledge specically look at the subject matter through the unique lens of the family office.

My first book, *The Complete Family Office Handbook* (Wiley/Bloomberg, 2014), revealed the complex landscape of the family office realm and captured some of the building blocks to starting, operating, and managing a family office. During the data capture for that book, I learned the variety of family office types and diverse approaches to building a family office. Similarly, I discovered with writing and editing this book that there is a wide diversity of approaches to direct investing. There is not a one-size-fits-all approach to family office or to direct investing. Everything has to be tailored to you, and this book provides a foundation for readers to create their own unique approach.

This book is designed to appeal to the novice as well as the expert direct investor, and consequently covers a broad array of content and fictionalized cases. The book is organized into three sections. Part I provides a high-level overview of direct investing and the family office context. Part II discusses the steps and process of deploying capital into direct investments. Part III provides some additional unique perspectives on direct investing. Specifically, Chapter 1 lays a foundation on direct investing in the context of family offices. Chapter 2 discusses the increased presence of private capital into directs. Chapter 3 shares the interest in co-investing and club deals, and, finally, Chapter 4 outlines the various private equity strategies and where direct investing may fit. Chapter 5 is the beginning of Part II and outlines the various steps to execute on a direct investment. Chapter 6 discusses the steps to create a direct investment thesis. Chapter 7 shares the importance of sourcing, deal flow, and screening and deploying capital into direct investments. Chapter 8 elaborates on the deal structures, terms, and portfolio construction. Chapter 9 shares what happens after the capital has been deployed and the investment monitoring, exit strategies, and harvesting of returns. Chapter 10 is the start of

Part III and examines the CIO perspective to direct investing. Chapter 11 looks at direct investing with a lens to Millennials' perspective on impact investing. Chapter 12 shares the Sustainable Cycle of Investing Engagement model (SCIE model) as a possible approach. Chapter 13 closes with describing the international approach to direct investing.

Direct investing is not for the faint of heart nor is it for every investor. A quick disclaimer is required to remind readers of the tremendous risks associated with the potential rewards of direct investing. The contributing authors and I are not endorsing that everyone should be direct investors. On the contrary: The reality is very few may want to embrace this approach to investing even if they are technically qualified. There are more losers than winners when investing in this manner, so operating with your eyes wide open to the downside risks of this type of investing is imperative. We hope this book will be a useful resource and guide to aid direct investors as they consider how/whether to deploy private capital into this niche area of private equity.

Part III and examines the CIO perspective on direct investing. Chapter 11 looks at direct investing with a lens to Millennials' perspective on impact investing. Chapter 12 shares the Sustainable Circle of Investing Engagement model (SCIE model) as possible approach. Chapter 13 closes with describing the institutional approach to direct investing.

Direct investing is not for the faint of heart and it is not for every investor. A quick disclaimer is required: to find readers of the tremendous risks associated with the potential reward of direct investing. The distributed authors and have no vendetta that everyone should be direct investors. On the contrary. The reality is very few may want to embrace this approach to investing, even if they are technically qualified. She's are much leaner than visitors when investing in this matter, so investing with your eyes wide open and the downside risks of this type of investing is full active. We hope this book will be a useful resource and guide to aid the conversation as they consider how whether to deploy private capital into this important use of private equity.

Acknowledgments

This book took a village to write, and there are many to thank for their involvement. First to the direct investors and advisors who shared their stories—this book is only possible because of your trust. Thank you to my family and especially my husband, John, who provided constant support and encouragement. Thank you to all the contributing authors who shared their experience, wisdom, and technical expertise in their respective chapters.

The contributing authors and I would like to share our appreciation to (in alphabetical order) Abdulwahab Ahmad Al-Nakib, Adam Goodfriend, Align Private Capital, Alex Lamb, Alex Scott, Alexander Monnier, Amy Fulford, Amy Hart Clyne, Andrew Pitcairn, Angelo Robles, Ann Kinkade, Anna Nekoranec, Anna Nichols, Anne Hargrave, Annette Franqui, Barbara Hauser, Barry and Nate Wish, Bengt Niebuhr, Benjamin Kinnard, Benji Griswold, Bill McCalpin, Bill Woodson, Blakely Page, Bob Casey, Bob Gould, Bob Rice, Bobby Stover, Brian Smiga, Bryce Stirton, Carolann Grieve, Caroline Davis, Carolyn Friend and Jamie Weiner, Charlotte Beyer, Chris Battifarano, Chris Cecil, Chris Chandler, Chris Cincera, Christin Cardone McClave, Claude Kurzo, Cynthia Lee, Daniel Goldstein, Darcy Garner, David Barks, David Guin, David Herritt, David McCombie, David Nage, David Shrier, David Wood, Dennis Jaffe, Diane Nakashian, Dianne H. B. Welsh, Dirk Junge, Don Carlson, Donald Sull, Doug Borths, Drew Mendoza, Elizabeth Fennell, Elizabeth Keller, Ellen Perry, Ellen Singer, Eric Knauss, Erwin Latner, Euclid Walker, Falko Paetzold, Family Office Association, Family Office Exchange, Family Wealth Alliance, Fran Lotery, Francois de Visscher, Fredda Herz Brown, George Blurton, Ginny Neal, Grant Kettering, Greg Curtis, Gregory T. Rogers, Gunther Weil, Hirotaka Takeuchi, Howard Cooper, Iñigo Susaeta Córdoba, Ira Perlmuter, Iris Wagner, Ivan Sacks, Jack Reynolds, James Gifford, Jane Flanagan, Jason Brown, Jay Hughes, Jean Brunel, Jeffrey Yin, Jennifer Eaton, Jennifer Kenning, Jesus Casado, Joanne Pace, Joe Calabrese, Joe Lonsdale, John Benevides, John Davis, John Rogers, Jolyne Caruso, Jon Carroll, Jon Van Manaan,

Jonathan Lidster, Josh Lerner, Joshua Nacht, Juan Luis Segurado, Juan Meyer, Juan Roure, Judy Green, Julie Alberti, Julie Kerr, Julio Gonzalez, Justice Rines, Justin Zamparelli, Karen Koepp, Karen Neal, Karen Rush, Kathryn McCarthy, Laurent Roux and Lori Zalbowitz, Lee Hausner, Liezel Pritzker, Ligian Ma, Linda Mack, Luke Gilgan, M.J. Rankin, Marcia Nelson, Margret Trilli, Maria Elena Lagomasino, Mark Haynes Daniell, Maya Imberg, Meredith Brown, Michael Balt, Michael Murray, Michael Sallas, Michelle Osry, Mindy Rosenthal, Natasha Pearl, Nate Hamilton, Nava Michael Tsabaris, Nikki Gokey, Noelle Laing, Omar Simmons, Pam Friedlander, Patricia Angus, Patricia Chadwick, Paul Karofsky, Paul McKibben, Peter Brock, Peter Senge, Phil DiComo, Phil Strassler, Phillip Edwards, Preston Root, Preston Tsao, Proteus, Ralph Wyman, Rebecca Gerchenson, Rebecca Henderson, Rebecca Oertell, Regine Clement, Renee Kaswan, Rhona Vogel, Richard Millroy, Rick Cott, Rick Stone, Rino Schena, Robert Blabey, Robert Kaufold, Robert Krugel and Konstantin Braun, Roger King, Ronald Mayers, Sam Altman, Sam Bonsey, Sam Weatherman, Sami Karam, Santiago Ulloa, Sara Hamilton, Sean Davatgar, Sean O'Shea, Smart Energy Capital, Stacy Allred, Steve Campbell, Steven Casey, Steven Hirth, Steven Weinstein, Summerly Horning, Susan Babcock, Susan Remmer Ryzewic, TAG Energy Partners, Ted Staryk, Temple Fennell, The Alberleen Group, Tom Handler, Tom Livergood, Tom Mahoney, Tready Smith, Tula Weis, Victoria Vysotina, Ward McNally, Warner Babcock, Wealth-X, Wendy Craft, Will McEnroe, Will Trout, William Kambas, and Yirhan and Irena Sim.

Thank you to the many additional individuals involved who requested to remain anonymous.

THE COMPLETE DIRECT INVESTING HANDBOOK

PART I

Direct Investing and the Family Office Test

CHAPTER 1

Introduction to Direct Investing

Investors have more and more options than ever before for methods to deploy capital in the aim of generating financial returns. Today many family offices, high-net-worth individuals, and institutional private equity investors have amassed wealth through private company ownership.

Many of these successful business-building investors are looking for more avenues to deploy large investments in private equity–oriented investments. Today, for many investors, from early stage *angel* investors who deploy tens of thousands of dollars through mega funds with billions of dollars under management, the strategy is the same: Invest in the ownership *directly* of a privately held company or illiquid asset like real estate, and sell your ownership interest for a profit at some point in the future.

Where historically extraordinary wealth has been created through building and owning equity in privately held enterprises, options range from public securities to esoteric hedge fund strategies. Investors can typically access any type of investment that meets their objectives defined in a risk-versus-return profile. As investment risk increases, the opportunity to generate outsized returns also increases. With innumerable choice for investors, from longstanding established asset classes through newly formed financial instruments, there continues to be a sustained interest in a form of investing referred to as *direct investing*.

Direct investing may be defined as investments that meet the following criteria:

- The investor is making the decision to participate in a specific investment that is closely held (not publicly traded).
- The investment capital is funded directly by the investor (from a balance sheet under their control).
- The investor will own an operating asset through a direct investment that has unique and specific operating requirements.

Investment strategies designed to capture the value created through private company ownership have typically been the domain of private equity (PE) and venture capital (VC) funds. "The MoneyTree™ Report by PricewaterhouseCoopers LLP (PwC) and the National Venture Capital Association (NVCA) based on Data from Thomson Reuters" revealed that "venture capitalists invested $48.3 billion in 4,356 deals in 2014, an increase of 61 percent in dollars and a 4 percent increase in deals over the prior year. In Q4 2014, $14.8 billion went into 1,109 deals."[1] To gain exposure to the outsized returns offered by these funds, family offices and ultra-high-net-worth individuals have invested as limited partners in a blind portfolio of fund investments. These funds, on one hand, may offer exceptional return expectations but also require large capital commitments that are illiquid for the long term with little visibility into the underlying companies for the investor. These funds also charged investors management fees and carried interest. In 2014, there were 33,429 Regulation D offerings reported on Form D filings, accounting for more than $1.3 trillion, with approximately 301,000 investors participating in these offerings.[2] To achieve high returns in the PE market as a limited partner, investors must gain access to the top-performing funds that are rarely open to new investors. This leaves family offices struggling to generate returns by investing with mid-tier fund managers, in turn making direct investing into specific deals more and more attractive.

Direct investing is not a strategy that is one-size-fits-all or for that matter appropriate for all investors to consider. At the end of any investment process, investors have an illiquid investment in an operating company and "own" the business, including the operational and execution risk associated that all companies are subject to regardless of size, sector, or stage.

This is, however, an attractive investment strategy for investors who:

- Have meaningful capital to deploy relative to the market in which they intend to build a portfolio
- Have the ability to sustain significant losses and are allocating a percentage of their overall portfolio that reflects the reality that some of these types of investments do not work out
- Are operationally minded and prepared to participate in active company investments as opposed to passive investments
- Have a unique advantage as an investor in terms of a track record of success in certain industries or markets, and can be defined as a "value-added investor"

Many investors can generate very attractive returns and outcomes through deploying capital into growth-oriented private companies. One aim of this book is to help investors identify the various approaches for participating in direct investments. There are countless examples of investments in private companies that fail. There are also examples of extraordinary successes although statistically rarer in occurrence. Through the book's research, interviews, and case studies we strive to better understand the dynamics of the direct investment risk/return profile, provide a framework for how to scrutinize opportunities, and feature perspectives from industry experts and showcase some current trends and strategies.

With the growing investment options that are available to investors, direct investing is not just a trend, but historically is a fundamental economic engine for growth, innovation, and monetizing the rewards of entrepreneurship. An important intention of this book is to be a comprehensive resource on the topic of direct investing that is beneficial to the seasoned practitioner and the less experienced investor alike.

2008: A Wakeup Call for Investors

With the contractions on the private equity markets in 2008 came an increased scrutiny by investors into their holdings and an investor mind-shift about public markets. What were some of the lessons learned from one of the most catastrophic market crashes in history? A *Wall Street Journal* article chronicling the lessons learned post-2008 identifies six key lessons learned: (1) Ignore Wall Street's optimistic projections. (2) People in charge may not know much more than you. (3) Debt is dangerous. (4) We are more risk adverse than we think. (5) Simple is beautiful. (6) Cash isn't trash.[3] There are a few more that the private investor and family office gleaned. When it came to investing in PE funds, the crash of 2008 triggered a host of liquidity issues for PE firms as the direct investing marketplace virtually dried up overnight. In particular, limited partners were unable to control the timing of divesting of assets and although many would be inclined to hold, or even reinvest, in an operating company during an economic downturn, they could not drive the timing of an exit as a limited partner in a fund.[4] This meant their capital was "benched" or locked up under the provisions of the fund, inhibiting them from exiting and deploying capital at the bottom of the market.

Some of the lessons learned from 2008 highlighted previously, coupled with the frustrations of lockups for funds, certainly contribute to an increased interest by investors to make a direct investment into a privately held operating company or real estate asset where there may be increased control, visibility into company operations, transparency into reporting, and niche, off-market opportunities for growth and appreciation.

Does the current focus and attention by investors on direct investing indicate that this is a new category of investing or a temporary trend? I believe that this is *not* a trend, but rather that building wealth through business ownership is the most fundamental basis for how great wealth has been amassed throughout modern history. From early industrialists, such as Ford, Du Pont, Getty, Carnegie, Rockefeller, and Firestone, building and investing into operating companies has been the backbone of the U.S. economy. And advancing from the industrial revolution, business owners like Pritzkers, Gates, Jobs, Bezos, Branson, Schultz, and Page still seek new innovations, process, technologies, products, and services that drive economic growth. Great fortunes have been amassed through building and growing business and the wealth realized through owning privately held equity.

Role of the Family Office and Private Investors

The private investor most focused on in this book is the family office. The definition of *family office* varies widely and often depends on whom you ask; however, the general rule of thumb is that they are entities to manage wealth for multiple generations. Some are more investment focused, while others may be designed to prepare family members to collectively manage, sustain, and grow their wealth. Family offices are the first line of defense to manage the various risks that wealth exposes families to. In addition to offering potentially a wide array of services such as tax, fiduciary, and compliance needs; investment management, risk management, estate planning, and trust administration; philanthropic advisement and financial education programs for family members; and family governance and wealth transfer planning, the family office typically has a higher purpose to create continuity and cohesion for families around their wealth. Those who may be familiar with the concept of the family office may not know how to identify whether it is right for their families or their client families, and those questions are expanded in *The Complete Family Office Handbook* (Hoboken: Wiley, 2014).

In the United States, the Securities and Exchange Commission has increased oversight of the family office and enacted the Family Office Rule, which defines a single-family office as "any type of qualifying entity that provides investment advice to a single-family including traditional family offices and private trust companies."[5] The definition is still fairly broad, but the reality is regulatory bodies are also closing in on putting more definition around these organizations in order to monitor and track their advisory practices. What does this really mean? The increased scrutiny on Wall Street post-2008 has shredded the proverbial kimono from many family office outfits, requiring them to make a determination of the need to register. Although the exact number of family offices is not known, Family Office Exchange estimates that more than 5,000 families in the United States have family offices, and that there are at least twice that number embedded inside private operating companies.[6] This number is an estimate and no grounded research on family office has occurred in earnest due the fact that the definition tends to vary. Consequently, it is difficult to put too much weight on it, but data points on the ultra-affluent are available and Wealth-X studies indicate that there are approximately 211,275 ultra-high-net-worth individuals (UHNWIs) with $30 million or more in net worth.[7] (See Figure 1.1.)

In the family office market, a notable legacy of wealth has been spawned through entrepreneurship and business ownership. From the inception of wealth to generate significant returns in a privately held company to warrant the setup and creation of a family office to the evolution of the family office and its investments to hold onto or deploy additional capital into privately held investments—the role of the family office can vary dramatically. So what is the appetite of family offices and private investors in the direct investing marketplace? With the increase in the deployment of capital across the investment landscape, research for this book reveals that private investors, family offices, ultra-high-net-worth individuals, and qualified buyers have an increased interest and capacity to make sizeable investments across multiple sectors when it comes to directs. J.P. Morgan and the World Economic Forum

8

FIGURE 1.1 Wealth-X's World Map of Wealth

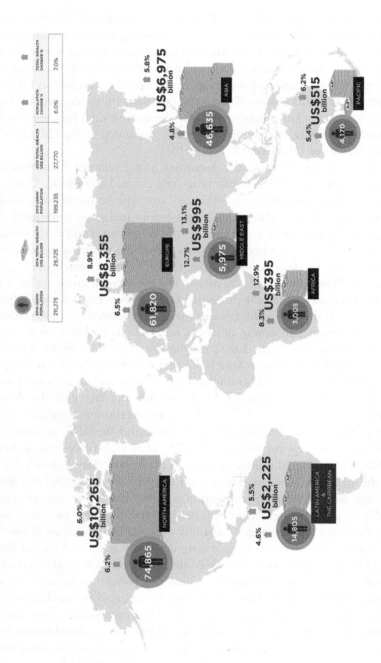

2014 UHNW POPULATION	2014 TOTAL WEALTH US$ BILLION	2015 UHNW POPULATION	2015 TOTAL WEALTH US$ BILLION	POPULATION CHANGE %	TOTAL WEALTH CHANGE %
211,275	29,725	199,235	27,770	6.0%	7.0%

NORTH AMERICA 74,865 ▲ 6.0% US$10,265 billion 6.2%

LATIN AMERICA & THE CARIBBEAN 14,805 ▲ 5.5% US$2,225 billion 4.6%

EUROPE 61,820 ▲ 8.9% US$8,355 billion 6.5%

MIDDLE EAST 5,975 ▲ 13.1% US$995 billion 12.7%

AFRICA 3,005 ▲ 12.9% US$395 billion 8.3%

ASIA 46,635 ▲ 5.8% US$6,975 billion 4.8%

PACIFIC 4,170 ▲ 6.2% US$515 billion 5.4%

Source: Wealth-X World Ultra Wealth Report 2015–2016

in 2016 surveyed 81 families, of which three-quarters had a net worth of at least $1 billion. Collectively this group of family offices represented over $200 billion in global wealth. They learned that we asked how family offices put assets to work; 65 percent noted investing in direct private equity and real estate.[8] Yet, the question remains: Is the direct investment space a prudent space to invest?

The direct investment space is not a panacea for all family offices and private investors. It is fraught with pitfalls and unforeseeable risks; yet for many family offices whose time horizons will certainly outlive one or more generation's lifetime, these possible downside risks can be qualified and managed, as these investors have distinct characteristics that broaden the overall opportunity set. For example, family office investors may be able to generate adequate returns to cover lifestyle needs and expenses on more traditional investment strategies that afford them the opportunity to take high risk that can yield high-return capital into direct investments. In other words, they have a much longer-term perspective for an investment than a traditional strategy or fund might have, which allows them to invest at both ends of the spectrum.

Key to this investment model is that the investor will participate as an owner of the investment for the life of the investment. Many times the focus is spent on the upfront activities and little attention is given to the operating needs that will be required for many years. The questions to focus on are:

- Why are family offices more focused on direct investing? (The answer to this we discussed earlier.)
- What are the opportunities and risks?
- What are the key drivers?

The Opportunity

There is no doubt that the intrigue and interest in direct investing is perhaps at an all-time high. In fact, a *Forbes* article notes that individual private investors and family offices are the "rising power in the private equity," as private investors and family offices are increasing their commitment to private equity at a time of record low interest rates, attracted by the private equity opportunity for double-digit returns that are not correlated to their public stock portfolio. In fact, Palico research, the online private equity fund marketplace, found in 2012 that family offices "account for 8% of the world's $4 trillion in private equity assets under management. That family office share is double that of just five years ago."[9] Virtually no investment or wealth management conference can refrain from discussing direct investments. The interest for investors, both private and institutional, is top of mind. The direct investment opportunity is attractive for many reasons. First, it may provide uncorrelated returns to traditional public market investments. Second, these investments have the ability to generate vastly larger returns than traditional publicly traded equities or bonds. Third, they tend to align with building and growing one or more businesses, particularly within founder family offices where the source of wealth was a function of starting. Direct investing for entrepreneurially minded investors becomes a logical outlet for deploying capital. And the opportunity of direct investing has several best practices learned and key considerations to assess its viability for each investor.

Best Practices

Over the many years of private investors engaging in direct investing, several best practices and lessons learned have been identified. Family Office Exchange (FOX) has captured their own list of best practices that they have gleaned from the Direct Investing Network (DIN) that they run for their active investor members. First, they found that investors lean to investing in deals where their capital gives them a strategic advantage. Perhaps they have first hand knowledge of a sector from prior business ownership and experience, or geographical or cultural experience, say, investing abroad, or perhaps they have an important peer group of investors or network that can bring a demonstrable edge to the investment. These advantages can be major considerations for where and how to put the family office capital to work.

Second, FOX identifies the importance to stay in "Circles of Competence," leveraging one's ability to be flexible. In other words, FOX sees a best practice to take advantage of their flexibility. From the check size to the deal size, the investor preference to the time horizon or sector, family offices, unlike PE funds or pension funds, are not governed with the same strict investment mandates. Third, FOX finds that family office investors have to make direct investment strategically and diversify them as their assets deployed in this area scale. FOX finds their family office investors have a strategic rationale for investing in the direct investment, but as the broader wealth of the family expands, so too should the diversity of the direct investment mandate and even the investment size.

Fourth, funds can play an important role particularly where the family office investor does not have expertise or access to market information. Although not all family offices will invest in private equity funds, for segments where due diligence, access to information, or direct experience in the sector is meager, PE funds can be a valuable tool in the investment toolbox. In conjunction with a broader asset allocation, PE funds can play a productive role for some family offices. Sara Hamilton shares, "For example, U.S. families often use funds for exposure to international or emerging market countries. Healthcare, pharma, or high technology sectors, where industry information tends to be highly specialized and barriers to entry are high, are other examples of areas where families emphasize their use of funds (or experienced co-investors). In addition, being an LP in a fund not only can provide you with valuable market information about where companies are transacting, industry trends, and market cycles, but can open up investment opportunities in an industry where relationships and information can be your most important assets."[10]

Further, FOX found that family offices should seek strong growth opportunities with high returns to the invested capital by the family office. They provide certain retail chains or franchises as an example of a model with highly positive unit-level economics and marginal returns for each new location opened. Family offices may find these investment opportunities attractive due to their asset intensiveness, stable cash flow, and replicable growth model. Another best practice FOX found is to utilize tax-advantaged structures whenever possible and preferable. Employing top tax counsel, family offices can own assets and manage them in a highly tax-advantaged manner relative to their overall portfolio of assets.

Another best practice FOX revealed is that there is an opportunity to capitalize on the changing demographics of wealth and business ownership. It is well documented that there is a sea change of wealth transitioning from one generation to the next; however, where has the most wealth in recent decades been created? Research from Wealth-X determined that 46 percent of wealth created in the last 20 years came from three primary sectors in the United States: financial services, real estate, and food service. Among these top three industries, 60 percent of business owners are over 65.[11] As family firms and business transition, there are great opportunities for direct investors into these domains.

Finally, FOX identifies co-investment with peers and partners with solid domain expertise as a best practice. A means to an end, co-investment is an important outgrowth of the interest in the direct investing space. Nate Hamilton notes, "For some families, it is a way to leverage capital, due diligence, and sourcing capabilities within areas where they already have existing core competencies. However, several of the most sophisticated investors cited co-investment deals as opportunities to partner with families that know more than they do in a particular sector or industry."[12] The FOX report indicates that the industries where families seek to partner with co-investors include healthcare, technology, real estate, and energy. More on co-investment strategies is covered in Chapter 3.

Key Considerations

The best practices from Family Office Exchange highlight some invaluable lessons learned and align with several key considerations gleaned from the research for this book. The following section provides further considerations for deploying capital into directs. Because there is no crystal ball to forecast the future when it comes to directs, it is important for the investor to analyze and form an independent view as to why an investment will perform well before deploying capital. The most successful investors profiled in this book are able to create a tempered view of the potential positive outcomes of an investment and be very disciplined in forming a view as to why an investment will not perform as expected. Assessing, managing, and pricing risk is a daily function for direct investors. To follow are several key considerations for investors considering or deploying capital into direct investments.

Recognize that direct investing is not a cost efficiency for PE fund investments. Making a direct investment outside of a VC or PE fund many times will be costlier to the investor up front. Most independent investors decide between hiring full-time resources internally to lead their investments or hiring outside consultants or experts. Yet the rationale to invest in direct investments in order to reduce fees as justification to invest in this manner is fraught with folly. Chapter 2 explores further the direct investing landscape and specifically the family office's role in this domain. Chapter 3 provides a broader understanding of co-investment strategies and club deals and the strategic opportunities of collaboration with co-investors.

Be a learning investor and look to trusted, strategic advisors and co-investment opportunities for greater intelligence. Another important consideration attractive to certain family offices and private investors is that they often provide a unique insight and operational support for an investment. Following the theme that these investors have created wealth through successfully building companies in the past, direct investors tend to be very operationally minded and active in a portfolio of operating companies. The term *value-added investor* applies to this approach where successful investors likely have cultivated a network of experts that can bring knowledge, advice, or step into an operating role or that provide a segment of the expertise that gives them deeper insights from operating experience than the lay investor. Many times we talk about the direct investors' "unfair advantage," or the fact that they have a leg up or superior intelligence of how to navigate a specific sector or strategy. What makes the investors' contribution of capital more attractive to a company or management team is the likelihood that the investors bring industry, market, product, people, investors, or lender relationships that the management team would not have access to on their own. When deployed effectively these value-added characteristics of the direct investor provide for a distinct advantage for a privately held company. Chapter 4 discusses the various private equity strategies and walks through the private equity life cycle.

Have a clear investment process and thesis. Where investors are planning to execute on a handful of deals in any given period, it is recommended for the investor to have a disciplined investment rigor where they seek input from internal and external experts and not bear the investment decision alone. In this situation the upfront work to get into an investment is significant and many times will drive up costs to hire industry experts to assist with due diligence. This is, however, money well spent if part of a process is designed to mitigate risk by picking the right investments, valuing them correctly, structuring the appropriate terms, and backing the right management team. Chapters 5 and 6 introduce the process of direct investing and how to develop an investment thesis.

Bet on the jockey, not the horse. This phrase denotes the importance of valuing the leadership and management above all else when considering any direct investing opportunity. This brings up the final point that the process of direct investing has two sides, the investor and the management team. There is a reason that the private equity market rallies around the cry of "bet the jockey, not the horse" — the "jockey" being management and the "horse" being the business or the sector. The operational risks for these types of investments are a major factor that may lead to a failed investment. But the management team also desires to have a quality investor the same way an investor requires a quality management team. Often the means to deploy capital may not be enough of a strategic advantage. Do their values, ethics, business acumen, leadership style, and experience match their role and the opportunity? There are incredible business opportunities all around us, but they may be all for naught if the key leadership is not the proverbial right jockey for the job.

In Chapter 7, the book investigates further sourcing, vetting, and analysis of a direct deal, and the due diligence on the leadership is also a key component of this analysis.

Pay attention to the terms and structure of the deal. No matter how much you may know about the deal and its opportunity, the key terms and structural considerations are where the rubber meets the road. Understanding which provisions are most important to you and why, where you fall in the cap table, and what your upside and downside risks are is critical when it comes to the deal terms and structure. Chapter 8 explores in more detail the "art of the deal" when it comes to structuring, terms, and portfolio construction.

Be prepared that direct investments are operationally intensive. There are a variety of considerations the family office and private investors need to take into account when considering direct investing. The single greatest risk to owning an operating company is execution risk. Execution risk is the risk that a company's business plans and thus the investor's associate capital will not be successful when they are put into action. The dynamic in the direct investing marketplace is one of collaborating with management teams who will be driving the day-to-day management of an operating business. These are investments that ultimately require significant care and feeding and it is very common that investors underestimate the scope of involvement required in making an investment a success. Despite going into an investment with the best intentions, there may be situations where a president or CEO needs to be terminated and, in particular with a smaller company, the investors many times will be the most likely candidate to fill the operational void when a decision like this must be made. Chapter 9 covers the operational oversight considerations, exit strategies, and how best to harvest returns.

Hire slow and fire fast. The difficult truth in the direct investing universe is that bringing on new employees in any business is not a sure thing. Take time to properly vet and conduct due diligence, background checks, and probe deeply into references before moving forward. Consider a first 90-day plan so that new hires are clear about alignment, goals, and metrics for evaluation. Conversely, when problems arise and there is a demonstrated pattern of infractions, do not fool yourself that somehow the employee will be turning over a new leaf. This is not the time to make excuses but rather to gather a plan for consequences and perhaps an exit. Personnel issues in direct investments can make all the difference with achieving intended growth plans. Chapter 10 provides some key insights on this front through the lens of the direct investing CIO.

Direct Investing means different things to different generations. Millennials are keen on direct investing; however, research indicates that theirs goals are not just about profits, but about progress. The desire to leave the world better than what they were born into is a common theme among the Millennial research, and they are finding opportunities through impact or socially responsible investing into directs a means. Chapters 11 and 12 explore the Millennials' role in direct investing, specifically impact investing and the SCIE model as a means to deploy impact-related investments into directs.

Direct investors are thinking globally, not just locally. Direct investing is more commonly done in your "geographical backyard"; however, increasingly investors are exploring more opportunities abroad to take advantage of dislocations in the marketplace. Yet, global direct investors beware—the bounty that exists is often connected to regulatory, cultural, legal, and international business standards unique to each geography. What applies for a direct investment at home likely does not apply when investing in emerging markets. Chapter 13 closes the book with insights, examples, and lessons learned from investing in directs abroad.

Direct Investing is not for everyone. Direct investing can be a roller coaster; from increases in operational intensity and oversight to disappointments with meeting milestones or requirements for additional follow-on capital. Despite writing a book about direct investing, we are keenly aware that direct investing is a niche, not the norm, and certainly not appropriate for most UHNWIs or family offices. Conversely, the majority of family offices should assess several considerations from risk to time horizon, to diversification, to appetite for volatility in a closed environment, to having to step into an active leadership role should the investment veer south. Thus, think long and hard before committing capital to this segment of private equity. A best practice is for family offices to ask the questions, "Does the direct investment strategy complement or play to the family office's strengths?" and "What ultimately are we attempting to achieve and for whose benefit?"

Conclusion

This chapter provides the basic tenets of direct investing, including the definition of direct investing for the purposes of this book and the background of direct investing. This chapter discusses the important wakeup call that 2008 provided and the ramifications it had on the direct investing marketplace. Further, this chapter more broadly defines the primary audience for this book, the family office, and the role of the family office and private investors in direct investing. Finally, the chapter discusses the opportunity direct investing presents and some of the best practices when it comes to deploying capital into direct investments. The chapter closes with some key considerations for deploying capital into direct investments. Now that a foundation for direct investing has been formulated, Chapter 2 will expand on the opportunity, attractiveness, and broader investor considerations for the nuances of direct investing.

Notes

1. "The MoneyTree™ Report by PricewaterhouseCoopers and the National Venture Capital Association based on Data from Thomson Reuters" or "PwC/NVCA MoneyTree™ Report based on Data from Thomson Reuters," National Venture Capital Association 2015, nvca.org/pressreleases/annual-venture-capital-investment-tops-48-billion-2014-reaching-highest-level-decade-according-moneytree-report/.
2. Scott Bauguess, Rachita Gullapalli, and Vladimir Ivanov, "Capital Raising in the U.S.: An Analysis of the Market for Unregistered Securities Offerings, 2009–2014" (October 2015), www.sec.gov/dera/staff-papers/white-papers/unregistered-offering10–2015.pdf.
3. Brett Arends, "Six Lessons You Should Have Learned from the Financial Crisis: Are We Any Wiser Than We Were Five Years Ago?" (September 22, 2013), www.wsj.com/articles/SB10001424127887324665604579081223815849080.
4. Limited partners are limited to the extent of the partner's share of ownership, but also limited partners generally do not have management responsibility in the partnership in which they invest and are not responsible for its debt obligations.
5. www.natlawreview.com/article/sec-adopts-final-definition-family-offices-exempt-investment-advisers-act.
6. Barbara R. Hauser, "The Family Office: Insights into Their Development in the US, a Proposed Prototype, and Advice for Adaption in Other Countries," The Journal of Wealth Management 4 (2001): 15–22; M. Rankin, "Wealth Management: A Brief History and Evolution of Family Offices," unpublished white paper, presented at the Family Firm Institute Pre-Conference Wealth Advising Seminar, October 5, 2004.
7. *Wealth-X World Ultra Wealth Report 2015–2016*.

8. *Inside the Single Family Office Today,* an in-depth look at how some of the world's wealthiest families are managing their fortunes and legacies, conducted by J. P. Morgan and the World Economic Forum, 2016, p. 8.

9. Forbes 2015, www.forbes.com/sites/antoinedrean/2015/07/28/individ ual-investors-and-family-offices-are-the-rising-power-in-private-equity/ 2/#14bd1d363aaf.

10. Nate Hamilton and Sara Hamilton, Family Office Exchange 2016 whitepaper, "Private Capital Perspectives: The Emerging Presence of Private Capital in Direct Investing."

11. Fox Wealth Advisors Forum, 2013.

12. Nate Hamilton and Sara Hamilton, Family Office Exchange 2016 whitepaper, "Private Capital Perspectives: The Emerging Presence of Private Capital in Direct Investing."

CHAPTER 2

The Emerging Presence of Private Capital in Direct Investing

Contributing Authors: Nathan Hamilton and Sara Hamilton

How has the presence of private capital impacted the realm of direct investing? Is there strong affinity and alignment between family office investors and the opportunities that arise in investing in privately held businesses? This chapter outlines the specific market of family offices and their unique preferences and vantage point on direct investing. Specifically, Family Office Exchange (FOX), a globally recognized private membership organization for family offices, provides proprietary research and demographic data on family offices as investors of private capital. The chapter further describes the unique benefits of private capital versus institutional capital to the direct investing marketplace. Finally, the chapter concludes some of the opportunities that family offices observe in the growing direct investment space.

This chapter was adapted from the whitepaper entitled "The Emerging Presence of Private Capital in Direct Investing," published by Nate Hamilton and Sara Hamilton, Founder and CEO of Family Office Exchange, in May 2016.

The Family Office Marketplace

There is no question that private wealth owners control a substantial amount of the world's capital. Figures released in a 2014 Wealth-X report estimate that globally there are over 56,500 families worth over $100 million, with private wealth estimated to be in excess of $21 trillion in U.S. dollars. In North America, there are almost 15,000 families with over $100 million, with investible wealth of $6.69 trillion. In addition to their core operating business, 60 percent of those families hold an average of 12 percent of their investible wealth in private equity, equating to $480 billion in assets. And the remaining 40 percent are more active investors who hold 30+ percent of their investible wealth in private equity, which equates to another $1.2 trillion, bringing the North American total investment in private equity to an estimated $1.68 trillion in private wealth.

There is no effective measure for the exact size of the family office marketplace, due to the very private nature of family enterprises around the world. FOX estimates that almost all multigenerational business-owning families embed some of their personal wealth management in a "virtual" family office inside the operating business, which means the number of virtual family offices is estimated to be proportional to the number of family companies with revenues over $200 million a year. The impact of private business owners on the local and global economy is unquestionable, and their commitment to direct investing represents an opportunity worth being fostered by all who care about growing our global economy.

The asset allocation surveys conducted by Family Office Exchange over the past 10 years provide key insight into the role of private equity within the average family office's asset allocation strategy. These surveys are sent out to over 700 family office contacts on an annual basis. Recent studies have shown that allocations to both direct private equity and investments in private equity funds have been increasing as a percentage of total assets in investable portfolios, for about 40 percent of the family office market.

Family offices have indicated in surveys that the volatility experienced in the downturn of 2008–2009 caused them to rethink their approach to private equity, which is a potential reason for the increased direct investment activity over the last several years. As Figure 2.1 indicates, the allocation to private equity has moved from an average of 7 percent in 2005 to an average of 12 percent in 2015.

In contrast to average allocations shown in Table 2.1, FOX surveys have identified a subset of family offices with a strong commitment to private equity (defined as an allocation of 20 percent or higher to private equity),

FIGURE 2.1   Equity Check Size and Direct Deal Team Size Indicated by Family Office
Members

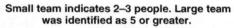

Small team indicates 2–3 people. Large team
was identified as 5 or greater.

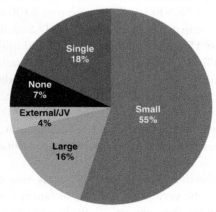

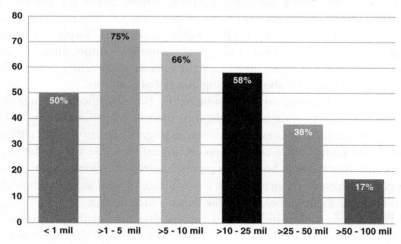

Equity Check Size: "Interest by Deal Size" refers to the amount
of equity invested by each family in their average deal.

Source: FOX Surveys *n* = 135

and this subset of survey participants clearly demonstrates the growing trend
toward an increasing allocation to direct investments in operating companies
where owners can sit on the board and have a direct impact on the future
direction of the business. FOX found that families focused on PE held more
funds than direct investments in private equity in 2011–12, but that the

TABLE 2.1 Family Office Exchange Benchmarking Surveys of Family Offices

2005 Year-End Average Asset Allocation $n = 48$	Category	2015 Year End Average Asset Allocation $n = 55$
13%	Cash	8%
14%	Fixed Income	12%
30%	Home Equities	31%
7%	International Equities	62%
9%	Hedge Funds	11%
3%	Private Equity Direct	3%
4%	Private Equity Funds	9%
14%	Real Estate	10%
1%	Real Assets	2%
5%	Other	2%

Source: Family Office Exchange Global Investment Survey

allocation to direct investments jumped to 22 percent of overall allocation by the beginning of 2015, outpacing investments in funds by a 2-to-1 ratio (see Table 2.2).

The Unique Benefits of Private Capital

Despite high levels of direct investing activity among family offices, families report rarely being in competitive situations with other family investors, as opposed to private equity funds and independent sponsors. Families highlighted the unique benefits of their capital relative to traditional institutional investors, and it was clear they emphasized these differentiators when competing against more traditional sources of capital. Ahead is a set of commonly cited strengths or characteristics that private capital investors provide in a transaction and some brief detail on each.

Long-Term Time Horizons

Family investors have the ability to invest for longer periods of time, which is often described by the coined term *patient capital*. However, because some

TABLE 2.2 Active Investors with 20 percent or more in Private Equity

Category	2011 Year End Average Asset Allocation $n = 11$	2014 Year End Average Asset Allocation $n = 12$	2016 Year End Average Asset Allocation $n = 15$
Cash	5%	5%	11%
Fixed Income	10%	7%	11%
Home Equities	20%	22%	21%
International Equities	13%	8%	8%
Hedge Funds	14%	8%	6%
Private Equity Direct	**12%**	**22%**	**22%**
Private Equity Funds	**14%**	**13%**	**8%**
Real Estate	8%	7%	10%
Real Assets	4%	2%	3%

Source: Family Office Exchange Global Investment Survey

family investors can also buy in and out of a deal opportunistically if they so choose (which may be more difficult for an institution), the more appropriate term may be nonprescriptive in timing rather than simply "patient." Without fundraising considerations, families also report being able to better optimize the timing of exiting an investment. This flexibility allows them the ability to get paid for illiquidity, entering higher-return deals with longer payoff periods. In addition, because their investment cycle is not tied to a fund, there is less pressure on professionals to deploy capital and close deals. For families with an existing business that continues to bring in cash flow, there can be less internal competition for funds that might otherwise be allocated to another division or asset class. This can give investment professionals more time to more carefully pick their targets and points of entry.

Deal Structuring Advantages

Private investors are able to provide more flexibility in structuring deals than institutions driven by fundraising cycles and stricter structuring rules. This can unlock value and create positive outcomes for buyers and sellers. For example, family investors interviewed report being more willing to leave control and ownership in the hands of a competent management team than the institutions they often found themselves in competition with. They also report a willingness to set larger, longer-term earn-in options for management teams, instilling a greater sense of strategic partnership with the company. Other structuring techniques mentioned included committing to provide follow-on capital or reinvesting earnings into the business if certain earnings or growth thresholds are met. Though some of these strategies may be offered to target companies by many institutional investors, family investors reported having a more convincing story because of the limited number of constituents family investors are ultimately responsible for serving, and the decision-making authority and flexibility this provides.

Sourcing Advantages

Increasingly, management teams and sellers are drawn to the idea of a patient, strategic family investor. The opportunity to partner with an investor that can be tapped for follow-on investments and make evaluations of what's best for the long-term growth of the business irrespective of a fundraising or market cycle can be an attractive value proposition. Strategically, many wealthy families bring the experience of having grown a business and a valuable Rolodex of contacts. To the seller of a family business, there is often the perception that family office investors will better understand the business owner's values and more effectively maintain the core philosophical principles or cultural traditions of the founders.

Tax-Advantaged Returns

Long holding periods reduce tax leakage and can create powerful compounded returns for private investors over time (see Table 2.3). This can enhance their returns and ultimately the value created by the business for its other investors and management team. Unlike institutional investment funds, whose tax profiles are most suited for the GP/LP legal and tax structures, private investors can utilize flow-through tax ownership structures like limited-liability corporations (LLCs) to avoid a double taxation on earnings at both the corporate and shareholder level. Families may also be able to more effectively use depreciation tax shields or match passive losses with passive income to reduce tax liabilities. More generally, sophisticated families report being able to come to the negotiating table with their own tax professional. This gives them the freedom to structure their interest in a deal in the most tax efficient manner, maximizing options and providing flexibility to the greatest extent possible.

TABLE 2.3 Supplemental Exhibit: Institutional vs. Family Capital

	Institutional Fund	Family Capital
Time Horizon	Focused on IRR • Short-term holding periods and focus on liquidity events • Short-term decisions in managing operations • Pressure to maximize leverage	Focused on long-term whole-dollar return • Intergenerational wealth-building focus • Utilize time horizon arbitrage and get paid for illiquidity • Use less leverage, lower risk
Alignment	Fee structures incent maximizing funds under management over value creation • Fund management considerations impact decisions • Sense of urgency to "put money to work"	Principal mentality • Aligned with management to make long-term operating decisions • Ability to optimize exit timing without fund considerations
Flexibility	Fixed life funds with inflexible mandate • Forces sale of good companies with significant additional upside and fully underwritten risk profile • Static investment strategy in a fluid market	Total flexibility • Structure creative "win-win" transactions that help sellers achieve their objectives • Ability to respond to fluid market dynamics
Approach	Transactional, financial returns focus	Family business roots/operating orientation • Business building approach • Understand unique family business dynamics
Tax Sensitivity	Driven by tax-exempt investors • Deal structures optimized for tax-exempt institutions • Churning assets is very tax inefficient for taxable investors	Optimized for taxable investors • Dramatic long-term value implications

Source: Used with permission from Rick Roeding, Orchard Holdings Group, LLC ($n = 135$)

Increased Interest in Private Equity

Core reasons for the increasing interest in direct investing by families is the general misalignment of interests and incentives between family office investors and traditional blind-pool fund investments. Many of these factors are not new, and they do not prevent even extremely sophisticated families from continuing to invest as LPs in fund structures or commenting on the merits of certain fund investments. As a result, we attribute the increase in direct investing to two other factors observed during our interactions with families. The first is that the financial crisis not only highlighted the lower-performing, more illiquid funds in the marketplace, but it was also a catalyst for families to rethink whether they could rely solely on the institutional fund market to provide the same historical returns going forward.

Second, families became more aware of their key competitive advantages as sources of private capital, and thus may now be more willing to consider direct investing. This may be compounded by the escalating competitiveness and maturity of the private equity industry, where it has become increasingly important to offer a differentiated form of capital in order to win deals. The result is families are considering a more strategic asset allocation between funds and direct investments.

To identify the set of industry trends most prevalent among family offices, the authors used a number of sources that included surveys, in-depth interviews with family offices, and industry news and research. Using these sources, the team identified a number of broader industry trends, which we discuss in what follows.

Families are increasing their exposure to direct investing: A 2012 study released by the Wharton Global Family Alliance of 106 families in 24 countries indicated family offices had increased their direct allocations to private companies and real estate to 11 percent in 2011 from 6 percent in 2009. In addition, increasing interest among family offices in direct investing has been one of the catalysts for the creation of several direct deal platforms over the last few years. Most of these firms report that they serve a large number of direct private investors who are increasing their exposure to direct private equity.

Families are more often seeking to recruit investment professionals to work for the family office: Though many single-family offices continue to outsource the investment management of the assets, families are increasingly hiring investment professionals to manage assets in-house directly for the family. Sixty-eight percent of families in the 2014 FOX Global Investment Survey of 120 families have chief investment officers. Within the staff managing the private equity allocation, some professionals report managing both the fund and direct investments while other families separate the teams that manage direct and fund investments. As Figure 2.1a highlights, 73 percent of family offices who have a direct deal team maintain small or single-person direct deal teams, which may explain the eagerness to engage in co-investing for the purposes of leveraging the capabilities of other private investors.

FIGURE 2.2   Industry Preferences of Family Offices Active in Direct Investing

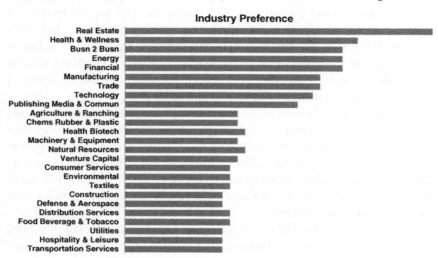

Source: FOX Surveys $n = 135$

Families surveyed are willing to write a range of equity check sizes into deals. Figure 2.1b summarizes the typical equity check size range, the majority of whom will write checks in the $1 million to $25 million range. As expected, the greater the check size the higher the likelihood a family is interested in leading or controlling the deals they participate in.

Family offices vary widely in the amount of industry focus within their direct private equity strategy: As Figure 2.2 illustrates, many families characterize themselves as "opportunistic," looking across nearly every industry for investment opportunities. Though this trend does not necessarily typify the most sophisticated family office investors, as a whole the population remains willing to evaluate opportunities across a variety of sectors. Many families report a willingness to invest in markets adjacent to their core expertise rather than move completely outside of it.

More sophisticated investors are willing to take a second seat in a private equity transaction than in the past, particularly behind a smart co-investor: FOX investor surveys indicate that about 80 percent of family office investors are happy to take a non-controlling but significant interest behind a lead family, institutional investor, or other private business owner. In addition, more family investors are also openly seeking knowledgeable co-investment partners, particularly when they can add strategic value to a deal. This represents not only a shift from the last 20 years for those that would only do control

FIGURE 2.3 Preferred Role in a Direct Investment Transaction

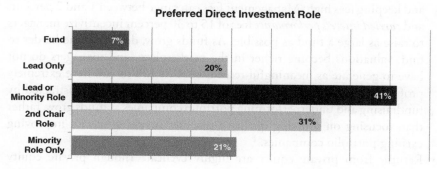

Source: FOX Surveys *n* = 135

deals, but may also differentiate private capital from traditional private equity fund investors where there is less flexibility. Figure 2.3 summarizes the roles that families are willing to play in their direct investments.

Families are finding it increasingly difficult to find "value" investment funds at compelling value: According to data from Mergermarket, U.S. merger-and-acquisition deals totaled $277.8 billion in the first quarter of 2014, a 56 percent increase year-over-year. Furthermore, the exit value of private equity firms was the largest since the second quarter of 2014. Pitchbook recently reported an 11.8× Median EV/EBITDA multiple for transactions in March 2014 and median transaction multiples in excess of 10.5× in every month of 2014. The abundance of historically cheap funding, the increasing competition within the private equity industry, and the influx of capital from sources like independent sponsors, middle market funds, and family offices are being reflected in fully valued companies and assets.

Some of the other relevant reasons cited by families who have increased their direct-investment activities are detailed below:

- Private equity firms use the pre-tax internal rate of return (IRR) as the primary metric for performance evaluation: This return benchmark does not always align with the taxable investor's long-term goal of wealth creation. Though multiple of invested capital (MOIC) is also commonly used to evaluate performance, an institutional fund manager's ability to raise his or her next fund is most frequently dependent on their track record of realized IRR to its limited partner (LP) investors. This emphasis on IRR can perpetuate behaviors such as selling winners too early to lock in gains, particularly if there is doubt about the likelihood of the other investments in the portfolio to pay off.

- Institutional funds are continually raising larger funds, chasing larger deals, and keeping fees high: Management fees can range between 1 and 2 percent, and *carried interest performance* fees of 15 to 30 percent incentivize managers to raise as large a fund as possible. As funds grow, deals become harder to find, valuations become richer in the marketplace, and managers do not have to generate as meaningful returns to their LPs to still have extremely profitable businesses. In addition, GPs are more likely to be distracted by fundraising and underperforming portfolio companies as funds grow, rather than focusing on sourcing quality deals, and investing in and improving existing portfolio companies.

- Returns from private equity are highly cyclical: Though private equity has historically been through several boom-and-bust cycles, private equity funds raising outside capital may be more susceptible to the cyclicality of the industry than private direct investors. For example, managers that have raised money are unlikely to return money back to investors at the peaks of the market when fundraising is easiest and valuations are highest. Investment professionals at institutions are paid specifically to deploy capital, often in very narrow industry verticals. Family office investment professionals, in contrast, have less pressure to put capital to work, and are typically not raising outside capital that may influence when they invest and when they sell. They may also have more flexibility to invest across industries and avoid sectors that the bulk of the institutional community is investing in.

- Private investors are most concerned with post-tax returns: Figures 2.4 and 2.5 illustrate the powerful compounding effects that avoiding fundraising

FIGURE 2.4 20-Year Hold vs. 5-Year Fund Recapitalizations

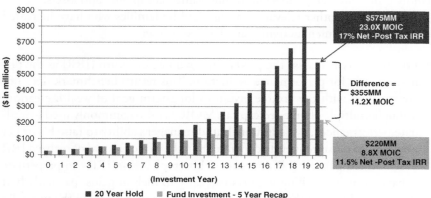

Note: Assumes $25mm initial investment in year 0 at 25% annual return, 20% carry and 25% tax rate.

FIGURE 2.5   20-Year Hold vs. 7-Year Fund Recapitalizations

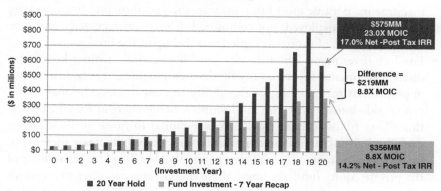

Note: Assumes $25mm initial investment in year 0 at 25% annual return, 20% carry and 25% tax rate and no management fee. IRR calculations are net of carry and taxes. Assumes two 7-year fund cycles and one 6-year fund cycle for a total of 20 years.

cycles can have on a private investor's return over the course of a 20-year period. In both examples, we assume a 20 percent annual rate of return, a 25 percent tax rate, no annual distributions, and a 20 percent performance carry. We ignore management fees for the purposes of this illustration, as a family will likely have a similar overhead expense supporting a direct investment team within their family office. In addition, in order to isolate the effects of the fund cycle, the model pays out the same 20 percent performance carry fees the same year in both examples, making the assumption that a private investor would also pay 20 percent of profits to its investment team. We will discuss compensation practices within family offices later in the chapter. Figure 2.4 illustrates an investment with a 20-year time horizon, with four recapitalizations that occur once every five years. These returns were compared against an investor able to hold that same investment over the course of 20 years, with the value of the investment compounding tax-free over the life of the investment.

Figure 2.5 highlights an investment with a 20-year time horizon, with three recapitalizations occurring, the first two every seven years and the third after six years. In both cases, we assumed distributions made to an LP fund investor after 20 percent of fees in the form of incentive-based carry, and 25 percent in taxes, are immediately redeployed back into a new blind pool fund. These assumptions may overstate the returns of the fund investment for two reasons. One, it may be difficult to redeploy capital back into a fund that can perform consistently as well as the first one. Two, fundraising cycles are rarely timed perfectly. Often capital is committed to a fund for a meaningful period of time before it is deployed into actual investments. Because most funds measure their performance from the time when capital is deployed, not committed, it may not accurately represent the true amount of time that capital was tied up in the fund.

- Fund co-investments often do not provide the same distinct benefits as direct investments: Private equity funds often provide direct co-investment opportunities to their LPs, or the ability to contribute additional equity capital side-by-side with the fund without being charged fees. In theory, this allows funds to raise enough equity capital to invest in their largest deals, and gives families the opportunity to selectively increase their exposure to certain companies while leveraging the due diligence capabilities of the private equity fund. At times, these transactions can offer tremendous value to a private investor. However, as a substitute for quality active direct investing they can also present limitations. For example, co-investments are often done on an accelerated timeline that may not allow a family office the ability to do its full range of due diligence. For a private investor, because the investment is part of a fund, it can be subject to many of the same issues that relate to exit timing and tax inefficiency. In addition, there is some evidence that suggests that co-investments actually underperform committed fund investments; 2014 research by Lerner and Ivashina indicates that co-investments are more likely to occur at market peaks than at market troughs, where the deals are largest and valuations may be the highest.

- With direct investing, private investors enjoy more flexibility to time the market, minimize cyclicality, and customize risk exposure: Direct investing provides families the discretion and transparency that is difficult to achieve in traditional blind-pool funds. A direct investment team may be able to select deals and industries with more appropriate risk, or structure deals with an amount of leverage the family is more comfortable with.

Conclusion

This chapter reveals compelling research and insights from Family Office Exchange (FOX) on the increasing role of private capital in the direct investing market place. There are several advantages that family offices have over their institutional brethren with respect to allocating private capital to direct investing, including: (1) longer time horizons, (2) deal structuring, (2) sourcing, and (3) tax advantage strategies. Various sources confirm the trend of the increased interest in direct investing for family offices.

FOX identifies the misalignment of interests and incentives of blind-pool investment funds with family office investors and the strategic opportunities that private capital affords as major drivers for the increased interest in directs. Although the deal teams are typically small (two or three people), the majority will write checks between $1 million and $25 million. Family offices surveyed by FOX identified real estate as the top sector to invest, with the majority (80%) indicating they would take a non-controlling, however significant investment behind a lead investor. Co-investment opportunity or club deals are of increasing interest to the family office and UHNW constituents, which is discussed in greater detail in Chapter 3.

CHAPTER 3

Co-Investment Strategies in Direct Investing

Co-investment strategies increasingly have become a popular means of entering direct investments. In this chapter, the concept of co-investment is defined and discussed as it relates to investing in direct investments. The chapter expands on what is driving the demand, popularity, and opportunity in co-investing with insights from the Family Office Exchange. Further, the chapter discusses the different roles of co-investors and how these roles interrelate, such as how and why individuals new to co-investing might consider that co-investing is appropriate for them. There are different ways of co-investing, such as participating in club deals, that appeal to different preferences, which will also be discussed in this chapter. Finally, the chapter concludes with a short case and some of the pitfalls and challenges that also come with this way of investing.

Defining Co-Investing and Providing Context

If you were to ask investors to define co-investing, you would likely receive different answers. According to Daniel Goldstein, a seasoned senior executive and board member for families of wealth, family businesses, and private trusts, there really is no precise definition of co-investing. He shares, "As with many other terms (such as hedge funds and impact investing), I find the term to be potentially so wide reaching in its scope that it becomes meaningless to use, beyond stating the obvious that there is more than one single investor. It is only meaningful to frame the context by a longer definition of the type, size, and scope of the co-investments being discussed. Only then will there be the possibility of finding who the right partners are with whom to co-invest."[1]

However, many academics and institutional investors define co-investment as when a private equity fund opens up a specific opportunity for a limited partner (LP) to invest alongside the general partner (GP).[2] This happens far less frequently, approximately only 10 to 20 percent of the time (accounting for less than 5% of the total dollars invested), according to estimates by David McCombie. He adds that the overwhelming majority of this allocation is absorbed by larger, institutional investors and mostly because among their current investors, the fund is typically oversubscribed.[3] As it relates to accredited investors and family offices, we offer a more expansive and simplified definition of co-investing as two or more separate investors deciding to invest alongside one another in a direct investing transaction.

Insights on the Popularity of Co-Investing

Nate Hamilton and Sara Hamilton published a 2016 whitepaper entitled "Private Capital Perspectives: The Emerging Presence of Private Capital in Direct Investing" that shares more about the latest interest and trends in co-investing (which are featured in Chapter 2).[4] They find that while approaches to co-investing vary widely across families, family investors do want the opportunity to participate when attractive direct deal opportunities arise. They further found in their research that families prefer to stay with a smaller cohort of investors rather than invest with lots of different co-investors. This preference, according to the Hamiltons' observations, may also apply to co-investment rights into funds or with other institutional investors, not just families.

Interest in Co-Investment Strategies

There are several reasons why private investors and family offices recently have taken more interest in co-investment approaches to direct investing.

Co-investment increases access and ability to leverage the strengths of partners, whether those strengths are financial or nonfinancial. As discussed earlier in this book, the rationale for direct investing may vary among taking the opportunity to diversify, become uncorrelated to the public markets, take advantage of high growth opportunities, drive entrepreneurial activities, and engage in tax and/or multigenerational wealth transfer planning. These are just a few of the reasons why an investor may decide to gain exposure to directs in their portfolio. Co-investment may be a means to that end and a strategy by which to execute a direct investing mandate. But what drives an investor to seek out co-investment partners rather than investing alone?

Let's look at co-investing from two perspectives: (1) the neophyte co-investor and (2) the expert co-investor. First, the beginner or less experienced direct investor can learn more of the direct investment process by co-investing with more seasoned direct investors. Whether seasoned or not, co-investing means getting access to greater deal flow through co-investment partners. Co-investment partners bring expertise in due diligence and evaluation whether because of their proprietary knowledge of certain industries or because of their financial savvy in dissecting balance sheets and business plans. There is also greater access to human capital as people are brought in to work with portfolio companies on strategic development and management oversight. There is greater access to resources as outside partners are brought in to supplement in-house human capital capacity. Partners may bring to the table greater access to networks, distribution, and control and reporting systems, not to mention invaluable tacit knowledge about how a particular segment works. Increased deal sourcing also creates the opportunity for greater diversification in a direct deal portfolio. Partners extended into diverse geographic regions and sectors bring possibilities that might have been difficult to find otherwise. Finally, newer co-investors may be able to gain specific knowledge, niche expertise, or operational excellence from a co-investor that they lack themselves. Having a co-investor with specialized knowledge, more deal experience, and a proven track record also increases the likelihood for a positive outcome of the co-investment opportunity, along with compensating in areas where the less sophisticated investor is not as strong. Typically, less sophisticated investors will be in a minority-stake capacity. This concept will be discussed further later in this chapter.

So why do some more expert investors decide to co-invest? Before we get to those reasons, it is important to acknowledge that many sizeable private investors actually do not co-invest because they believe (1) that they have the capital to invest on their own; (2) that they have the industry or segment sophistication, track-record, and operational knowledge to invest without partners; (3) that adding co-investors to a deal may dilute the investor and the long-term outcome (in the case of smaller deals); and (4) that the added complexity of additional investors (from a governance standpoint) will not be advantageous.

Yet, there remain several situations where a sophisticated investor desires to co-invest. For example, there are the direct investment deals that might be so large in financing (whether debt or equity) that a sophisticated investor will look for co-investors to fill out the deal. Other reasons for sophisticated investors to desire to co-invest include wanting to diversify their portfolios into areas where they may not have the operational or segment expertise. They may be strong with doing directs, but see the incredible value of involving a strategic partner who has deep operational knowledge, who is an operator and can execute, and who may have strategic networks that might help distribution of a product, or in-country knowledge if the company is out of their home country. Further, sophisticated investors may also see substantial opportunities with a direct deal, but also see associated hurdles and risks. In the cases where they are eager and interested in being part of a deal but do not want to assume all the risks of doing so, they may share those risks with one or more investors. These are just some of the real reasons expert direct investors also like to co-invest.

Roles of the Co-Investor

There are many roles or "hats" that a co-investor might wear in the co-investment process, including deal originator, network facilitator, lead investor, minority investor, and strategic expert investor. This section provides a fuller description of each of these roles.

Deal Originators

These individuals bring the deals to the table. Deal originators may be private investors, brokers, bankers, incubators, universities, deal clubs, or online platforms. Direct deals also may be events sourced through crowdfunding. David Nage, managing director at Ponvalley, a private investment family office, clarifies that Ponvalley wants to be catalytic with their investment and sees the possibility for all investments to have an impact. "We believe that all investments, good or bad, have an impact. We want to only do good and unearth the areas of greatest need to make the most positive change with the funds we are allocating,"[5] shares David. Ponvalley has substantial direct investing experience and has participated in transactions as the deal originator, the lead investor, and/or minority interest investor. Sometimes the deal originators are in fact the family office or private investor, and David may review, vet, analyze, and assess the quality and probability for success of the deals presented to him from the deal originator. When searching for a deal, David looks for companies that are fixing a problem in society, are run by good people, and are focused on turning a profit. To find such a company, he looks for companies that exhibit eight key characteristics:

(a) [involve] building a platform or product addressing a real need in society (e.g., having a meaningful mission beyond simply creating the next social media platform);

(b) a battle-tested management team;

(c) a total addressable market (TAM) north of $10 billion domestically and $50 billion globally (ideally there's a large TAM unless it solves a specific needed problem that unlocks other social need or value);

(d) a "defensible moat" through protected intellectual property or lack of direct competitors;

(e) the ability to capture clients through organic marketing or intelligent utilization of things like search engine optimization;

(f) business model innovations like those in the direct-to-consumer space;

(g) substantial retention of users/clients and high return user data; and

(h) mindfulness of its monthly burn ratio and focus on reaching a state of positive cash flow.[6]

It must be noted, however, that even when these factors are present, it takes time to develop trust in a deal and the associated parties. In David's words, "You can't trust someone until you both put on your dancing shoes and see how you tango."[7] In other words, trust develops over time, although this process can be accelerated through mutual connections or reputation of the individual introducing David to the deal. Many times, David shared, he will take a call and look at a deck because the originator is a friend of a person in his inner circle, whereas deals that are sent to him from unknown or weak connections (e.g., via a LinkedIn connection) are less likely to be reviewed.

As described, the role of deal originator involves many intricacies and exercises of judgment. Thus, the deal originator, in essence, is someone who is in the position to allocate funds to companies that are changing the world in positive ways. In this way, according to David, deal originators play a vital role in creating a better world for our children and help advance the success of our society. He explained, "It is my opinion that private wealth and family offices are the actual change agents, as we are mobilizing our vast networks, actively putting dollars to work, and helping businesses operate successfully in service of innovation."[8]

Network Facilitators

Network facilitators are akin to Malcom Gladwell's *connectors*, those individuals who are adept at building relationships and bringing together strategic parties. These individuals thrive on connecting others to co-invest, but do not necessarily originate the deals. One might find these individuals in various places, from private networks and forums to professional advisory boards, to conferences and events, and even in online communities. Angelo Robles, CEO and founder of the Family Office Association, a private family office membership organization, convenes forums for investors on a multitude of family office and investment topics, from real estate to life sciences and bio-pharma, from fintech and edtech to multi-strategy, among many other topics. Angelo runs as many as 12 events and attends hundreds more each year with approximately 300 different families and single-family offices. These education and networking forums allow possible investors to learn about different areas of investing and also attract investors to listen to business concepts and industry developments. Private safe harbor forums like those the Family Office Association hosts for its members offer a wonderful opportunity for families and single-family offices to connect with their peers and listen to and meet finance thought leaders on many investing subjects. This is time efficient for many families and single-family offices, allowing them to collect the thoughts of their peers as well on a variety of topics of mutual interest and on forum speakers.[9] But be advised, Angelo is not a broker-dealer who takes a placement or finder fee. Instead, he operates a membership organization for families and single-family offices. Finance and investing are but two of the many topics he covers within his organization's national programs. In contrast, being a broker-dealer or even connecting investors to opportunity requires such individuals to be registered representatives and hold licenses in order to raise capital. Most private membership executives or network conveners are not holding these licenses, but some may. Be sure to ask.

Sponsor

The sponsor is typically the lead investor and in the driver's seat. As a result, this stakeholder may play several key roles, such as creating the deal, being the deal originator, and/or taking a majority stake in the direct investment opportunity. Sometimes, the sponsor is very selective and introduces the deal only to a select cadre of potential investors. Recent research conducted for this book indicates that approximately one-quarter (26.4%) desire to hold the controlling interest in the direct investment and about half (45%) desire to be the sponsor (see Figures 3.1 and 3.2). These investors can be active or

FIGURE 3.1   Sponsor vs. Minority Co-Investment Strategies

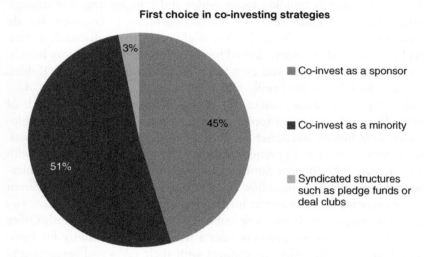

Source: Tamarind Partners Direct Investment Survey, 2016

FIGURE 3.2   Seeking a Control Position

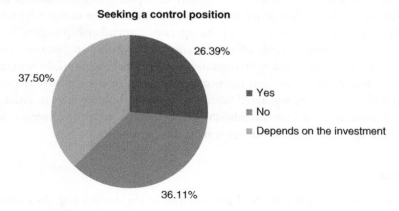

Source: Tamarind Partners Direct Investment Survey, 2016

passive from a standpoint of strategic and operational interaction versus purely financial participation. Sean O'Shea, managing principal at Sienna Capital Partners, a real estate investment banking and private equity boutique, shares that regardless of whether the sponsor is active in the day-to-day operations of the investment, the sponsor almost always is involved in major decisions such as refinancing or dispositions. This is important because having control of the capital structure and exit timing can fundamentally have the greatest impact on overall investment returns.[10]

Minority Investor

The minority investor tends not to be the deal originator; however, they may take an active role, such as taking a board or managerial position, to the other extreme of rather passively cutting a check and waiting to see the outcome of the investment. Approximately half of investors (51%) desire to be a minority investor in a co-investment structure and one-third (36%) indicated that they are not seeking a control position when it comes to co-investing (see Figures 3.1 and 3.2). Tom Mahoney, senior managing director, head of Tangent Alternative Markets, senior managing director of Tangent Capital Partners, and head of Tangent Alternative Markets, works firsthand with both lead and minority investors. Tom shares,

> In our experience, one motivation for family office minority investors is that they are often seeking to reduce the average fee drag on their overall alternative fund IRRs, by co-investing alongside the investment fund sponsors in direct portfolio investments (often through "sidecar" special-purpose vehicles that are unpromoted for limited partners, or which bear lower management fees and/or carried interest). Another key consideration is often to try to develop investment staff expertise in direct investments in deal structuring and due diligence, by learning to the extent possible from the lead sponsor's best practices, and in many cases also by taking a board or observer seat in the portfolio company, especially where the family office co-investor may have some domain expertise in the company's industry sector which the lead sponsor deems value added. In other cases, where the family office investor is not a limited partner in one of the private equity, venture capital or hedge funds leading or "clubbing" the deal, they may participate as a minority investor through a direct relationship with the corporate issuer, or be introduced to the deal by an investment bank representing the issuer in raising capital for the transaction. In these cases, family office investors typically derive comfort that the deal has been appropriately vetted by recognizable alternative investment managers (e.g., Blackstone leading a buyout syndicate or Sequoia Capital leading a late stage

venture round). Absent such "brand name" endorsement of the business and revenue model of the investee, as well as importantly the valuation and terms of the investment, many family offices (even multibillion-dollar ones, with large professional investment staffs) will often decline to participate in the deal.[11]

Many times, co-investors might play multiple roles, so it is wise to outline those roles early in the process, as they typically have implications when it gets down to structuring the deal and negotiating terms. As in any business arrangement, it is essential to have clearly defined roles, rights, and expectations that are written into agreed-upon terms at the outset of forming a co-investment partnership.

Going Solo: Why Co-Investing May Not Be Your Choice

Although co-investing offers many benefits and options, it is not the right choice for everyone. The *co* in co-investment means that you will always be affected and influenced by your interactions with your co-investor(s). This dynamic introduces countless potential risks. Different partners often have equally different viewpoints regarding what time horizon is suitable for building greater value, or with some wanting to harvest investments over a shorter term and others preferring a longer term. Co-investors also may have very different ideas about whether to hold, exit, sell, go public, or acquire or spin off assets. There can be different expectations regarding when to write off investments and when to provide follow-on funding. Different partners have their own individual liquidity needs and pain points that may have nothing to do with the co-investment or the co-investment partners. Exiting at a time when one co-investor does not want to can bring tax implications and reinvestment risk. Emotions can come into play when one party falls in love too much with an asset or lets ego cloud his or her investment judgment. When an investor is acting alone, that investor is able to make all investing choices according to his or her own preferences. In cases of co-investing, each party must take into account all partners' preferences.

Each phase of the deal introduces specific challenges. For example, deal origination can introduce inequities among partners. Key questions to ask are whether deals are being cherry-picked or whether bad deals are being dumped on co-investors. Are there conflicts of interest in evaluating assets and contributions to deals? Are there inequalities in the division of labor on who is sourcing deals, diligencing them, and carrying out the execution of the deal?

Issues also may exist surrounding confidentiality, branding, exposure of family name, and liability of affiliation with parties who operate in other areas beyond your knowledge and certainly beyond your control. These issues can translate into adverse performance. Lily Fang, Victoria Ivashina, and Josh Lerner further found in their review of 20 years of direct private equity investments by seven large institutions that co-investments underperformed the corresponding funds with which they co-invested while solo transactions outperformed fund benchmarks. A leading cause of underperformance is that investing partners often are given only a limited time frame for completing due diligence, leading to situations where deal originators offer low-quality deals and investing partners have insufficient time to discover the problems.[12]

In other words, the reasons for caution are many when considering co-investing, and co-investment may not be suitable for any one investor. As a result, it is crucial for would-be co-investors to outline clear objectives regarding why they want to co-invest and spell out a clear profile of their desired partners. The next section more deeply discusses the potential benefits and drawbacks of co-investing.

The Perils and Pearls of Co-Investing

Throughout this chapter, we have mentioned that co-investing offers certain benefits as well as decided drawbacks. This section reviews some of those drawbacks (perils) and benefits (pearls) in more detail.

One peril is that even when you think you know your co-investors, they may surprise you. As with your friends, significant others, children, and other loved ones, your co-investors will likely make some unanticipated decisions or have unexpected reactions to events over the course of the investment. They may even have a few skeletons in the closet.

For example, it is difficult to identify partners who share similar outlooks on holding period, liquidity, and long-term visions for the investment.[13] For a family investor, this can be particularly challenging, as often the most experienced potential partners in a deal are institutions, which can present some of the same challenges as fund investments. To mitigate these risks, family investors should seek appropriate corporate governance protections, and gauge potential partners' views using specific questions such as: What are the liquidity requirements of your private equity portfolio? How do you define the time horizon? When do you believe is the right time to sell the business? How would we make decisions when partnerships are involved? Are there any related-party transactions (conflicts of interest)?

In addition, experienced co-investors typically ask potential partners how they are likely to deal with problems, such as liquidity constraints, corruption, or replacing a management team. Ultimately, investors cannot cover every contingency beforehand, but in the end, a family must use its best judgment to determine whether a partnership will work well throughout the life of the transaction. Adequate due diligence on all prospective partners and enhanced communication can limit these potential problems to the greatest extent possible.

For a family making a direct investment alongside an independent sponsor, fund, or another family investor, they should maintain a disciplined process for evaluating the track record and compatibility of a potential partner. A family leading a transaction can expect the same amount of due diligence to be conducted on them, and must be prepared to address difficult questions regarding their backgrounds before obtaining capital commitments. Though circumstances vary, the same investor seeking capital has often sourced the transaction and may be seeking compensation for sourcing the deal or for prior due diligence.

Due to the challenges in selecting suitable partners, it is important to engage in a due diligence process with co-investors before embarking together on an investment—and to be aware that this important process cannot be shortchanged. Research from the Family Office Exchange found that the due diligence process needed for individuals to orient themselves to other possible co-investors was "time-consuming, and presents a number of risks and rewards."[14] Moreover, no matter how thorough or effective your process, always keep in mind that you may have missed something or that your partner may change. While these missed issues or unanticipated changes do not have to be detrimental for the investment, it is important to maintain a cautious optimism about your investing partners rather than simply believing you know everything there is to know about them.

A second peril to be aware of is that investors of private equity funds and certain co-investment structures often have different agendas than asset managers. This reflects, according to Lily Fang and colleagues, the classic principal–agent problem where the intermediary may behave in its own interest, rather than that of the investor. In practice, this can mean that fees may grow at the expense of growth in returns, managers may aggressively invest at market peaks when expected returns are only moderate at best, and managers further may exit transactions prematurely to facilitate fundraising. This may occur primarily with fund investments, which is why investors often want to invest directly so they can actively select each investment. These potential pitfalls underscore the importance of assuring in advance and on an ongoing

FIGURE 3.3 Importance of Aligning Managers' and Investors' Interests

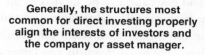

Generally, the structures most
common for direct investing properly
align the interests of investors and
the company or asset manager.

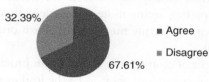

32.39%

■ Agree

■ Disagree

67.61%

Source: Tamarind Partners Direct Investment Survey, 2016

basis that investors' and managers' interests are aligned. Similarly, in Tamarind Partners' Direct Investment Survey, 67.61 percent of respondents agreed that the most effective direct investing structures align investors' and managers' interests (see Figure 3.3).

At the same time, co-investing is not without its benefits, as family investors are able to realize a number of powerful benefits from co-investing alongside independent sponsors, other families, or funds. Many of these benefits are particularly relevant for private investors, who may naturally possess less capital or operating resources than some of their more institutional counterparts.

First, as with many situations in life, there is strength in numbers— although, in co-investing, it is important to remember that strength is found only in strategic numbers. In other words, as this chapter has explained, it's not as simple as more investors meaning better results. Instead, what is needed to bring the advantages of co-investing into reality are more investors who are aligned with each other and who bring the intellect, connections, and subject matter or domain expertise to realize desired returns. When complementary parties are brought into a deal, co-investors can use their skills, industry experience, relationships, and intellectual capital in synergistic ways across all phases of a transaction. Robert Wiltbank pointed out, for example, that when more than one venture capitalist is involved in a new deal, the lead investor gains more viewpoints to help vet a deal. Moreover, these types of deals prompt the various venture capitalists involved to engage in collaborative behaviors as well as cooperative and reciprocal checks that enhance the outcomes for all.[15]

Co-investing also makes it possible to leverage the larger set of strengths, capabilities, and resources present with multiple investors. For example, all parties are able to leverage collective capital to invest in larger transactions, and leaving dry powder for follow-on investments in the company. Collective due diligence capabilities and costs also can be applied to the deal, increasing the number of investment professionals evaluating a deal and reducing what can be costly sums of time and money an investor might otherwise spend alone on vetting a transaction. Finally, co-investors can benefit from the sourcing capabilities of other parties, seeing more transactions than they might otherwise find on their own and having more potential exit opportunities over the life of the transaction.

Yet another benefit of co-investing is that it can provide opportunities to invest in areas where you may not want to be the lead or sponsor. Recall that sponsors act as the drivers of the deal, playing various operational, strategic, and leadership roles as varied as originating the deal, taking a majority stake, and having a controlling interest. While there are advantages to these roles, you may not possess the connections, capital, experience, or subject matter or domain expertise to be effective. In such cases, a strategic partner can serve as the sponsor as well as provide you with the opportunity to gain exposure to and take advantage of deals you otherwise may never hear about.

Vetting Co-Investors

Once you have made the decision to move ahead with co-investing, it is important to define and carry out a due diligence process on your co-investors and identify which data points are most meaningful. Tom Handler, JD, PC, is a partner at Handler Thayer, LLP, and chairman of the Advanced Planning and Family Office Group. Tom noted that it is human nature to underestimate our exposure in any given situation and, therefore, it is important for co-investors to soberly assess the risk they are undertaking by joining with partners and entering into deals.[16]

At the risk being repetitive (but, then again, it should be the theme of this chapter), the first step in any evaluation—whether that involves evaluating a deal or a potential investing partner—is to set out with clearly defined objectives. Your due diligence processes then will reflect the criteria, parameters, and ranges established in those objectives. The process and development of a thesis are discussed in greater detail in Chapter 5, Family Office Considerations to the Direct Investment Process, and Chapter 6, Designing a Direct Investment Thesis.

Some areas to consider are the same as evaluating any partner. A starting point is to confirm that the potential partner has a direct investment thesis and to understand what that thesis is. Specifically, it is important to confirm that any potential partners are clear about their role in the co-investment, their objectives, their desired time horizon, and liquidity needs.

Second, evaluate the financial profile of the partner. What is their net worth and their basic asset allocation and liabilities? It is important that the investment is the right size for your potential co-investors. That is, it should not be so small and insignificant for them that it never earns their attention. At the same time, it should not be so big for them that they will be hindered by fear of loss in making decisions or lack the staying power to ride out the investment. Moreover, it is important that they have the liquidity to add follow-on funding or agree to dilution terms at preset valuations in order to allow new funding as needed.

Third, examine their track record. Track record reveals a lot about your prospective partners, such as whether they have very limited direct investing experience or have done a number of deals. Keep in mind, however, that most direct investors deploy on average 0 to 2 deals a year (see Chapter 5, Figure 5.5). This means you are unlikely to find partners who have extensive experience numbering in the hundreds.

Once you determine how much experience they have had, examine the specific co-investment deals they have engaged in to understand how the deal emerged and how it evolved. Specifically, what was your prospective partners' involvement along the way? What decision points can they explain to show the value they added to that investment? Can their story be independently corroborated?

Moreover, what do their past co-investing partners say about them? If you are able to know past deals and other players who have participated in those deals, it is not out of bounds to learn more about the roles co-investors played in those deals. For example, some parties prefer to be silent financial investors while others prefer to be activist drivers that play an integral role in the monitoring and oversight. It is important to know your partner's preferences and orientations before entering into a co-investment arrangement so that you can assure you are aligned and complementary.

Fourth, evaluate what the investors uniquely bring to the table in terms of strategic leadership, managerial or functional expertise, technical knowledge, and other assets. Are they good at the financial/legal structuring of deals? Do they have deep operational expertise in running, managing, and growing these types of companies? Do they have key expertise on the exit or harvesting of the company, such as with important industry relationships? Do they have in-house counsel they could use to review contracts?

Fifth, before entering into any co-investment, it is additionally important to learn about potential partners' sourcing, due diligence, and vetting processes, including whether they work with an internal team, outsource the process to direct investment consultants, or utilize a combination of approaches. Given the importance of due diligence and the fact that co-investing partners do not always have the opportunity to thoroughly vet opportunities,[17] it is essential that all parties involved have adequate mechanisms in place to vet deals.

The final critical step is to evaluate potential partners' character, values, and business ethics to assure they are aligned with yours. Background checks using social media, newspapers, and public records to check criminal, credit, bankruptcy, and legal history can be useful in doing so. One investor, for example, was careful to learn about his co-investors' personal relationships. His philosophy was that if any potential partners treated their significant others badly, they were unlikely to be good co-investors. After all, if they treated their loved ones poorly—by cheating on them, for example—why would they treat business partners well? Even when you do not find egregious issues in a potential partner's background, cultural mismatch is still a possibility. Tom Handler points out that in his work he has seen families who have been "doing business 60 or 70 years in a certain way. If they're going to do a direct deal with another family that operates in a completely different manner, that's just likely not going to be a good scenario."[18] He advises getting to know the potential partners' perspectives, tolerance to risk, tolerance to publicity, and privacy needs. If alignment is not assured, he warns:

> The deal still might go very well, and the yield could be very good, and yet this very private family now finds itself in the public news or the public sector, and suddenly they now have to purchase hostage and kidnap insurance, a higher level of security and on and on.... Anytime there's a disconnect in the [co-investors'] cultures, they are just opportunities for something to go sideways.... It's just a very different way of doing business, and it's a recipe for catastrophe. So you need to have some sense of whether these people can function together. It's not just a deal—you still have the family, and the family culture and the family business behind it. There are just more factors to be considered.[19]

Club Deals

Although investors seemingly have innumerable options for investing in private equity, three of the most common avenues for doing so are investing in a private equity fund, internally replicating a full private equity firm, and participating in individual club deals.[20] According to David McCombie, founder and chief executive officer of McCombie Group, LLC—a collection of influential families actively seeking to invest long-term capital into established family-owned businesses—participating in individual club deals means investing in individual opportunities on a deal-by-deal basis in conjunction with other investors. Investors also may enjoy some involvement in the deal, such as holding a board or advisory board position. Typical club deals range from $5 million to $50 million. McCombie asserts based on his experience that strong club deal investments should average yields of 15 to 20 percent when accounting for all fees. He further offered a rule of thumb that gross returns are typically 4 to 10 percent higher than what actually will be returned net of fees and gross returns should be underwritten at 20 to 25 percent or above for lower-risk buyout investments and 25 to 35 percent for higher-risk growth investments.[21] Direct investments by families are only on the rise, and McCombie states that when families invest in private equity directly, 99 percent of them will do it via a club deal format.

As discussed earlier in the chapter, the term *co-investment* can have multiple meanings, and what one person thinks of as a co-investment, McCombie acknowledges is often more of a club deal. McCombie emphasizes, "Fund co-investments are extremely rare. Funds generally open up co-investments only to their current co-investors, unless the deal is extremely large and the funds cannot absorb the whole investment themselves."[22] He further points out that for every dollar of co-investment rights you have, you will need to invest approximately $20 million into the fund. In other words, "You're going to need to invest a tremendous amount in funds to get a material amount of co-investment rights when they merge."[23] Further confusing matters is that club deals and co-investments functionally have the same characteristics— that is, both involve a third party that has the authority to run the investment and you are deciding whether to participate in an individual deal. In a club deal, the governing third party is another family or independent sponsor, whereas in a co-investment, the governing third party is the fund or independent sponsor. In other words, when people say, "I'm co-investing with another family," often what is functionally occurring is that that other family is running the club deal as the sponsor or lead investor, and the other person is simply investing alongside them.

A final note is that as club deals involve entering into a deal with one or more partners (like other types of co-investing), the same due diligence considerations with regard to the deal and the investing partners apply.

Key Considerations of Club Deals

An ideal club opportunity has three characteristics in common: (1) strong deal fundamentals, (2) a qualified sponsor, and (3) a fair and aligned structure that minimizes risk, assuring a proven management team committed to the venture is in place. Ideally, the investor will also be able to enter at below-market terms.

McCombie offers several recommendations to enhance the possibility of outsized returns.[24] First, it is important to ensure that valuation multiples relative to earnings are reasonable—using historic earnings as an indicator. The relative attractiveness of a deal also should be evaluated in light of alternative industries that money could be deployed into (e.g., tech companies may be overpriced relative to pharmaceuticals). Whenever possible, deals should be obtained in an off-market fashion to avoid a speedy, formalized sales process that tends to undermine due diligence, compromise terms and structures, hike up prices, and reduce returns.

Management teams that have a strong commitment to the venture and a strong track record of execution comprise a final key ingredient for club deals. The most appropriate managers are those who previously ran the firm or who are being brought in for the purpose to take the helm post-closing. Given that club deals typically involve smaller businesses, it is critical to identify and fill key talent gaps as part of due diligence. In particular, it is inadvisable to continue a deal where top leadership roles in the company are vacant.

A qualified sponsor can greatly enhance the success of a club deal. Most top sponsors are experienced C-suite-level industry executives in their late forties or fifties or private equity professionals in their mid-thirties to late forties who previously worked for a top private equity firm and chose to go independent. Additionally, most sponsors work in pairs or small teams of three or four. One key characteristic to look for in a sponsor is that they are candid about both the strengths and weaknesses of a deal and also believe in the deal enough to invest a significant percentage of their total net worth (i.e., 10–50%) into it. The sponsor also should have deep subject matter expertise and connections within the relevant industry. This can be invaluable for identifying and originating off-market opportunities, underwriting deals, filling management and board positions, making connections with potential customers and suppliers, and ensuring that the company is operated optimally. Sponsors additionally should have experience with smaller, lower-middle-market funds versus marquee megafunds to improve chances that the sponsor has the diverse set of entrepreneurial skills needed to support the venture's success. Sponsors need to be willing and able to assume a variety of different roles and responsibilities (e.g., origination, execution, operational consulting) to help minimize transaction costs from third-party professionals.

Having a favorable deal structure can enhance value by providing downside protection derived from shifting the risk of underperformance to other parties. McCombie explains that ideally the seller assumes some of the downside risks, as they are best positioned and most knowledgeable about their former business. Specific tools to reduce risks and align performance incentives include earn-outs, seller notes, and requiring the seller to reinvest a portion of their proceeds.

As mentioned earlier, any investor should have a clearly defined mission as to why they want to co-invest with parameters addressing in what, how, and with whom. There are a few additional issues to carefully consider:

Know the deal, not just the partners. Understanding all the details—from legal and financial to intellectual property and market—is critical to successful investments. Questions to consider include: Whom does it come from? How long has it been shopped around, at what price, and why did someone not take it beforehand? Is there a carry or promote? How is the incoming investment divided (cash vs. other) and how are the resulting returns divided (pro-rata, performance fee, hurdles, waterfalls, clawbacks, etc.)? What are the expectations? What time horizon is given for the deal? What would spur follow-on funding, and how much would be given and when? What would cause a write-off to occur and how would that be structured? What are the different scenarios and do the terms adequately provide for all foreseeable contingencies? What conflicts of interest exist? Does one co-investment partner hold an advantage such as holding senior status on debt or getting back some of their investment by selling services to the investee company? Knowing your co-investors' backgrounds is paramount. Take care to do an equal amount of homework on the deal and do not simply rely on your co-investor's prestige, track record, or reputation.

Skin in the game does not equal success. Over and over, I hear that because certain investors have some (or all) of their capital invested, this means they are "watching the ball" (or some other euphemism), suggesting they will take better care in the investment. This may simply not be true. Just because you are driving a car does not mean you are a good driver. You may be distracted, emotionally charged, asleep at the wheel, or intoxicated. By the same token, an investor may be emotionally clouded and trying to convince others to commit the same folly. The investor may load too much risk or not fully comprehend the risk inherent in the investment. It *is* a telling sign when someone lacks the conviction to invest in proportion to others or refrains from investing at all. However, one's decision to invest should not be overrated in its importance.

Having investors equally invested is not always a good sign. Be wary when evaluating a co-investment opportunity where there is no clear sponsor or lead investor. Clear investor leadership is often an important component of strong co-investment relationships. For example, four investors who each have 25 percent equity may be a recipe for conflicts and stalemates. It even can be better to have a suboptimal leader or strategy than none at all. Lead investors play an important role in the sourcing, vetting, structuring, terms, and rights for a deal.

Risks of Club Deals

Consistent with the success factors for club deals, risks concerning the deal, the sponsor, and the structure require attention. The key risk concerning any deal is underperformance. Therefore, it is important to assure the deal provides both strong fundamentals with structural elements to protect downside risk. Measures to do so include assuring that the purchase price is reasonable, cash flows are realistic, industry dynamics and trends are supportive of future success, and a qualified management team is in place. It is additionally important to consider how the investment may perform under various scenarios and to note the key assumptions underlying the deal.

Sponsors exert a substantial amount of influence over a deal's success once it is closed. Therefore, it is important for you to be able to trust that sponsor once the deal closes. In order to do that, adequate due diligence in advance of the deal is essential. Red flags concerning the sponsor to be watchful for include use of semantics and technicalities that misrepresent the deal, lack of transparency or candidness when answering questions, or inability to verify the sponsor's background or track record, or evidence that the sponsor has differing risk tolerances and views of the world compared to your own. Aside from these red flags, you should also examine the sponsor's track record (e.g., roles, level of involvement, performance, value added) in similar investments. Take care to examine both successful and less successful past deals and to verify the sponsor's claims. Throughout the process of due diligence, you should also evaluate whether the sponsor exhibits good judgment and trustworthiness, evidenced by a thorough due diligence process, conservative assumptions in their underwriting, transparency about a deal's benefits and drawbacks, responsible stewardship, and your own personal comfort with the sponsor.

The key risk concerning a deal's structure is whether it is fair and maximizes alignment of all parties' interests—meaning that the terms assure that any one stakeholder (e.g., sponsor, management) succeeds only when you succeed. Key measures for doing so include making sure that interests are aligned in both upside and downside scenarios and that fees are reasonable, and assuring that the due diligence process is not shortchanged.

Mini Case Study

An excellent case of aligning the interests of key strategic co-investors is found in the example of a group of four Italian families who engaged in a family office co-investment opportunity.[25] The deal was substantial, involving shipping goods into a particular marina in a harbor, putting them on trains, and then shipping them to their various points of delivery. One family served as the deal originator and they brought in the three other families—one controlled the marina in the harbor, one operated a large shipping enterprise, and one owned the trains. One of the families also was well connected politically. By strategically selecting the families involved and assuring they had complementary strengths and assets, each brought substantial strategic and operational value to the partnership, placing all families on equal footing.

Moreover, through their arrangement, they were able to eliminate a wide range of risks that can undermine co-investments. For example, they were able to cut out the investment bankers and typical financiers that would be involved. Understanding the value each provided, the families looked out for each other in the transaction, and everyone enjoyed favorable pricing. Their valued political and industry connections as well as the sheer importance of these families enabled them to clear many other obstacles they might have faced.

Additionally, each of these families had extensive co-investing experience, further enabling them to leverage past best practices and lessons learned in the current deal. The co-investment of these families created a synergy that increased the collective strength of each individual investor. Because of their unique domain expertise, their power and influence in these diverse sectors coupled with the political influence they could exert, these families created tremendous value by coming together in a co-investment structure.

Conclusion

Co-investment approaches to direct investing are of increasing interest to novice and seasoned as well as private, institutional, and family office investors alike. Much of this interest has arisen due to benefits such as being able to leverage collective capital, due diligence, capabilities and costs, capabilities sourcing, and strategic competencies. However, co-investing is not for everyone. To be effective, would-be co-investors must outline clear objectives regarding why they want to co-invest, spell out a clear profile of their desired partners, and take measures to thoroughly vet potential partners and deals. Assuring that the right partners, deals, and structures are selected so that all parties' interests are aligned will do much to help reduce risks and promote positive outcomes.

Moreover, while true co-investment is rather rare, direct investments with one another by families are on the rise, and most families' co-investments will be through club deals. A desirable club deal will allow families to enter at below-market terms, have favorable structures that minimize risk, assure a proven management team committed to the venture is in place, and have a qualified sponsor for the deal. As with any investment, club deals introduce certain risks that need to be managed. However, when strong club deals are found, they are expected to average yields of 15 to 20 percent—suggesting they are worthwhile.

Notes

1. Interview with Daniel Goldstein, August 2015.
2. Lily Fang, Victoria Ivashina, and Josh Lerner, "The Disintermediation of Financial Markets: Direct Investing in Private Equity," *Journal of Financial Economics*, 2014.
3. Interview with David McCombie, founder and chief executive officer of McCombie Group, LLC, September 2016.
4. Nate Hamilton and Sara Hamilton, "Private Capital Perspectives: The Emerging Presence of Private Capital in Direct Investing," Family Office Exchange, 2016.
5. Interview with David Nage, managing director at Ponvalley, August 2016.
6. Ibid.
7. Ibid.
8. Ibid.
9. Correspondence with Angelo Robles, CEO and founder of Family Office Association, August 2016.
10. Interview with Sean O'Shea, managing partner at Sienna Capital, October 2015.

11. Interview with Tom Mahoney, senior managing director, head of Tangent Alternative Markets, January 2015.
12. Lily Fang, Victoria Ivashina, and Josh Lerner, "The Disintermediation of Financial Markets: Direct Investing in Private Equity," *Journal of Financial Economics*, 2014.
13. Nate Hamilton and Sara Hamilton, "Private Capital Perspectives: The Emerging Presence of Private Capital in Direct Investing," Family Office Exchange, 2016, p. 13.
14. Ibid., p. 13.
15. Robert Wiltbank, "Investment Practices and Outcomes of Informal Venture Investors," *Venture Capital: International Journal of Entrepreneurial Finance* 7(4), 2005.
16. Interview with Tom Handler, partner, Handler Thayer, LLP, Advanced Planning & Family Office Group, August 2016.
17. Lily Fang, Victoria Ivashina, and Josh Lerner, "The Disintermediation of Financial Markets: Direct Investing in Private Equity," *Journal of Financial Economics*, 2014.
18. Interview with Tom Handler, partner, Handler Thayer, LLP, Advanced Planning & Family Office Group, August 2016.
19. Ibid.
20. David McCombie, "The 15 Questions You Need to Answer before Participating in Any Club Deal," 2016. The McCombie Group, LLC.
21. Ibid.
22. Interview with David McCombie, founder and chief executive officer of McCombie Group, LLC, September 2016.
23. Ibid.
24. Ibid.
25. Interview with Interview with Tom Handler, partner, Handler Thayer, LLP, Advanced Planning & Family Office Group, August 2016.

CHAPTER 4

Private Equity Strategies: Characteristics and Implications

Contributing Author: David McCombie

The term *private equity* is often treated as a catchall, used interchangeably to describe a broad variety of investments. Such loose use of the phrase fails to capture the range of nuanced business ownership strategies it refers to and risks branding an entire asset class with characteristics and implications that are typically relevant to only a particular subcategory. In reality, however, private equity refers to an array of investment strategies each with a unique risk-return profile and differing core skillsets for success. Moreover, certain strategies are more prevalent among families who invest directly.

This chapter aims to help family offices and the advisors who serve them better understand the nuances of the various subcategories of private equity.

This chapter was adapted from the whitepaper entitled, "Private Equity Unpacked," published by David McCombie, CEO McCombie Group LLC, that was updated in July 2016.

Ultimately by understanding the characteristics and implications of each asset class, the reader should be equipped to make an educated choice regarding the most relevant and appropriate strategy for their unique profile. Specifically, this chapter covers real estate, early-stage investing such as venture capital and seed investing, as well as growth capital, buyouts, mezzanine financing, and distressed investing. Each section looks at the different characteristics of the type of investment from cash flow characteristics to risk-return profile, use of leverage, and skillsets for investors implementing these strategies, as well as the size, duration, and nature of the investment.

What Is Private Equity?

From a technical perspective, private equity is nothing more than making investments into illiquid non-publicly traded companies (i.e., companies not regulated by the SEC or a comparable regulatory body). It is the umbrella term for an asset class that can be segmented into six broad investment strategies: (1) venture capital, (2) growth capital, (3) mezzanine financing, (4) buyouts, (5) distressed investments, and (6) real estate. The first five strategies correspond to the progressive stages of a business's natural lifecycle, illustrated in Figure 4.1, while the latter is subject to its own set of development stages.

Nearly a decade after the Great Recession, private equity has still not fully recovered from its 2007 peak, when global capital raised reached $681 billion.[1] Despite bouncing back from a 2010 low of $299 billion, only $527 billion was raised in 2015 (representing a slight decline from the prior year). While Figure 4.2 shows the relative share of various private equity investment strategies institutionally, family offices tend to have a different allocation mix when investing directly.[2] The most prevalent strategies that families invest in directly are real estate, venture capital, growth capital, and buyouts. Given their more technical nature, distressed investments and mezzanine loans are generally a less prevalent strategy among family offices.

Each private equity strategy possesses a unique risk-return profile and characteristics that have implications regarding the nature of the ideal target, the deal structure, and the necessary investor skillsets typically required for success. As depicted in Figure 4.3, risk-return profiles typically decline across business lifecycle stages with the exception of distressed, which deviates from this trend due to the level of uncertainty involved. Recent empirical data suggests that the relative risk-return profiles may not always hold (particularly over the short term), insinuating that certain asset classes are systematically more attractive than others.

FIGURE 4.1   Private Equity Strategies across the Business Lifecycle

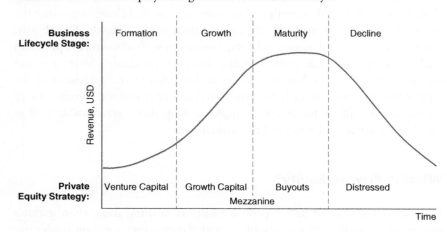

FIGURE 4.2   Number of Private Equity Funds and Corresponding Capital Raised by Strategy, Q2 2016

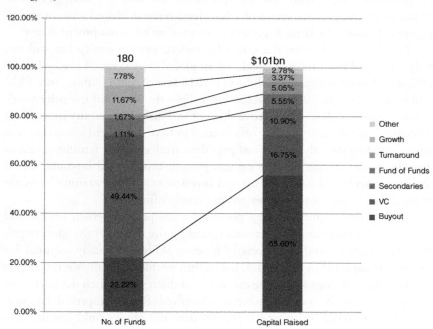

FIGURE 4.3 Illustrative Risk-Return Profiles by Private Equity Strategy

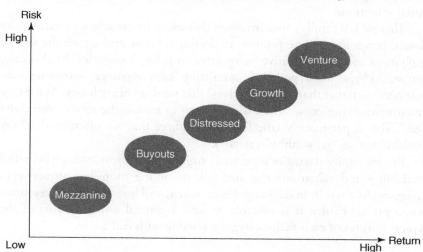

Unlike institutional funds that typically have strict investment parameters limiting the kinds of assets they can consider, family offices are in the unique position of being able to be flexible. While there may be situations where it is advantageous to consider reallocating into more favorably priced categories, there is obvious value in asset class expertise that typically manifests itself in superior deal sourcing, negotiation of terms, and pricing, among other forms. In fact, empirical studies show that a 20 percent increase in asset class diversification in private equity funds results in a 6 percent fall in IRR.[3] As a result, if investing directly, it is best practice to focus direct investments on a particular category and its immediate adjacencies (and gain exposure to the other strategies through fund commitments), as observed by most institutional funds, which commit to a strict investment mandate or thesis, which will be covered in Chapter 6. Moreover, it is difficult to mentally recalibrate when assessing opportunities across categories because of the respective mindsets required to analyze each. In particular, risk tolerances for individual deals, in theory, generally decline as you move across the private equity continuum from highly speculative earlier stage deals (i.e., venture capital) toward more mature companies with stable financial histories. The higher risk levels and failure rates of the former are compensated by the potential for much greater upside. If you applied the same liberal risk perspective from venture capital—where success is predicated on hitting a few homeruns and tolerating a majority of failed deals—to buyouts of established companies, you're likely to do poorly given the much smaller margin for error inherent in their higher initial valuations.

That said, if family office investors do seek to invest across private equity classes, it would be more prudent to do the opposite and err on the side of applying a more conservative perspective to riskier categories. In this case, you would be, at worst, guilty of committing "false negatives"—turning away "winners"—rather than "false positives" that result in heavy losses. As the sage investment saying goes, "The easiest money to earn is the money you don't lose." This is particularly true for family offices that are often in the "stay wealthy" versus "get wealthy" category.

Private equity strategies experience unique investment cycles where deal availability and valuations rise and fall, becoming more/less attractive to investors. As a result, in deciding where, when, and how to allocate resources across private equity, it is valuable to have a general understanding of the typical features of each major category, starting with real estate.

Real Estate

Family office investors often utilize private equity investment structures to gain real estate exposure. In fact, this is by far the most prevalent direct investment for most families given the "intuitiveness" of the asset class, derived from their preexisting familiarity with buying and selling personal homes, and the perceived safety of owning a "hard asset." Moreover, real estate permits a wider range of equity check sizes: from under $100,000 for a single condo rental unit to hundreds of millions for a large office building. Like private equity in the realm of operating businesses, real estate offers a diverse array of risk-return profiles. Broadly speaking, there are three main strategies for investing in real estate, each with its own profile and differentiated skillset for success. *These include core, value-add, and development real estate investing, which, when examined together, represent a spectrum of increasing investor involvement and risk-return tradeoffs.* (See Figure 4.4.)

Investors typically move from a capital preservation to a wealth generation posture when transitioning from more passive *core* to more hands-on real estate *development*. Because of this dynamic, real estate fund managers typically only receive flat management-based fees for core strategies while charging a mix of management and incentive-based fees for riskier value-added and development investments.

In practice, preexisting real estate properties are valued using capitalization rates (which are essentially the reciprocal of the earnings multiples used

FIGURE 4.4 Real Estate Investing Continuum

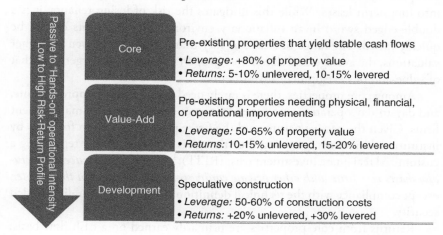

to value operating businesses). These "cap rates" are applied to historical net operating income (real estate's functional equivalent to EBITDA) to determine a price. Such cap rates are positively correlated with macroeconomic drivers like inflation and interest rates and are informed as well by more localized and deal-specific factors like real estate inventory, tenant quality, tenant industry concentration, and so forth.

Core Investing

Core real estate investing resides at the low-risk/low-return end of the continuum. It typically involves investments in preexisting office, industrial, multifamily, and/or retail properties that yield stable cash flows and are located in major metropolitan markets. A diversified core portfolio generally includes a broad range of property types or geographies, specializing in one dimension and diversifying across the other. That said, when families make these investments privately, they often concentrate with regard to both dimensions, given capital constraints and preference for familiarity. Family offices typically "get their feet wet" with the simpler core strategy and over time consider higher risk-return options.

Core properties aspire to generate stable cash flows through high occupancy levels. This typically involves higher-tier properties filled with tenants who have good credit. Nevertheless, some subprime residential properties, such as low-income housing, can be considered "core" because of the financial backstop provided by public subsidies. Commercial properties are generally occupied by national chains, such as CVS Pharmacies, that are locked into long-term leases. While this mitigates the risk of losing tenants, it is a double-edged sword in an inflationary environment, since rents cannot be quickly raised. The range of sizes can vary dramatically, but given its higher valuations, the average deal size of core properties tends to be larger than that of value-add or development investments.

Among core properties, there is rarely need for significant improvements, and day-to-day operations are generally outsourced to property management firms. Given the passive nature, and the fierce price competition for deals by institutional investors, pursuing this strategy is akin to privately replicating a customized real estate investment trust (REIT).[4] *As a result, core investing actually shares very little with other private equity strategies described in this chapter,* except compliance with the technical definition that it is not a publicly traded security.

Returns from core properties are primarily earned on a cash flow basis; less emphasis needs to be placed on property disposition. Unlevered returns for core properties typically range from 4 to 8 percent because of the minimal risks involved. As in a leveraged buyout, returns on equity can be bolstered through increased use of debt in the capital structure. As a result, success is contingent on securing the lowest cost of capital. Overall, core real estate can take on significant debt loads—leverage ratios typically range from 70 to 85 percent—given its sound fundamentals, and therefore deliver levered returns averaging 10 to 14 percent. Achieving this upper range of leverage requires supplementing senior debt from banks, institutional investors (i.e., insurers, pensions, etc.), and mortgage-backed security instruments with higher interest rate mezzanine facilities.

Core returns, while robust, are typically part of a broader wealth preservation, rather than a wealth creation, strategy. Core properties are in fact viewed often as an inflation hedge. Empirical analysis suggests that rental income closely tracks inflation in relatively low inflationary environments, though this relationship may not persist during periods of extreme inflation stress. For example, rental income growth in the United States did trail in the period of high inflation from 1977 to 1982.

Value-add Investing

Value-add investing makes up a wide range of strategies that fall in between conservative core investments and more speculative development projects. As the name implies, value-add investments typically feature an improvement of the physical, financial, or operational characteristics of the underlying property. Traditional examples of value-add investments include properties that require physical renovation or market repositioning (i.e., changing property offerings to a higher, more valuable use; this is sometimes accomplished through rezoning) or a combination of the two. This segment can also include distressed properties with poor cash flows because they are over-indebted or poorly run. As with distressed businesses, success in distressed properties requires patience and deep legal knowledge to unwind the various competing claims in order to own the property outright and to remedy any operational deficiencies.

Value-add investments tend to produce moderate income and rely most heavily upon property appreciation, which is ultimately realized upon exit. Unlevered returns from value-add investments range between 8 and 12 percent. Value-add strategies use moderate leverage, given the higher volatility and lack of availability of many kinds of debt financing, such as mortgage-backed securities. Debt loads are typically in the range of 50 to 65 percent, resulting in levered returns of 15 to 20 percent.

Development Investing

Development represents the highest risk-adjusted return potential within real estate. It typically involves speculative construction from the ground up and the completion of unfinished projects. Unlike the other real estate categories, which have some historical precedents to validate demand levels, risk comes not only from the pricing/income side, but also from initial costs—significant uncertainty may exist regarding construction cost and timing overruns. Additionally, developers often have a herd mentality, which creates booms and busts from spikes in inventory. As a result, volatility in investment performance is high. Moreover, returns are predicated upon exit since profitability is only reached once the development is built and stabilized with tenants. Once a property is stabilized, there are fundamentally two options: investors can either sell or convert it into a core property through a recapitalization (typically with bank financing).

Unlevered expected returns for development investments are typically at least 20 percent—this is lower than venture capital, despite some risk parallels, given the greater underlying salvage value of the property that makes total losses less likely. Moderate bank leverage, typically ranging from 50 to 60 percent of development costs, boosts levered return on equity to 30 percent and above. Note that once a property is completed, its collateral basis steps up from the property's cost to its value, supporting significantly greater debt.

Skills for success in development include construction project management as well as a deep understanding of the local market's unique characteristics and anomalies. Choosing reputable partners with complementary expertise is also very important. Together, they should be positioned to directly add value by leveraging key relationships that can minimize the likelihood of construction cost and time overruns (stemming from zoning, environmental, and code review bureaucracy), and can expedite the sale/leasing of units at the most favorable rates.

Core versus Non-Core Real Estate Investing

Family offices seeking to invest directly into real estate should focus in areas where they can generate and capture greater value than a fund or public market alternatives. Typically these opportunities are in non-core properties since they allow for value creation on both the front- and back-end of deals. Regarding the entry price, value-added and development projects tend to be less competitive, which provides scope for greater upside. This is especially the case for families who have a long-term time horizon and can be patient enough to wait for opportunistic deals. Such prospects rarely exist within core investment strategies, which often pursue the same deals as REITs, and thus are exposed to the pricing efficiency of public markets. (Note that this may not hold true in emerging markets where no suitable public market vehicles exist.) Additionally, by nature of their active involvement, non-core investments are the only real estate opportunities that allow investors to add material value. As a result, a skilled family office investor can potentially do better than a fund structure since competition is not simply in the domain of picking the right deals but also revolves around vision and operational performance. Hence, greater potential exists to generate above-average net returns by investing directly in non-core assets, relative to core properties, which are likely to track the same low returns found in passive portfolios.

Venture Capital

Venture capital involves investing in innovative early-stage startups with an extremely high risk-return profile. These companies typically target existing markets that are ripe for disruption or address latent demand for products where no market previously existed. Generally cash flow negative, they almost always have outstanding questions regarding the viability of their underlying business model. Consequently, rather than earning returns from the ongoing operating profits, investors are generally exclusively dependent upon an eventual exit, typically occurring via sale to a strategic buyer or an initial public offering (IPO).[5] Moreover, given their pioneering nature, venture capital investments generally exhibit a binary success profile, either losing everything or yielding significant returns. In aggregate, "winners" must generate a significant multiple of capital invested—in excess of 10×—in order to compensate for the high number of failures.

Venture capital is best viewed as a series of progressive options that increasingly sheds light on the real value of the company. Investors stage their financing against the achievement of preset milestones with the intent of doubling down on winners, and perhaps more importantly, cutting their losses on less compelling opportunities. As in poker, an investor is faced with the option of paying for the right to see new information that will help them determine whether to continue to fund the enterprise or fold. With each round of financing, the company should make progress toward informing or eliminating key uncertainties regarding the soundness of its fundamental business model (e.g., Does demand exist? Is there a significant willingness to pay? Will partners be willing to work with us?). Valuations are fundamentally driven by the ability to address key reservations regarding the investment's long-term potential.

In practice, venture capital takes the shape of consecutive financing rounds starting with seed and angel financing, followed by a lettered series of institutional raises (Series A, Series B, etc.). The amount of funds raised (and corresponding valuations) generally increases across these financing rounds. While official data is scarce, anecdotal evidence indicates that the average seed round ranges between $25,000 and $200,000, with angel rounds averaging $250,000 to $1 million. Data shows that Series A rounds typically raise $1.5 to $3.5 million for a 15 to 25 percent equity interest, while Series B and C rounds average between $4 and $8 million and $8 and $15 million, respectively.[6] As startups meet their milestones and progress through additional rounds, their pre-valuations escalate 50 to 70 percent per round,[7] providing the headroom for founders to raise larger amounts of capital while experiencing relatively lesser levels of dilution. As seen in Figure 4.5, the entire lifecycle of a successful venture (i.e., from founding to exit) typically ranges from 5 to 10 years.

Seed versus Venture Capital

When discussing startup financing, the various stages of venture capital are often mentioned in the same breath. But, while they draw on similar strategies

FIGURE 4.5 Venture Capital Cycle

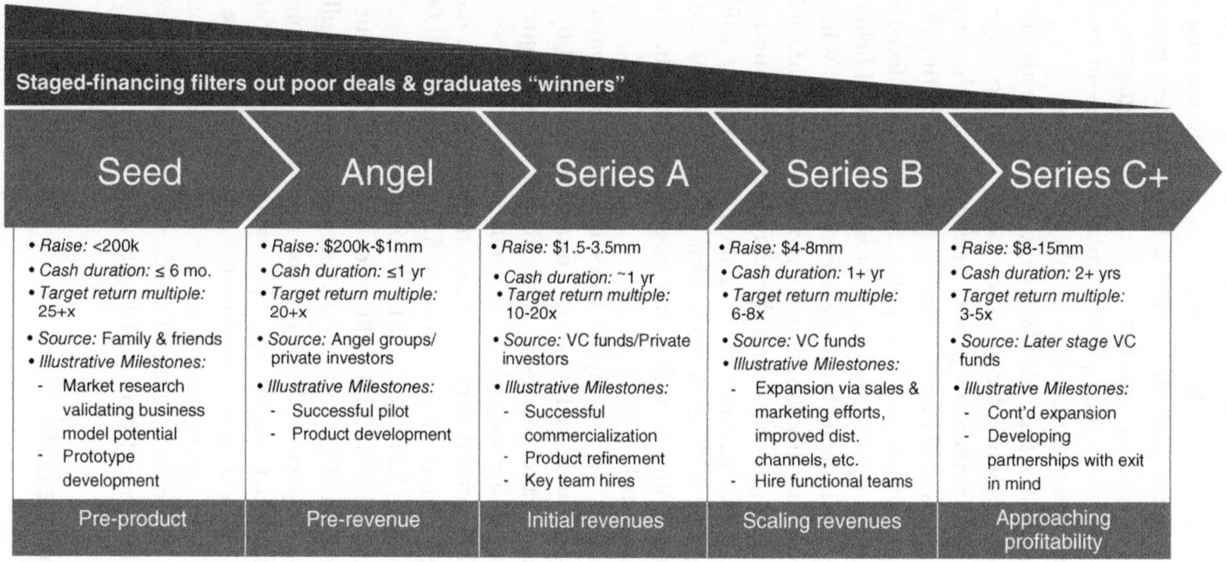

Staged-financing filters out poor deals & graduates "winners"

	Seed	Angel	Series A	Series B	Series C+

	• *Raise: <200k*
	• *Cash duration: ≤ 6 mo.*
	• *Target return multiple: 25+x*
	• *Source: Family & friends*
	• *Illustrative Milestones:*
	  - Market research validating business model potential
	  - Prototype development
		• *Raise: $200k-$1mm*
		• *Cash duration: ≤1 yr*
		• *Target return multiple: 20+x*
		• *Source: Angel groups/ private investors*
		• *Illustrative Milestones:*
		  - Successful pilot
		  - Product development
			• *Raise: $1.5-3.5mm*
			• *Cash duration: ~1 yr*
			• *Target return multiple: 10-20x*
			• *Source: VC funds/Private investors*
			• *Illustrative Milestones:*
			  - Successful commercialization
			  - Product refinement
			  - Key team hires
				• *Raise: $4-8mm*
				• *Cash duration: 1+ yr*
				• *Target return multiple: 6-8x*
				• *Source: VC funds*
				• *Illustrative Milestones:*
				  - Expansion via sales & marketing efforts, improved dist. channels, etc.
				  - Hire functional teams
					• *Raise: $8-15mm*
					• *Cash duration: 2+ yrs*
					• *Target return multiple: 3-5x*
					• *Source: Later stage VC funds*
					• *Illustrative Milestones:*
					  - Cont'd expansion
					  - Developing partnerships with exit in mind

	Pre-product	Pre-revenue	Initial revenues	Scaling revenues	Approaching profitability

in practice, it is worth noting that seed, angel, and later-stage capital usually differ in formality of structure, amount of funds raised, and risk involved.

Seed funding is a capital raise for very early stage—often pre-launch—businesses. The investment is meant to pay for preliminary operations such as initial market research and product development that position the company for a more formal capital raise soon thereafter, assuming results are favorable. Sources of seed capital typically include founders themselves, friends and family, and incubator/accelerator programs that invest for an initial equity stake. Seed capital involves significantly higher risk since investors make their decision whether to fund a project *entirely* based on the perceived strength of the business idea, and the capabilities, skills, and history of the founders. Rather than spending the effort to negotiate a valuation and the corresponding ownership stake, these deals are often structured as convertible loans that provide the right to convert into equity in the next financing round at a stipulated discount—typically between 10 and 25 percent.[8] The discount is intended to compensate these earlier supporters for the greater risk incurred relative to future incoming investors. Considering this period presents the highest level of risk for a startup and later-stage institutional rounds typically increase in value 50+ percent for each subsequent fundraise, this is generally a poor risk-adjusted return relative to waiting to invest at a later period.

While not universal, most successful ventures raise additional intermediate funding from "angels" (accredited investors) that enable them to gain sufficient operational traction to garner the attention of formal venture capital funds. Typically this capital is used for further product development and initial operating expenses, though significant questions about the viability of the business model often remain. By this point, investments are almost always structured as preferred stock, and typically mandate a preferred return (expressed either in terms of accrued interest or as a multiple of the original investment—e.g., 1.5✕), which must be achieved before the common shares can participate.

Later-stage investments typically are dominated by institutionalized venture capital funds. These discretionary funds typically manage a minimum of $100 million assets under management, which they allocate across a portfolio of approximately 20 ventures.[9] Note this does not mean each company is allocated the $5 million average. The vast majority will only receive $1 million or less before the "plug is pulled," enabling money to be reallocated to double down on the successful startups as they achieve their milestones.[10] Cumulatively, these "winners" may receive over $10 million in capital allocations. Over the past decade, venture capital funds have systematically moved toward larger, later-stage deals, because of the perceived superior risk-return tradeoff.

Additionally, the larger deal sizes can better accommodate their fee structures, including the significant overhead of professional staff.

Characteristics of Venture Capital Investments

As shown in Figure 4.6, venture capital investments are concentrated among patent-dependent technology sectors (such as biotech, computer technology, etc.) and consumer Internet firms.[11] The reason for this is these industries generally share a common set of underlying characteristics, which are well suited for the targeted return profile. *Ideal venture capital investments occur in businesses with the potential to achieve most or all of the following characteristics: (1) significant market size, (2) fast growth, (3) defensible market position, (4) high gross margins, and (5) low capital intensity.*

As a general rule of thumb, professional venture capitalists limit their consideration to markets that have the potential of reaching a minimum of $200 million in annual revenues. Given the reality that captured market share will rarely exceed 50 percent, this size is necessary to yield the outsized investment returns sought by the category.

FIGURE 4.6 Venture Capital Industry Mix, by Number of Deals

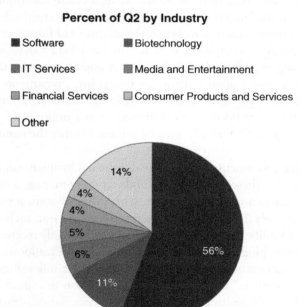

Percent of Q2 by Industry

■ Software   ■ Biotechnology

■ IT Services   ▨ Media and Entertainment

▨ Financial Services   ▨ Consumer Products and Services

▨ Other

Additionally, growth is paramount to justify the lofty acquisition prices that these ventures receive upon sale. Given the exorbitant cost of winning in a fierce marketplace (i.e., product discounting, sales and marketing expenses, etc.), anticipated growth should be driven from growth of the overall market rather than stealing market share from current incumbents. As opposed to traditional small businesses, intellectual property-based startups are rarely constrained by geographic barriers, and therefore can experience explosive yet cost-effective growth, accessing broader national and international markets.

Having market power also enables a firm to sustainably defend its position from new entrants and other competition. This strength can derive either from structural barriers, such as patents, or from brand loyalty to a differentiated product. Although often overrated, first-mover advantages can sometimes handicap later competitors, particularly if the market benefits from network effects or has a tendency toward standardization.

Moreover, the potential for high gross margins is important to substantiate such significant valuations. As a general rule, good investment candidates exhibit margins over 70 percent. Some products, such as software, have margins approaching 100 percent, as there is little to no incremental cost to producing additional items, once initially developed.

Similarly, low capital intensity enables the scalability that allows significant growth without a corresponding increase in capital invested. In order to minimize the amount of committed capital, companies should have positive working capital cycles (typically achieved via little to no inventory), require minimal headcount, and remain "asset light," preferring leasing over ownership of property or equipment. While this asset-light strategy does preclude obtaining bank financing and leaves little salvage value if the venture fails, it helps facilitate the high return on equity targeted by venture capital investments.

Core Investor Skillset

Family office investors investing in venture capital should be directly adding value to their portfolio companies by assisting them to reach their growth potential. These efforts typically include introducing companies to new customers and partners, helping them recruit world-class engineering, technical, and managerial talent, and coaching them on how to expand and professionalize various corporate functions (e.g., marketing, sales, HR, legal). Interestingly, we observe a skills paradox here. While venture capital is a financial activity, successful investors in this space are characterized by a solid set of soft skills that are grounded in qualitative directional improvements, rather than precise financial engineering. Taking the opposite angle on this issue, the causes of poor performance in new ventures are widely attributed to deficiencies in human capital, often taking the form of ineffective senior management. *In sum, while having the right management team will not guarantee success in venture capital, the wrong one will almost undoubtedly preclude it.*

One important related factor to consider is management's alignment with an investor's exit objectives. While management's goal is generally to maximize the value of the company via an eventual exit, differences in expectations often occur. Any indication that the founder will irrationally hold out (because of emotional attachment or unreasonable valuation expectations) is a cause for concern given the investor's minority position. Thus, investors are well served by a collaborative deal-making process that ensures all parties are on the same page. While forced-sale clauses and other legal protections can be helpful tools to avoid intractable conflicts, ultimately founder teams are expected to remain post-acquisition and, thus, their being onboard is typically a prerequisite for a successful exit. Consequently, nothing can replicate an aligned founder: Failing to address doubts up front will only lead to headaches down the road.

Core Risk Management Practices

Venture capital is almost always hit-or-miss and, like baseball, you miss more often that you hit. Aside from a plethora of legal protections negotiated within specific deals, three key lines of defense help to mitigate this high-risk profile: (1) staged financing, (2) portfolio diversification, and (3) conservative valuations.

Investors use *staged financing* for three primary reasons. First, it provides option value, minimizing losses in the event the business fails. Second, it motivates management to remain lean and to use capital efficiently. Finally, given the negative cash flow of startups, staging helps strengthen the hand of investors, ensuring founders remain responsive to their views.

While management can implicitly pursue alternative investors for their future capital needs, this is a lengthy and uncertain process. Obtaining additional capital from current investors is almost always faster and easier than having to raise funds from new outside sources. While a completely motivated new investor generally takes between 30 to 60 days to complete due diligence and legal formalities, a far greater amount of time is typically necessary to pique interest beforehand. Because of these dynamics, startups often err on the side of fundraising early (usually 6 to 9 months in advance of running out of cash) to ensure that they have alternatives if a current investor chooses not to participate.

The second line of defense in managing startup risk involves investing across a *well-diversified portfolio*. As a rule of thumb, 60 to 70 percent of venture capital investments are expected to fail, likely resulting in a total loss since little underlying salvage value exists, 20 percent are expected to roughly breakeven, and 10 to 20 percent are expected to hit it out of the park. Financial returns are predicated upon the outsized returns from these few homeruns more than compensating for all of the other losses. The ability to accurately predict beforehand which investments will be high-performing versus weak is nearly impossible, even among the most successful professionals. As a result, venture capital is a volume game—in order to increase the likelihood that an investor has committed to a few winners, they must deploy enough investments.

The prior risk management strategies, while critical, would be all for naught if investors buy in at the wrong price. As a result, the third and most important line of defense is *buying at a sufficiently low price* to provide a cushion against underperformance. Since startups generate losses over the near-term, their valuations cannot be based upon traditional discounted cash flow techniques. Furthermore, there is rarely fundamental salvage value that can anchor a startup's worth. Instead, returns rely almost entirely on an enterprise's exit potential. This stands in contrast from other forms of private equity, like growth capital and buyouts, in which returns derive from both capital appreciation and operating profits.

While heavily dependent upon market cycles, every industry has its own relevant industry benchmarks, which drive the exit potential of a firm (e.g., price per unique monthly viewer, subscriber, patient, etc.). As a result, strategic emphasis is often placed on maximizing these affiliated metrics, even if it comes at the expense of interim profitability. Given publicly available information, there is often a surprising consensus among experienced investors regarding the potential value of a company if it achieves its goals. Yet estimating potential exit value is more art than science, since it fundamentally is driven by assessing the realistic likelihood of management achieving its stated targets. Even with the best of intentions, there is a clear tendency to underestimate the likelihood of setbacks and the ferociousness of competition. One useful tactic is to cross-reference sales projections against verifiable reference points, such as estimated market share, or to compare expected growth relative to analogous industries (e.g., this consumer electronics venture is assuming customer adoption faster than the iPod, etc.). The latter tactic is particularly valuable when assessing ventures creating new products where no market previously existed. Accounting for all of these factors, an investor must develop his or her own perspective regarding a plausible exit value.

Given the sky-high prices paid for startups with little to no profit, many family office investors view them as a speculative house of cards. Nevertheless, incumbents can often achieve profitability when plugging these products and services into their preexisting infrastructures (given both their superior economies of scale and widespread sales and distribution networks). Moreover, many purchases are viewed as strategically valuable to the buyer for more than their future expected cash flows. Facebook's high-profile purchase of Instagram for $1 billion seems irrational if based purely on the numbers, since the startup did not even have revenues. However, many industry experts have speculated that the move was done to preempt the actions of future competitors and to signal to the market its commitment to winning in the vital mobile space.

As stated before, even high-performing venture capital funds derive nearly all of their returns from just 10 to 20 percent of their portfolio investments. Accounting for fees and the average six-year lifespan of most venture capital investments, an early-stage fund would need to return to investors 5 to 6 times their initial capital in order to achieve its aggregate IRR goal of at least 25 percent. Because of the inherently high rate of failure, an investor therefore needs to target a return multiple of 10 to 20 times (equivalent to an approximately 50 percent IRR hurdle rate over the average deal lifespan) for any particular deal. As shown in Figure 4.7,[12] early-stage deals need relatively higher multiples to compensate them for the greater risks incurred as well as to provide a buffer against the inevitable dilution from future financing rounds.

Given the estimated potential exit value, investors then work backward from their target return multiples to calculate an entry price (by dividing potential exit value by this target multiple). The calculated output is a "post-money" valuation, which determines the amount of equity received for a given capital contribution.[13] Because of the high hurdle rates and extended timeframes, demand for precision in estimating exit valuations is relatively unimportant, particularly in the earliest stages when expected multiples are highest. Being directionally correct is sufficient, as there is little difference between benchmarking against an eventual exit of $175 million or $200 million. For such an enterprise, an investor seeking a target return multiple of 20× for a $1 million investment corresponds to receiving 11 versus 10 percent equity in the company, respectively.[14] Ultimately, the agreed-upon

FIGURE 4.7 Relative Valuations Based on Expected Multiples

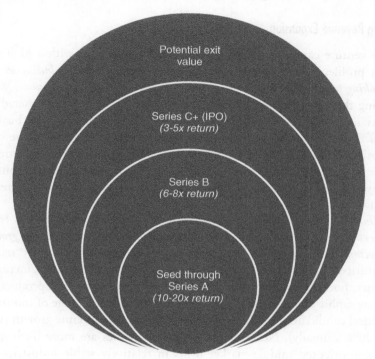

price and terms are highly dependent upon negotiating leverage, market factors, and the perceived urgency (desperation) for funding.

Given the magnitude of resources needed to run a venture capital portfolio with a high degree of success, many family offices choose to gain exposure to the category through fund structures. One alternative to retain control and still be exposed to a roughly similar risk-return profile would be to pursue an angel strategy, investing smaller amounts across a high number of startups.[15] Nevertheless, when accounting for the opportunity cost of their time, many investors decide this approach is not justified. Most families achieve subpar risk-adjusted returns in their venture capital investments (many happy to just break even). Families seem to like the venture capital asset class because of the relatively small check sizes, the prospect of potentially hitting it big with an exciting new venture, and the ability to engage younger generations, who tend to have a lot of interest in startups and have grown up with technology.

Growth Capital

Funding Revenue Expansion

While venture capital is geared toward investing in firms with a high risk-return profile, *growth capital seeks already proven, profitable businesses that are looking to scale operations, either organically or through acquisitions.* When reaching this stage in their lifecycle, companies should have eliminated any doubts regarding the viability of their underlying technology or business model. Instead, investors are fundamentally assuming the risk of the value proposition's scalability and management's ability to execute. The primary goal is no longer to fund new product development and refinement, but the expansion of distribution and marketing resources to achieve broad market penetration.

Though running lean and efficiently is also important, the greatest return on investment in growth capital is typically achieved by emphasizing growing the bottom-line through top-line revenue growth. Because of their relative immaturity, growth capital targets have significant headroom for increasing revenues, both through market share gains and expansion into product line and geographic adjacencies. Investments can span a wide range of industries, with ideal candidates experiencing faster-than-average revenue growth (more than 20% annually). Nevertheless, target companies are more likely to be execution-oriented middle-market firms in relatively stable industries that observe linear success patterns.

Size, Returns, and Duration

Growth capital investments are often larger than venture capital infusions, ranging from $5 to $100 million in equity commitments. Capital concentrations are higher in this space, with funds targeting only 8 to 12 deals at a time, because of the larger deal sizes and lower need to diversify relative to venture capital. Levered target hurdle rates remain high, however, at approximately 30 percent, with unlevered returns generally ranging between 17 and 20 percent. Given the sounder operating fundamentals of this category, a growth capital investment can sometimes yield strong returns on a cash flow basis alone. Yet, the finite lifespan of private equity funds mandates an exit, which occurs either through an IPO or sale.

A successful growth capital cycle typically lasts 3 to 6 years, and with few exceptions, capital is disbursed in full upfront. Growth capital strategies are not characterized by a phased-financing approach since investors typically have majority control and, thus, there is no further influence they can gain by rationing funds. If majority control is untenable, investors generally negotiate control-like protections into the shareholder's agreement, such as "forced sale" clauses.

Growth Capital's Catch-22

The strategy of growth capital is to court already successful, cash flow–positive firms and take them to the next level. However, a catch-22 exists, since the best investments are typically into companies that are not seeking outside capital. Current owners often grow complacent with their company and its trajectory, particularly if performance is already strong. Moreover, given the positive cash flow nature, they retain the option to self-finance growth. Consequently, it is not uncommon for investors to have to woo compelling opportunities for months or even years before successfully closing. Investors should be wary of target companies that seem too eager to receive a capital injection, as this may signal deeper structural issues regarding the quality of their earnings. Ultimately, many current owners turn to growth capital as a means to "take some money off the table" by selling a portion of their shares while still maintaining exposure to further upside.

Valuation Implications

Valuations are determined by traditional techniques such as discounting future projected cash flows or using comparable transaction multiples applied to historical earnings (i.e., EBITDA). Given the lower margin of error inherent in the higher initial valuations and the risk of hidden preexisting liabilities, growth capital investors must be more conservative than venture capitalists from a risk tolerance standpoint. Consequently, skill in due diligence and legal structuring tends to be relatively more important.

From a structural standpoint, growth capital can be viewed as a hybrid between venture capital and buyouts, since it typically combines injecting additional capital into the company to fuel growth while simultaneously "buying out" a portion of management's shares. This mix of capital use has an implication when computing the company's post-money valuation and ultimately the associated ownership percentages. Figure 4.8 illustrates three different permutations of how $10 million could be deployed into a company currently valued at $10 million.

FIGURE 4.8 $10mm Infusion by Private Equity Strategy

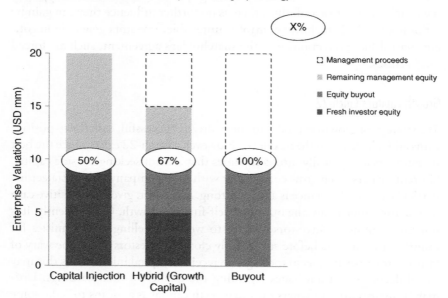

Unlike venture capital, where you start with a determined post-money valuation (computed based upon ownership percentage received in exchange for capital) and work backward to determine the corresponding pre-money valuation, here we do the opposite. Growth capital assesses the value of the company on a standalone basis (what it would have been worth without the capital infusion) and then adds the capital contributed into the company to determine post-money valuation.

When negotiating the terms of this hybrid transaction, it is important for investors to be collaborative in their deal-making approach. Unlike buyouts, where investors are incentivized to negotiate in a more transactional manner with outgoing owners (i.e., "squeezing every last penny"), in growth capital, you will need to maintain an ongoing working relationship with your counterpart. Thus, in the interest of maintaining a solid partnership, investors should go out of their way to demonstrate a willingness to seek a fair and balanced outcome from the onset. Growth capital investments present an excellent opportunity for family offices to exhibit their unique comparative advantage relative to large, institutional private equity funds. Business owners often view families as friendlier and more relationship-oriented partners. Moreover, families can provide long-term patient capital that is willing to fund future needs long after traditional funds would have chosen to exit.

Growth Skillset

Value add in growth capital generally derives from two reinforcing sources. First, earnings are boosted via aggressively growing revenues and improving operations. Second, the market tends to apply higher multiples to firms whose earnings exceed certain thresholds, otherwise known as "multiples expansion." For example, a company with $5 million in annual earnings may have been purchased for $25 million (5× multiple), and is eventually sold for $70 million after reaching $10 million in earnings (7× multiple). Part of this phenomenon is explained by professionalization of a company's processes, reporting, and controls (remember, many of these companies were initially run as informal family firms), which eases the burden of integration into a strategic buyer's corporate infrastructure.

This growth is achieved either through acquisitions where adjacent companies are bolted on or through the strategic pursuit of organic growth. *A solid corporate development skillset is extremely valuable.* While the former approach is best suited for former investment bankers or individuals with significant deal-making experience, the latter is best achieved by former strategy consultants or operators with marketing experience. Intimately understanding the industry landscape and end-customers' evolving needs is vital to discerning and capturing future geographic and product line expansion opportunities.

Buyouts

Buyouts represent most people's conception of private equity, as portrayed in bestselling books like *Barbarians at the Gate*, among others. In such deals, investors acquire controlling stakes of mature, cash flow–stable companies financed with debt, resulting in modest to moderate risk profiles. Negotiations are typically less collaborative and more transactional in nature than in venture or growth capital, as the seller typically cashes out completely, and if they remain, retains only a minority interest (i.e., less than a 20% equity stake). The equity contribution of the buyer, usually a single or consortium of private equity firms, typically ranges from $20 million to $2 billion and targets a levered return of over 25 percent. (This corresponds to an unlevered return between approximately 13 and 17%.) Given the sheer size of these deals and operational intensity required to manage them, funds generally deploy 5 to 10 buyout investments, leaving little margin for error. While buyout investments are often profitable, nearly all operating cash flows are dedicated to servicing the sizeable debt load taken on to purchase the company, as further described ahead. Financial returns are, therefore, achieved upon a successful exit, usually 3 to 6 years after the investment, via an IPO or sale to a strategic buyer.

Demystifying Buyouts

Targets for buyouts can be either private or public companies. While mega-buyouts of public companies receive most of the press headlines, these deals are rare since only a few funds (e.g., KKR) can execute them and, even then, public takeovers do not present the majority of their deal flow. In fact, Bain & Company reports that less than 5 percent of private equity funds are large enough to acquire billion-dollar companies. Instead, *the more common source of buyouts is smaller private companies* with the archetypical example being a firm selling out as a result of a generational transition in leadership. Usually, in this context, firm ownership is spread across heirs who are not capable or willing to assume the business and, thus, want to sell. Here, as in other forms of private equity, buyouts add value through increased alignment between managerial and shareholder interests. This is achieved by replacing passive family members/shareholders with a smaller group of new equity investors who have a greater motivation to monitor management performance. In addition to receiving equity or other similar financial incentives, top executives are strongly encouraged (if not required) to commit a significant portion of their net worth to the business.

Additional primary value sources in buyouts include use of financial leverage, as well as operational improvements, predominantly cost cutting. Each of these strategies and their corresponding skillsets are described in turn.

Leverage: Double-Edged Sword

Buyouts are often referred to as "leveraged buyouts" because they are typically levered 50 to 80 percent in order to minimize the amount of needed equity, boosting returns on investment. The exact amount of leverage taken on is determined by industry norms and deal-specific conditions such as the volatility of the company's earnings and quality of the underlying collateral (historically, total debt levels have averaged between 4 and 6 times the firm's EBITDA). All other things equal, the more stable the industry and company cash flows, the greater access to leverage investors have. Typically leveraged buyouts incorporate a variety of lenders. Secured lenders are collateralized against the hard assets of the company and a working capital pledge of its accounts receivable and, thus, receive a low interest rate. Unsecured lenders, such as mezzanine investors and revolving credit facilities, are not protected with collateral, are subordinate to secured debts, and typically offer a fixed interest rate. As a result, they are compensated with a higher interest rate. Many times these subordinate loans are financed by the seller himself as a substitute for a portion of the purchase price. Overall, these debts are generally nonrecourse to the financial sponsor or any of their other portfolio investments.

A leveraged buyout devoid of any operational improvements affects the liabilities and equity of a company's balance sheet, not the assets. A buyout simply rearranges the ownership structure, replacing most of the equity with a cheaper cost of capital and redirecting the savings to the remaining shareholders. In this context, value is not created, but instead transferred. In reality, increased leverage can also improve earnings generated through two main channels. First, the firm's taxes are reduced because of the increase in deductible interest payments, so greater operating income flows through to investors. Second, the continued pressure to service debt forces managers to operate as leanly as possible—a highly levered firm cannot afford any fat.

Despite its potential benefits, leverage is, nevertheless, a double-edged sword that can also amplify downside risks. Increased leverage can quickly lead to company instability should operating profitability decline. In this context, interest payments will eat away at earnings and, in the extreme case, result in losses just when there is little equity cushion available to absorb them, thus accelerating firm failure. Rising interest rates can cause similar havoc, in addition to reducing a firm's capacity to absorb and roll over debt. Moreover, it places downward price pressure on exits since future buyers will have to finance at higher rates. Unless performance is improved, success in leveraged buyouts is predicated on an environment of low or declining interest rates.

Leverage: Skill Implications

It is important to note that drastically increasing a company's leverage requires investors to have robust financial capabilities. Within the portfolio companies, a strong CFO must be in place to tightly manage finances and to manage the various lenders. In particular, they should be adept in navigating the company's finances without breaching covenants, and, in the event one is broken, skillfully renegotiating terms or seeking alternative financing. Solid financial modeling skills are vital to accurately projecting returns and valuation. While valuing a potential buyout candidate is theoretically straightforward on an unlevered basis, as it is based on traditional cash flow modeling and historical numbers, the addition of leverage requires intense analytics. Specifically, buyouts include various debt schedules, including some that revolve, meaning they are not tied to a fixed number of payments or payment amount, but rather assumed operational needs.

Operational Improvements and Value Creation

The days of using leverage to exclusively drive returns for buyouts are increasingly in the past, as financial engineering, once a black art, is now widely practiced. Increased competition for target companies with low debt profiles has narrowed the field for "easy" returns. *Thus, yields from buyouts are also increasingly stemming from profitability improvements.* While external consulting firms are sometimes used to recommend these improvements, private equity firms are increasingly building these capabilities internally.

Mature companies targeted by leveraged buyouts are typically prime candidates for cost-cutting initiatives. These are often the immediate routes to enhancing profitability. Focus is usually on limiting unnecessary capital expenditures and streamlining excess working and human capital needs that stem from inefficiencies neglected in the previous growth ramp-up. Usually this includes the implementation of measurement-based strategies like Six Sigma that focus on process improvement and reduction in cost volatility. Cost-cutting should be deliberately planned since long-term impairments to the financial potential of the firm will result in discounted valuations by future acquirers—as the saying goes, "You shouldn't cut your nose to spite your face."

Finally, buyouts supplement these efforts with efforts to expand sales, through many of the same tactics used in growth capital. Given the maturity of buyout targets, this typically involves the introduction of new products and entry into new geographies rather than share growth in existing markets. Because of the scale of revenue needed to materially boost profitability, these objectives are often met through acquisitions or strategic partnerships with existing businesses. As a result, leveraged buyout investors should also possess a solid corporate development skillset that can draw on successful experiences in targeting and integrating M&A candidates and joint venture partners.

Mezzanine Financing

Investors can also choose to invest in similar companies targeted by growth capital and buyouts, with a lower risk-return profile through mezzanine investments. Mezzanine capital describes a variety of debt instruments sitting between equity and secured debt (i.e., it can take many different technical manifestations). Typically it's structured as a fixed-term loan[16] (typically 5 to 8 years in length) that binds the company to regular payments and features a small grant of warrants, commonly called an "equity kicker." The kicker typically represents less than 5 percent of the shares outstanding and can be exercised by the lender if the investment turns out to be attractive. As a result, it provides a small amount of additional upside potential in addition to the contractual loan payments, akin to the proverbial "cherry on top."

Size, Returns, and Terms

Given its requirement to meet regular payments, mezzanine capital is clearly intended for companies well past the startup phase with stable histories of strong cash flows. Mezzanine loans typically range from $5 to $500 million, financing not more than 20 to 30 percent of a company's total value. Terms are usually more flexible than traditional bank financing—specifically, mezzanine lenders have a greater tolerance for higher leverage ratios. Interest rates charged vary between 12 and 15 percent. While interest can be payable on a straight cash basis, it can also just accrue (called *payment in kind*—PIK) or be a mixture of the two. In total, returns average 15 to 20 percent when including the value of the kicker. Given the safer risk profile of these debt-like cash flows, the returns of mezzanine are naturally lower than their equity fund counterparts.

Attractive Alternative for Owners

Typically mezzanine loan capital is a form of supplemental financing that businesses turn to because cheaper senior debt options have been exhausted—it is rarely used in isolation unless the company has few tangible assets to encumber. In fact, businesses often pursue mezzanine capital in an effort to secure senior loans on more favorable terms, since banks typically view access to mezzanine capital as a validation of the company's sophistication and soundness.

Mezzanine capital is an attractive source of capital for owners who want to accomplish a strategic goal such as an acquisition or expansion while minimizing equity dilution. Moreover, many owners utilize these loans as a preferred alternative to a partial buyout since they can still maintain ownership while taking some money off the table through a recapitalization.

Capital Stack Implications

Within the capital structure hierarchy, mezzanine financing is subordinate to most other forms of debt, but has priority over equity (see Figure 4.9). Being sandwiched in the middle of the capital stack is laden with its own unique set

FIGURE 4.9   Typical Capital Stack

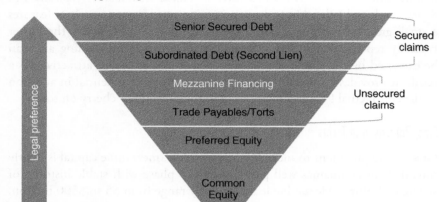

of risks. Should the company fail, more senior debt claims will be paid first, leaving the mezzanine lender exposed to the risk of being partially or wholly wiped out, if there is insufficient company value to cover claims. While mezzanine investors attempt to restrict their lending to firms with sufficient salvage value, it is far more valuable to select high-performing companies that have a low probability of getting into trouble in the first place. As long as the underlying firm is solvent, lenders are typically restricted from having any hands-on operational involvement. Nevertheless, negative covenants are typically put into place requiring affirmative lender approval before any significant changes are made or if the company is further encumbered. To further protect themselves, debt coverage ratios ratchet up influence should financial performance start to deteriorate.

In the worst-case scenario, should the company enter into bankruptcy or restructure, mezzanine lenders typically have the right to assume ownership. In such cases, they will generally seek to minimize losses by either working out the loan or quickly selling the company to a financial buyer that specializes in turning around distressed firms, a separate private equity strategy discussed later in this chapter. Ultimately, mezzanine investors are typically not operators and therefore prefer not to take control of operating businesses.

Transactional Skillset

Given the more arm's-length nature of mezzanine lending, the required skillsets are more skewed toward underwriting and valuation capabilities. Specifically, mezzanine lenders must be adept at sourcing high-quality borrowers with solid historical cash flows and sober expansion plans. In general, mezzanine lenders typically prefer situations with few preexisting debt holders, but this consideration may be attenuated if a company's value is sufficiently attractive.

Most due diligence comes prepackaged—already researched and digested by equity investors with a subordinated claim. Consequently, less emphasis is placed on researching strategic questions and more on modeling the sensitivity of returns to various financial, operational, and macroeconomic shocks. Additionally, significant effort is expended on legal due diligence to validate the status of the company's assets and any corresponding encumbrances.

Ongoing monitoring tends to remain relatively passive until any covenants are at risk of being breached, signaling a jeopardized economic position. Mezzanine lenders usually receive the same monthly financials and management reports provided to the board. While they sometimes assume a Board Observer role, they typically are satisfied piggybacking off the vigilance of lead investors. At a minimum, they should be meeting with executives once a year to check in.

Distressed Assets

Turnaround Culture

Distressed private equity is a strategy that profits from opportunistically buying and improving neglected businesses. It involves purchasing debt claims—nearly always at a discount—on a company that is cash flow negative and careening toward default in order to gain ownership, turn the company around, and sell it. Ideally, the source of distress derives from addressable internal problems (e.g., overleveraged balance sheet, cost overruns, etc.) rather than external factors, such as an obsolete business model. Often, these firms have strong fundamentals, but are in mature industries that are ripe for consolidation (e.g., manufacturing). All other things equal, companies with "encumberable" fixed assets are preferable to service firms highly reliant upon intangible assets (e.g., human capital).

Troubled companies are also especially in need of strong, reliable leadership, as they are characterized by a broken culture of widespread distrust that motivates stakeholders to curtail their exposure to the firm, destroying company value. For example, employees may be planning departures for more certain opportunities; customers may be reluctant to buy over concerns of honoring warranty claims; or suppliers may deny credit and require cash on delivery. At this point, operating the company as a going concern will require the balance sheet to be restructured through forgiveness of debt or conversion into equity.

Taking the Long View

Distressed private equity stands in contrast to hedge funds that intend to quickly flip undervalued claims for a profit. *Private equity takes a longer view, seeking to actually take possession and operate the business as equity holders.* Value is created by successfully addressing structural issues and returning the firm to profitability. Eventually, an exit via acquisition or IPO can be orchestrated.

Like leveraged buyouts, there is little room for error in distressed private equity. Investments typically range from $10 million to $1 billion, limiting funds to no more than 5 to 8 deals at a time, and command hurdle rates of 25 to 30 percent due to the level of uncertainty involved. From purchase of initial interests to exit, distressed deals typically last 3 to 7 years[17] and require investors to have both strong transactional and operational capabilities. Each skillset is described in turn within the context of the overall strategy.

Capital Stack Strategy

Success in distressed private equity is contingent on securing a valid creditor claim that eventually leads to ownership. This is a strategically intense process and this section is limited to only a top-level overview of it; a fuller treatment of distressed debt analysis can be found in books solely devoted to this topic.[18] That said, the first step when considering an investment in a distressed company is to inventory its assets and liabilities in order to determine which claims should be purchased. Since most companies have an array of formal and informal creditors, investors should rank all liabilities according to their legal priority compared against a conservative valuation. *The goal is to purchase at a discount a "fulcrum security," which is a claim that is marginally in the money.* Since full satisfaction of the amount outstanding cannot be guaranteed, the claimant will be granted ownership over the company. Buying into the right layer of the capital stack (see Figure 4.10), however, does not necessarily guarantee a successful takeover. Until a final court resolution or agreement to the contrary, current shareholders retain the option to extinguish debt by paying off the outstanding claims (both principal and accrued interest). This of course is an attractive consolation, as you receive full payment for claims that were recently purchased at a steep discount.

In general, available assets should be easy to inventory when examining a company's books; determining liabilities, however, is not as straightforward.

FIGURE 4.10 Illustrative Targeting of Distressed Debt Investment

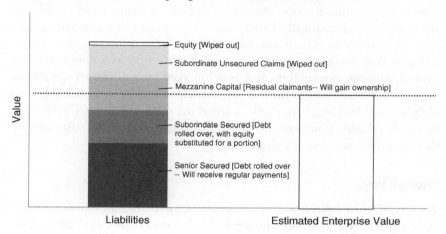

Given the poor reporting and controls often found in distressed firms, there exists a wide variety of potentially unknown creditors. Aside from accounts payable to a dispersed array of smaller service providers and vendors, which may have not been recorded properly, executives may have accepted or guaranteed unauthorized liabilities, which only become known after the fact. Moreover, future, unknown tort and product liability victims (e.g., asbestos) are also considered unsecured creditors. Courts typically create a reserve, which future victims can sue to access.

Existing creditors often have differing skillsets and interests. Very few are in the business of successfully navigating the uncertainty of a restructuring and ultimately operating a company. Most are satisfied with minimizing their losses and quickly returning back to business as usual. Consequently, this provides new investors with the opportunity to purchase claims at a significant discount relative to their "true value." Once a liability is selected and negotiated, investors must be capable of conducting a proper due diligence that verifies that the claim is valid and acknowledged by the debtor. For example, if an outstanding account receivable is purchased from "Joe the Plumber," you must be able to back up that the work was actually conducted and never paid for.

Valuation Implications

In order to maximize value, a company's future cash-flow-generating capability should be compared against the alternative of liquidation. If the assets have little prospect of generating profits, even on an unlevered basis, the conclusion may be that the firm should be sold off. Assessments of liquidation value can vary dramatically based upon the assumed sale conditions (i.e., "fire sale" versus an orderly process). Since cash flows are negative, historical cash flow modeling is irrelevant to valuing a firm as a going concern. Instead, earnings potential is often benchmarked (at a discount) against the value of similar, healthy firms that are unencumbered by unsustainable debt obligations. Moreover, historically accrued net operating losses (NOLs) can be highly valuable from a tax perspective to potential acquirers, who can use them to offset their own earnings.

Keeping It Simple

The ideal distressed deal is one that is complicated with the least number of material claimants. In this context, investors face less uncertainty as to which layer of the firm's capital stack they should buy into. Moreover, a voluntary restructuring is more likely since there are fewer participants that have to be collectively persuaded to accept an offer. If no agreement can be achieved between all parties voluntarily, a formal bankruptcy will be necessary. This can be a drawn out and expensive process, often taking years and burning through up to 5 to 10 percent of the firm's value through attorney's and other professional fees. However, one important advantage is that bankruptcy is the only mechanism to extinguish all liabilities, certifying the assets as unencumbered, which is valuable for firms that are suspected to have latent environmental or product liability risk. Regardless of the approach used to reorganize the firm, most creditors will accept the substitution of some equity consideration for their claims, rather than fully rolling over their loans onto the restructured entity, in order to enable a more sustainable (i.e., less leveraged) capital structure.

Typically, the most straightforward deal structure is akin to the "cash for keys" offerings recently made popular in the midst of the foreclosure crisis. Here an investor agrees to buy out the lender's claim (e.g., mortgage) at a discount and incents the distressed owner to voluntarily transfer ownership with a nominal payment, in order to avoid a formal bankruptcy proceeding. As a result, an investor's negotiating position should demonstrate a collaborative willingness to make the best of a sour situation.

Debt restructurings that involve multiple material creditors can be an especially complex process that risks devolving into a zero-sum game characterized by aggressive, transactional deal making. Typically, claimants at the top of the capital stack are incentivized to underestimate a company's valuation so they can push out other claimants and seize ownership of the company.

Alternatively, claimants at the bottom of the stack are incentivized to exaggerate the company's valuation so they can at least receive a partial recovery. Here again, a willingness to creatively sweeten the proverbial pot can help negotiations reach a mutually beneficial solution.

Finishing the Job

Wrestling ownership is only half the battle in distressed private equity. Recall that the real value is added in returning the company to profitability; thus, success in this space is also contingent on investors being savvy business operators. Turning a company around often requires significant cost cutting and refocusing the business strategically. Typically, this involves reducing excess capacity through consolidation or execution of an industry rollup strategy. Additionally, success is frequently dependent upon changing the business's underlying culture, which is usually characterized by low morale and insufficient skills because of an ongoing brain drain. The firm's best people systematically choose to leave for better opportunities, leaving behind the lower performers, who have fewer options. In this context, a distressed private equity investor is taxed with the double duty of being capable of resurrecting a lean company while recruiting and inspiring qualified human capital.

Conclusion: Putting It All Together

Family offices are increasingly investing directly and providing business owners with a better, more personalized capital solution. Rather than trying to compete head on with large institutional funds, they should capitalize upon their unique advantages, such as having a longer time horizon, the ability to provide more flexible terms, and their greater focus on values and relationships.

This chapter covered the wide spectrum of private equity options accessible and available to sophisticated investors and family offices. The prevalence, characteristics, and implications of these strategies are summarized in Appendix A found at the back of the book.

As we have observed, risk-return profiles generally decrease along the business lifecycle continuum—with the notable exception of distressed assets that more closely resemble startup financing given the uncertainty involved. As risks decline, investments sizes typically increase, a trend that is reinforced by greater access to leverage. Returns, and in particular growth from organic operations, often plateau, however, when businesses mature. Such contexts underscore the importance of key skillsets to create and sustain value, such as buying in at opportunistic valuations, generating efficiency gains, and broadening corporate development plans, among others highlighted. This is particularly important to family office investors because ensuring fit and harmony is often just as important as achieving stellar financial returns.

It is valuable to have a general understanding of the typical features of each major private equity category and their requisite skills to determine not only how much to invest, if at all, but also how to deploy that investment. It may be that reading this chapter has reaffirmed your desire to gain exposure to buyouts as well as venture capital, but helped you realize that your internal investment team is well positioned to only lead the latter. In that case, you would be best served by investing in venture capital directly and in buyouts through a more curated fund structure. Both strategies are fraught with nuances. With a better understanding of the private equity landscape and options for investors, the following section provides a broader discussion of the direct investment process.

Notes

1. Bain & Company, *Global Private Equity Report 2016.*
2. Preqin Quarterly Private Equity Update Q2 2016.
3. Ulrich Lossen, "The Performance of Private Equity Funds: Does Diversification Matter?" Munich School of Management, Paper No. 2006-14, June 2006. Paper calculates asset class diversification by using a Herfindahl-Hirschmann-Index (HHI) that assigns each portfolio company to one of the following financing stages: (1) seed and early stage VC, (2) second, expansion, and later stage VC, (3) buyout, (4) listed securities, and (5) other financing stage. HHI takes on the value of 0% for a fund, which is not diversified at all (i.e., a fund which invested only in one asset class) and the value of 100% for a perfectly diversified fund.
4. A REIT is a security that sells like a stock on the major exchanges and invests in real estate directly, either through properties or mortgages. Their revenues come principally from their properties' rents.
5. Despite the disproportionate attention received, less than 10% of successful VC exits occur via IPO (percentage is relatively greater for growth capital and buyout investments).
6. Wilson, Sonsini, Goodrich, and Rosati, "The Entrepreneur's Report: Private Company Financing Trends," Q1 2016 Ed. https://www.wsgr.com/publications/PDFSearch/entreport/Q12016/private-company-financing-trends.htm

7. Fenwick West LLP, "Silicon Valley Venture Capital Survey," Q1 2016 Ed.
8. New York Venture Hub, 2016 Trends in Convertible Note Deal Terms, Alon Y. Kapen, 2016.
9. Venture capital typically invests in 15 to 30 investments per fund.
10. As a general rule of thumb, for every $1 initially invested in a company, venture funds typically reserve an additional $2 to $3 for future rounds.
11. NVCA Money Tree Report, Thomson Reuters, Q2 2016.
12. Figure 4.7 adapted from Dermot Berkey, *Raising Venture Capital for the Serious Entrepreneur,* McGraw Hill, 2008.
13. "Pre-money" values can easily be calculated by subtracting the amount raised from this "post-money" valuation.
14. $200mm/20x = $10mm post-money valuation and investing $1mm implies 10% equity ($1/$10mm), while $175mm/20x = $8.75mm post-money valuation and investing $1mm implies 11% equity ($1mm/$8.75mm).
15. Given their early-stage bias, the risk-return tradeoff is typically a bit higher.
16. Borrower usually has the option to retire debt earlier by paying a prepayment "penalty."
17. Some deals may quickly be resolved, without ever achieving ownership, if the distressed company is able to raise the necessary funds to make outstanding claims whole.
18. For further reading see: Stephen Moyer, *Distressed Debt Analysis: Strategies for Speculative Investors,* J. Ross Publishing, 2005.

PART II

Direct Investing in Action

CHAPTER 5

Family Office Considerations to the Direct Investment Process

In Part I, an introduction to direct investing and discussion of the emerging presence of private capital in direct investing—including both co-investment strategies and various private equity strategies for private investors and family offices—were presented. In this chapter, I shift gears and focus on the mechanics of the direct investment process and the nuances of direct investing from the vantage point of a family office. This chapter first describes how the source of wealth may bring certain preferences to the direct investing interests and how that impacts the process and approach to deploying capital. Specifically considered is whether the source of wealth and internal bias impacts your approach to the process of direct investing and, if so, how. Also discussed are: (1) What are the strengths, weaknesses, opportunities, and threats

(SWOT analysis) of deploying a direct investing strategy for a family office? (2) How does your approach complement your broader strategy to your investment mandate? This chapter outlines and describes a three-phase process to help investors understand the full cycle of deploying capital to harvesting returns. Implications of the three phases for the family office investor also are examined. The chapter closes with a family office case study of deploying capital into a direct investment opportunity.

Source of Wealth: Lens of the Family Office

Family offices all have one thing in common: They are greatly influenced by the source of wealth and the influence it has on its key stakeholders. As it relates to the direct investment process, the investor's source of wealth tends to be an important factor in terms of sector interest as well as domain expertise. For example, if a family office made its wealth as a function of a technology business, they will likely have a greater interest as well as domain expertise to want to further invest in tech-related businesses. The same goes for real estate moguls, manufacturing enterprising families, and other types of investors. Not only does the wealth source drive a bias toward a certain domain, but it also may shape the preferences of income distribution and time horizon. For example, if the source of wealth in a family was real estate—specifically with certain properties yielding consistent current income—then the family may be less interested in direct investments that do not provide for a current income.

Not only does source of wealth influence the sectors where a family may desire to invest in directs, but how the family sees the opportunity. Having spent some time in Asia, I noticed that most of the wealth has been created in the last 25 years by gregarious, driven, Type A entrepreneurs. Commonly, when I asked about their investment interests and the role of the family office, these entrepreneurs responded that they wanted to continue to build wealth through the deployment of capital into direct investment opportunities. The mainland Chinese tycoons with whom I met were particularly bullish on the Chinese market and also expressed interest in offshore real estate investments. Most of these entrepreneurs with net worth above $1 billion saw the source of their wealth as an engine to continue building wealth. Hence, direct investments continued to subtly surface in many different conversations as a particular interest area.

Another takeaway about the influence of source of wealth relates to risk tolerance. For example, serial entrepreneurs who opportunistically have had great success in building wealth (despite some failures along the way) may have greater risk tolerance than individuals who have had only one major liquidity event. These latter individuals may have less appetite to allocate much if any of those dollars to private equity, as they are in the "stay rich" business versus the "continue to build and get rich" mentality. These family office investing mindsets influence how much, if any they would allocate to a direct investment portfolio. For example, a family office with a wealth preservation mindset and a highly conservative lens to investing is likely to dedicate less to direct investing, if at all, than one with a wealth-creating mindset and less conservative lens.

Finally, source of wealth matters when it comes to time horizon, age, and stage of the family office. For example, some multigenerational family office investors who allocate to directs see the opportunity to invest in direct investments at a low basis into generation-skipping trusts (GSTs), if the trust provisions allow, as a means of getting low-basis, privately held stock down to generations at an early age. With a 10- or 20-year time horizon in certain cases, these assets may grow exponentially, as young beneficiaries may have little need to access these assets until their adulthood. Be advised, however, that, as in any investment case, negative consequences can mount with gifting assets that may mushroom and grow beyond the founder's original wealth. Connecting with appropriate tax, trust, and estate planning counsel is critical. Thus, source of wealth may influence a family office's preferences regarding (1) where to invest, (2) how to invest, (3) risk associated with direct investing, and (4) time horizon for deploying capital.

SWOT Analysis for Direct Investing

An important exercise for a family office investor is to clarify the strengths, weaknesses, opportunities, and threats (SWOT) analysis for devising a direct investment strategy. For example, you may want to begin by identifying the strengths of the family, the source of capital, the domain expertise, the family office infrastructure, and the strategic knowledge of the family office. Next consider the potential weaknesses of the family office setup, infrastructure, talent, deal flow, sourcing opportunities, network, or strategic relationships that may thwart successful deployment of capital. After identifying strengths and weaknesses, take inventory of the opportunities to deploy capital into directs, including whether each opportunity (1) introduces rewards that offset the risks, (2) fits within the broader family office mandate, and (3) stirs enough interest, desire, and zeal to deploy capital in this manner. Finally, identifying all the critical liabilities or threats that exposure to directs may lead to will help clarify the negative impact that an exposure to directs may result in. Consider the SWOT template in Figure 5.1 as a reference point to create your own SWOT analysis for direct investing.

Through the exercise of creating a SWOT analysis, investors can start to understand the appropriate resourcing sources and approaches to consider when deploying capital into directs—along with how these align with their investment thesis. Chapter 6 covers crafting your investment thesis in greater detail. To follow is an overview of the direct investment process broken down into three main phases.

Three Phases to the Direct Investing Process

There are many excellent texts on deploying capital into private equity and alternatives. For example, there are various stepped approaches to direct investing illustrated in texts on private equity and venture capital from a number of academics and practitioners.[1] The *EY Family Office Guide* outlines a three-phase approach of making, managing, and monetizing on direct investments (see Figure 5.2). In their model, making the investment involves activities such as research, sourcing, evaluating, financing, and closing the investment. Managing the investment involves outlining strategic objectives, monitoring operations and financial results, and addressing capital market and governance issues. Monetizing the investment involves determining and executing an appropriate exit strategy. Throughout the process, the investment team enlists assistance from a support network of financing, tax, legal, regulatory, technology, process improvement, compliance, and other resources.

These various models are all relevant and valuable applications to the deployment process. I have reflected on these approaches and insights from David McCombie and others in order to adapt a three-phase model for family offices. The three phases outline a series of activities and steps a family office investor may take to deploy capital intro directs. The goal of this model is to provide investors with a rigorous, repeatable, and scalable process of checkpoints that empower investors to quickly eliminate those investment opportunities that do not meet their unique criteria.

FIGURE 5.1 SWOT Analysis Template for Reviewing a Direct Investment

Strengths	**Weaknesses**
Core domain expertise . . .	Ownership considerations . . .
Key attributes of your family office infrastructure . . .	Complexity . . .
Key resources or domain experts . . .	Conflicts of interest . . .
Network and connections . . .	Lack of talent . . .
Reputation or credibility . . .	Lack of domain expertise . . .
Co-investors . . .	Lack of risk tolerance . . .
Risk tolerance . . .	Wealth transfer constraints . . .
Serial entrepreneurial tendencies . . .	Lack of sophistication . . .
Governance . . .	Too expensive . . .
Sourcing or deal flow . . .	Poor deal flow . . .
Other: _____	Negative reputation . . .
Other: _____	Other: _____
	Other: _____
Opportunities	**Threats**
Intellectual property (IP) . . .	Liquidity . . .
Disruptive technology . . .	Lack of alignment . . .
Impact investing . . .	Monitoring, oversight, or information access . . .
New strategic or financial partners . . .	Need for follow-on capital . . .
Emerging markets or geographies . . .	Risk tolerance . . .
Scalability . . .	Lack of buy-in or support from investor(s) . . .
Vertical or horizontal integration . . .	Failure or worst drawdown considerations . . .
Wealth transfer, tax or estate planning considerations	Other: _____
Privacy and/or anonymity considerations . . .	Other: _____
Other: _____	
Other: _____	

Of course, the model is effective only to the extent it is implemented. Investors become vulnerable when they fail to adhere to such a rigorous process (I, too, am guilty of having made this mistake). Such mistakes can happen, for example, when an investor falls in love with a deal and makes emotional decisions or makes concessions to invest in an opportunity that is out of scope, fails to meet one's investment criteria, or lacks the proper structure, to name

FIGURE 5.2   EY Direct Investment Process

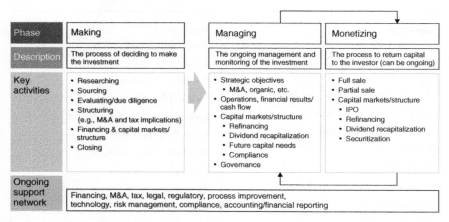

Source: EY Family Office Guide, p. 40

just a few of the common scenarios. However, it is invaluable to adhere to a strict mandate and process to source, vet, and analyze opportunities, structure terms, and eventually deploy capital.

The following adapted model involves three primary phases with several discrete activities under each phase:

Phase I: Due Diligence and Discovery

1. Discovering New Opportunities
2. Conducting an Initial Company and Management Review
3. Preliminary Vetting and Analysis

Phase II: Direct Investment Deployment and Governance

4. Direct Investment Governance Considerations and Formal Offer
5. Final Due Diligence, Terms and Structuring
6. Closing

Phase III: Monitoring, Oversight, and Exit Strategies

7. Post-Closing Oversight
8. Exit Strategies and Harvesting Returns
9. Postmortem

During each phase, the investor wears different "hats" and may need to involve additional outside resources such as an audit team, strategic partners, and/or domain experts to weigh in on the opportunity. The hope is that investors can more quickly eliminate those investment deals that do not fit their mandate. The due diligence, vetting, and analysis activities are discussed in greater detail in Chapter 7. Associated with each phase and series of sub-activities are the internal and external controls, including the responsible parties who are engaged, as listed in the "Ongoing Support Network" section (see Figure 5.2 and 5.3).

A Three-Phase Direct Investing Process

The following sections describe the three phases and accompanying steps direct investors can follow as they discover, analyze, structure, and execute an investment. Investors may customize these steps according to their own discretion; however, the need for outlining a consistent and repeatable process to guide the investment lifecycle cannot be overstated. Moreover, investors must fulfill the specific requirements of each step and secure any external resources needed to carry out each one successfully.

FIGURE 5.3　Direct Investment Process

"Investigator" Hat	"Decision-Maker" Hat	"Overseer" Hat
Phase I: Due Diligence and Discovery	**Phase II: Direct Investment Deployment and Governance**	**Phase III: Monitoring, Oversight and Exit Strategies**
Activities: • Discovering New Opportunities • Conducting an Initial Company and Management Review • Preliminary Vetting and Analysis	**Activities:** • Direct Investment Governance Considerations and Formal Offer • Final Due Diligence, Terms and Structuring • Closing	**Activities:** • Post-Closing Oversight • Exit Strategies and Harvesting Returns • Postmortem
Outcome: Making a formal offer or passing on the transaction	Outcome: Closing the direct investing transaction	Outcome: Exiting the company and evaluating the investment

Phase I: Due Diligence and Discovery

Phase I consists of discovering, initially reviewing, and thoroughly vetting investment opportunities. Successfully completing this phase requires having an active pipeline of high-quality possibilities in place and applying a rigorous, consistent, and repeatable process for sifting through these opportunities to identify the few that align with your investment thesis. This process will require being in contact with a range of sources of solid opportunities and, once a suitable opportunity is identified, being in close contact with the management team to gather the information needed to arrive at a sound investment decision. Throughout this phase, it is important to enlist the support of external advisors and consultants as needed to carry out the various steps. The following sections describe the tasks of this phase in more detail.

Step 1: Discovering and Sourcing New Opportunities

Before you can determine the best direct investment opportunities for yourself, you need to create an active pipeline of high-quality possibilities (see a full discussion of this in Chapter 7). In this context, *high quality* is defined as alignment between your investment thesis and the deal's characteristics. It follows that *quality* is highly subjective, meaning that one investor's treasure may be another investor's trash.

Figure 5.4 provides a depiction of how the direct investment process helps investors sift through the many possible investment opportunities available to them to zero-in on the few opportunities that are truly viable in terms of being an appropriate fit for them. As shown in this figure, the investor may discover hundreds of possible investment opportunities through its sourcing process.

FIGURE 5.4 Opportunity Funnel and Yield

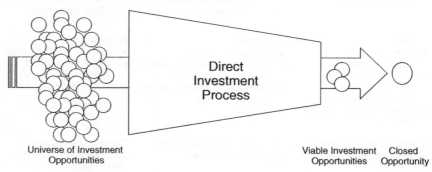

Universe of Investment Opportunities

Direct Investment Process

Viable Investment Opportunities   Closed Opportunity

These opportunities are then filtered and funneled through a rigorous direct investment process that ultimately identifies the few high-quality options that fit the investor's criteria and culminates in one closed investment. In this example, assuming that 100 initial opportunities were discovered, the process produced a yield of 1/100, which is statistically greater than typical venture capital yields, and in alignment with private equity ratios. Based on our survey of private family offices, 56 percent of family offices make 0–2 investments and 33 percent make 3–5 investments annually. This survey also found that only in 6 percent of the direct investment opportunities reviewed annually did the investor actually deploy capital.[2] See Figure 5.5.

Sourcing new opportunities is an ongoing activity. Moreover, because many family offices go through continual cycles of making investments and exiting existing investments, sourcing is occurring regardless of where an investor is in any investment cycle. Finding suitable opportunities on an ongoing basis is the lifeblood of a successful direct investment strategy.

All parties in a family office play a role in sourcing. Commonly, opportunities arise through introductions, referrals, and other proactive activities related to professional services firms, universities, conferences, investment pitch meetings, and other external entities. Opportunities that show promise typically are assigned a "deal lead" who will act as the main point of contact throughout the rest of the direct investment process. Specific activities are then planned and monitored through weekly direct investing team meetings. Be advised that not all family offices have a formalized process, and they may work with a third-party consultant or investment advisor to support

FIGURE 5.5   Annual Deployment to Direct Investments

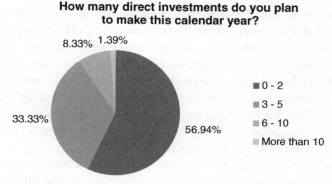

How many direct investments do you plan to make this calendar year?

8.33%   1.39%

33.33%

56.94%

■ 0 - 2
■ 3 - 5
■ 6 - 10
■ More than 10

Source: Tamarind Partners Direct Investment Survey, 2016

them with sourcing direct investment opportunities. For those managing the process in-house, consider using a deal-tracking spreadsheet as a way to monitor what opportunities are in the funnel and where they are in the process (see Figure 5.6).

Step 2: Conducting an Initial Company and Management Review

Once an opportunity is determined by the investor to have promise and a deal lead is assigned, the opportunity moves into Step 2 and is subjected to an initial company and management review. To begin this effort, one or more meetings are held with the management team presenting the investment or transaction for the purpose of learning more about the opportunity. It is important to gather as much information about the opportunity as early as possible to (1) discover reasons to quickly decline the opportunity and/or (2) have an informed discussion with the management team.

Commonly, investors request background information on the business, market, and individuals, including the business plan or offering memorandum, financial model and projections, and management bios. A management presentation also is typically shared at this stage, which may outline the company business proposition, operating history of the company, details of the investment transaction, and any relevant legal issues.

It is particularly important at this stage to evaluate the individuals involved in the business and to build rapport with the management team, given the criticality of these players to the investment's success. Investors should make special note of the corporate culture as well as the capabilities, personalities, and compatibility of the management team with the investor. Often, it is advantageous to meet with the management team at their place of business to best experience the work environment and interact with employees.

Following the initial management presentation and information review, the deal lead and any other individuals from the family office who participated in the meetings analyze the data regarding their views of issues such as the market opportunity, potential management team deficiencies post-transaction, capitalization table, risk assessments, exit opportunity, and transaction rationale. It is important not to rush the analysis, although the management team soliciting the investor likely will actively try to advance the process. Interacting with the management team and their advisors is a nuanced process that, when done well, can take substantial time.

Following a thorough analysis, the deal lead and team members consolidate their findings, report back to the family office, and make a recommendation on next steps. Although the investor now should have sufficient

FIGURE 5.6 Opportunity Tracking Spreadsheet

Opportunity	Date Added	Deal Lead	Source	Industry/ Sector	Stage (Active/Priority/ Track/Decline)	Transaction Description	Fit with Investment Thesis	Next Steps	Notes

information to decide whether to proceed with the investment, internal discussion and debate are common. Additional requests for meetings or information may be made of the management team if the family office determines that key details are still missing or unknown. If, at the conclusion of this step, the opportunity is not eliminated from consideration, the investment team will outline the key issues that need to be resolved and advance the deal into a more thorough vetting and analysis.

Step 3: Preliminary Vetting and Analysis

Preliminary vetting and analysis involves a more thorough examination of an investment opportunity and is conducted for those transactions that the deal team and investment committee agree merit further consideration. Often, this step can take several weeks or more than a month to complete, depending on the complexity of the business or opportunity. As with any step in the direct investing process, the investment committee should prepare to secure external assistance as needed from outside consultants and domain experts in conducting this step and composing the memorandum.

The results of this step are captured in an internal Vetting Memorandum that consolidates the deal team's findings to date, yielding enough information to make an informed investment decision and, if favorable, structure a term sheet and make an offer. As such, the memorandum serves as the formal, written communication with the investment committee and the deal team. This document normally remains on file for the duration of the investment, and we know of many situations where investors will go back and reference what was understood about the investment at the outset.

The memorandum generally contains seven main sections, each of which significantly informs the investment decision. First is the Executive Summary, which provides an overview of the company and transaction and outlines the aspects of the deal that support the investment thesis. Second is Industry Information, which identifies the market trends and dynamics that support the business's success or failure. This section also outlines precedent transactions and industry characteristics.

The third section is Company Information, which reviews the core business model, history, competitive positioning, products and services, customers and providers, and strategic growth plans. Fourth is an Operational Analysis, including a summary of how the company operates, logistics and supply chain, IT systems and infrastructure, intellectual property, and due diligence findings.

Fifth, an overview of Management and Employees is provided, including an organization chart, management team and their bios, and a management gap analysis that outlines the management team's deficiencies or weaknesses. A Financial Information section follows, which outlines the company's historical financial statements, projected financial statements, capitalization table, valuation analysis, and exit strategy projections. Importantly, rather than taking the management team's financial projections at face value, experienced direct investors generate their own projections in collaboration with and using information provided by the management team. We consider this a critical task that deepens all parties' understanding of the operating parameters and key assumptions the management team is operating against. One CEO described how much better and more informed he felt once he had a better understanding of his own business based on the perspectives and business experience that the investor shared through the process, despite not actually closing a transaction at all.

The closing section of the memorandum is Final Recommendations, which contains the deal team's recommendation whether to move forward. This section also includes risk assessments, a summary of the transaction, next steps, and—if the recommendation is to move forward—the proposed term sheet and structure under which the deal would be formed. On the contrary, if the team uncovers anything that would preclude endorsing the investment during the vetting process, the deal team will communicate with the rest of the team and indicate that a decline will be issued.

Based on this comprehensive memorandum, a formal internal review can commence and the investment committee can make a formal offer or pass on the transaction. Investment committee meetings can take many forms. Small offices with few people may have short meetings with little dialogue. Larger teams, like those found in private equity firms, have more structured committee meetings with detailed agendas and formal voting members. In our experience, the teams with long working relationships know the preferences of the investors and get into a rhythm with each other, resulting in expedited decisions.

Phase II: Direct Investment Deployment and Governance

The second phase in the direct investing process includes deploying the direct investment and addressing relevant governance issues. This phase includes activities such as preparing a formal offer and summary of terms that outlines the structure and parameters of the transaction under which the investor will close. Other activities in this phase include completing a more thorough due diligence process and finalizing the terms and structure tentatively agreed upon at the outset. The conclusion of this phase is closing the transaction, which signals the start of the investor's ownership in the interest and partnership with the management team. The following sections describe these steps in more detail.

Step 4: Direct Investment Governance Considerations and Formal Offer

When the deal team decides that an endorsement of the transaction is warranted, the deal proceeds to evaluate direct investment governance considerations and to make a formal offer. The investor will begin by preparing a formal offer for the company or management team. The offer will include a summary of terms (the Term Sheet) that will either be a standalone document or be part of a more detailed Offer Letter, Letter of Intent, or Memorandum of Understanding.

The Term Sheet outlines the structure and parameters of the transaction under which the investor will close (see Chapter 8 for a primer on important term sheet items). It is important to note that the composition of the family office and its key stakeholders may strongly influence the behavioral, financial, and legal issues involved in structuring the investment process of a family office.[3] Key terms to clarify include:

- Valuation or pricing of the transaction
- Governance and shareholder rights
- Exclusivity period to pursue the transaction
- Timing and closing date
- Listing of definitive agreements to be negotiated and executed at close
- Any employment agreements or corporate contracts to be negotiated and/or required to close
- Reporting requirements
- Capitalization table post-closing

Importantly, the Term Sheet at this stage typically is nonbinding and the accompanying documentation does not constitute the detailed closing documents. Instead, the purpose of these documents is to negotiate the key transaction details under which both parties agree to close (assuming nothing material changes about the current understanding of the business that would impact the terms), before significant time and effort is expended on final due diligence.

Successfully completing this step typically takes considerable time from both the management team and investment committee, and transactions fall apart during this process if the parties are unable to reach mutually agreeable terms. One area of contention often is valuation. Whereas the investor wants to negotiate a valuation as low as possible to capture greater economics of the operating company, the management team and/or prior owners want to value the business as high as possible due to both their own economic interests as well as their own commitment and investment in the venture. Coming to terms over valuation is a major hurdle in closing a transaction.

Step 5: Final Due Diligence, Terms and Structuring

Due diligence, the act of investigating a business before initiating a contractual or business relationship, is a crucial activity for an investor to perform. When effective, due diligence allows the investor to assess the opportunities, risks, upside potential, and downside risks of the target company being evaluated, thus leading to a more informed investing decision. The timeline for final due diligence is commonly 45–60 days. However, it is important to set a realistic time expectation upfront because both parties need to engage in a great deal of analysis during this step.

Although the overall process of due diligence actually starts much earlier when the investor first learns about the opportunity and gathers initial information, this process becomes increasingly more detailed and in-depth as the direct investing process progresses. Sometimes, this step is called "confirmatory due diligence" to signify that much of the due diligence has already been completed but that each party needs to confirm their findings before moving forward. When final due diligence is completed, the investors are clear to close the transaction.

During this step, both parties are actively analyzing all aspects of the investment about to be closed, as there is no turning back once the investment is made. The investor is ensuring that their assessment of the business is accurate while the management team is examining whether the investor is able to finance and effectively manage the combined business going forward. As part of this process, the investor may provide references to other management teams they have backed.

The deal team also involves and manages necessary third parties to assist with the final due diligence process, including the legal team that drafts the definitive agreements, the accounting team that reviews tax or financial due diligence items, and external consultants or experts that evaluate specific due diligence materials, among others. The deal team can create clarity throughout the process by organizing regular meetings and communicating with the various parties to assure that everyone is aware of the deal's status and outstanding issues.

Ultimately, the aim of due diligence is to review all pertinent information and to document and address all remaining issues in the definitive agreements. For example, if a salesperson crucial to the business is found to be lacking a valid employment agreement with the company, this agreement would need to be negotiated and agreed upon by the employee prior to closing.

It is helpful during this process to maintain detailed and organized records of information requests and their fulfillment. For example, a web-based information repository and tracking log can be helpful, such as that shown in Figure 5.7.

Step 6: Closing

Closing a transaction constitutes the final milestone in the direct investing process and involves collecting the final executed agreements and documentation. As with other steps, closing is carried out by both the direct investor and the company or management team. Closing items for an LLC typically include articles of organization, operating agreement and business plan, shareholder and definitive agreements, and resolutions authorizing investment. Closing items for a corporation include such things as the shareholders' agreement, share purchase agreement, and schedules to share purchase agreement.

The closing date is initially negotiated as part of the Term Sheet, and both parties will strive to hold each other accountable to this timeline. Delays can be initiated by either party, often due to critical issues discovered by either party during due diligence. For example, the investor may discover an issue that obstructs closing and need to postpone the closing date or withdraw from the deal altogether. It is important for investors to be aware that they should not be pushed to close without being absolutely ready.

Although this step signifies the conclusion of the direct investing transaction, it also signals the start of the direct investor owning a new interest going forward and, often, the initiation of a partnership with the management team.

Phase III: Monitoring, Oversight, and Exit Strategies

The third and final phase of the direct investing process involves monitoring and providing oversight of the investment, exiting the company in an appropriate manner and at an appropriate time, and evaluating the successes and failures of the investment. It is important in this phase to be aware that the majority of direct investing transactions fail due to execution risk, indicating that ongoing support and oversight from the investment team is often vital to a successful outcome. Moreover, although a variety of

FIGURE 5.7 Sample Due Diligence Tracking Spreadsheet

Opportunity Date			
	Review Committees	**Collection and Preparation**	**Investment Committee**
	Legal	Person A	Person A
	Accounting	Advisor A	Person B
			Person C

Due Diligence Materials Collection, Preparation, Review & Approval

Start Date	Event/Activity	Responsible Parties	Company Resources	Dependencies	Delivery Method	Target Delivery Date	Submitted Y/N
dd/mm/yy	**Due Diligence Checklist (Primary Activity)**	Deal Team Legal Accounting	Management Team Legal Advisors	Completed Diligence Checklist		(30–45 days)	
dd/mm/yy	DD Checklist "Corporate Organization" Section				Upload to VDR		✓
	DD Checklist "Capital Structure" Section			Capitalization Table Employee Option Plan	Upload to VDR		✓
	DD Checklist "Management & Employees"			Management Bios	Upload to VDR		
	DD Checklist "Business" Section			Quality Systems Summary	VDR and Physical DR		✓
	DD Checklist "Sales & Marketing" Section			External reports from Distributors, suppliers, vendors	Upload to VDR		
	DD Checklist "Property" Section				Upload to VDR		
	DD Checklist "Legal" Section				Upload to VDR		
	DO Checklist "Contracts" Section				Upload to VDR		
	DD Checklist "Financial Condition" Section				Upload to VDR		
	DD Checklist "Regulatory Review Items" Section			On-site Data Room Meeting dd/mm/yy	Physical Data Room		
	Investment Committee Sign Off of Due Diligence						

approaches are available for harvesting returns and exiting the investment, the most suitable approach for any one investor will depend upon the objectives and interests of the many stakeholders involved. Care should be taken to understand these objectives and agree upon exit strategies early in the direct investing process. Finally, conducting postmortems is a critical practice for improving the success of each investment transaction. Chapter 9 discusses in greater depth key considerations when it comes to monitoring, exit strategies, and harvesting returns.

Step 7: Post-Closing Oversight

Once the transaction closes, many investments require ongoing support, monitoring, and oversight. These investments typically have a lifecycle of 5 to 10 years and are an illiquid asset with value created through good operations. Notably, the majority of direct investing transactions fail due to execution risk, with statistics indicating that less than 20 percent of investments in the private equity market ever generate any return for investors. One cause of these failures is that many family offices neglect to identify the support that the investment needs to be successful between closing and an exit or liquidity event.

Although it is impossible to mitigate all the risks in a direct investment, even with the most advanced processes, it must be noted that family offices are uniquely positioned to provide operational support to their portfolio investments. In brief, there are four considerations that should be attended to in this step:

1. *Executing against the agreed-upon business plan:* At closing, a business plan is typically agreed upon in writing. This plan provides both a roadmap or playbook for the company to follow and metrics by which the company's success and failures will be judged. The investor can play a central role in monitoring the company's adherence to the plan.
2. *Governance and board of advisors:* Direct investments exhibit high failure rates; therefore, success often heavily relies on the management team's ability to execute. It follows that the investor is motivated to assure that the management team remains effective and supported. Having a seat on the company's board may be a way to be involved more closely by an investor.
3. *Additional funding needs:* Often, earlier stage growth companies will require additional investment capital before a liquidity event. Even more established businesses often require additional financing to fuel growth

or acquisitions. Therefore, investors should be prepared to invest more money in additional rounds of financing as needed.

4. *Exit strategies:* The ultimate goal of a direct investment is to monetize it, whether that occurs by selling it to a strategic or financial buyer, collecting dividends over the long term, or executing an initial public offering. Although each of these exit strategies involves a different approach to managing the business, the investor plays a key supportive role regardless of the strategy. For example, the investor may offer the management team access to strategic relationships or manage the process leading up to an exit event so the management team can stay focused on operations.

There is no clear consensus among direct investors regarding how the deal team or investment team should be involved after closing. Sometimes, family offices have specialized transaction professionals who cease their involvement at closing. In other cases, the deal team takes an active operational role in the company after closing. Although there is no right or wrong approach, investors should align their approach with the competencies and capabilities of their deal team.

Step 8: Exit Strategies and Harvesting Returns

The objective of any direct private investment will be to participate at some point within a certain expected time frame from the date of the first investment in a liquidity event. Companies can pursue a variety of exit strategies and means for harvesting returns, such as selling the enterprise to another buyer, selling shares back to the company or to another individual investor through a secondary transaction, collecting dividends, or executing an initial public offering (see Chapter 9 for a more complete discussion of exit strategies).

A critical starting point is to assure that objectives and interests among the minority stakeholders, majority stakeholders, and management team are aligned, especially as it pertains to interim cash distributions and an exit time frame. These objectives have implications for what kinds of companies are invested in — for example, investors who desire cash flows through interim distributions would not invest in early growth stage companies, whereas investors who want to exit within a certain time frame might avoid investing in closely held family businesses that may provide distributions but lack a clear path to monetization. It is important to be aware that corporate lifecycles also will influence and shift the company's growth and payout potentials over time. For this reason, exit strategies should be discussed and agreed upon early in the direct investing process, with such plans clearly documented within the closing documents or business plan. This advice is particularly critical for minority stakeholders, who often have limited ability to influence decisions and exit strategies once the deal has been closed.

Advisors and other external resources tend to be invaluable during this process. For example, hiring an investment bank or other advisor to coordinate this process can provide invaluable insight to structures, transactions terms, and expected valuations. These advisors can play key roles in activities such as identifying potential buyers, preparing company summaries and descriptions, drafting confidentiality agreements, collecting and evaluating nonbinding indications of interest from buyers, and coordinating with interested buyers.

It is worth reiterating that many exits are not achieved due to seller expectations being misaligned and one of the areas where family offices need to develop discipline is in negotiating a satisfactory exit and not holding onto an investment beyond the highest point of its value as a private company. Therefore, investors and the management team should take care to address the various exit strategies considerations mentioned here and discussed more fully in Chapter 9 from the outset of the direct investing process.

Step 9: Postmortem

A common practice in several fields is conducting a postmortem following the completion of projects to learn from the successes and failures of the past. Due to a variety of reasons, from a reluctance to examine one's own failures to a desire to move forward, to thinking there is no time for reflection, postmortems often are only superficially conducted, if they are conducted at all.

Conducting a postmortem for each investment is crucial step that allows the investor to understand more granularly what most impacted the investment outcome's success or failure. For the investor wanting to make each direct investment more effective and successful than the last, this process can help identify gaps in the process, missteps by management, or false assumptions from the beginning about the market, company, and/or opportunity. Therefore, although it can be difficult to admit shortcomings in oneself or one's process, a postmortem is a vital path for learning from the past, developing best practices, and devising and executing more successful strategies moving forward.

Making the postmortem as easy and nonthreatening as possible for those providing the information is one way to improve the likelihood that it is completed and that the results are valuable. Collier, DeMarco, and Fearey advised that the most effective postmortem processes have clearly documented procedures and guidelines; gather confidential, positive, and blame-free feedback from participants; include a means for incorporating lessons learned into standard operating procedures moving forward; and balance the time and costs of conducting the postmortem with its benefits.[4]

Specific steps include creating and distributing a survey about the investment, collecting objective investment information, conducting a debriefing meeting, and publishing the results within the family office, investment team, and management team. It is important to focus the data collection and analysis on those metrics and areas of the direct investing process that will offer the greatest improvement opportunities in the future. Once these findings are compiled, analyzed, and documented, these should be translated into best practices and operating procedures that will enhance the investment team's approach on successive deals. Collier et al. emphasize that the postmortem is effective only to the extent that it translates what "everybody knows" (lessons learned from the investment) into what "everybody does" (revised practices moving forward). As a result, you can make adjustments in your process or approach, fine tune your investment thesis, and/or make tactical and/or strategic changes to your future direct investments.

Case Study

A case study provided by Warner Babcock, chairman and CEO of AM Private Enterprises, an independent advisor to families and their enterprises, illustrates the direct investing process.[5]

In this case, the direct investing process began when AM Private Enterprises identified the opportunity through a proactive, intensive national search. The specific investment was a startup venture in the scientific instrumentation and diagnostics field, based on a revolutionary technology breakthrough developed at a Department of Energy laboratory. Although the venture and management team was very small, the business was expected to grow into a $1 billion enterprise, as it had very broad medical applications.

AM Private Enterprises found the opportunity for one family member who was investing on his own and who played the role of sponsor. Although no other co-investors were brought in initially, the plan was to bring in other high-quality outside investors later in the life of the investment.

The opportunity fit well with the investor's criteria, which were developed collaboratively with the special investment advisor and venture manager. Specifically, it was believed that the opportunity would enable the investor to achieve his financial and personal objectives, as it involved direct investment as a founding investor in an early-stage, leading-edge technology venture in a personal area of interest. This opportunity also would allow the investor to gain experience outside the family business in building complex, successful entrepreneurial businesses. Expectations were that the venture might grow very fast or very slowly; therefore, it was important for the investor to be patient and allow the company to build in the right way and on the right time horizon.

AM Private Enterprises assisted a venture manager in the family office in screening and vetting the opportunity. In structuring the investment, care was taken to establish milestones with ratchets along with certain protections and policies.

Post-closing, the venture manager in the family office monitored investment on a routine basis with periodic reports, visits, and board representation. Ultimately, the venture merged with another small private company. At the time of this publication, the merged venture has a total value of approximately $250 million and is still growing.

As part of the postmortem, AM Private Enterprises helped document and assemble lessons learned from this successful investment experience. Babcock emphasizes that direct investing is a complex, long process that can be highly lucrative when done right. Key takeaways he offers from this experience are:

1. Develop a disciplined, deliberate plan and process for direct investing, taking care to devote the time and resources necessary to close, grow, and exit the investment the right way.
2. Create a top team of internal and external highly experienced advisor(s) and professionals. Include people with operating backgrounds and attract great co-investors, board members, and management. Work to build goodwill with the various stakeholders throughout the process.
3. Be proactive in sourcing deals nationally. This will support the investors in attracting great opportunities that allow them to focus on building a successful business long-term.
4. Throughout the process, it is important for investors to perform their own high-quality due diligence and to move carefully, taking care to read and understand all documents and structure deals. Investors also need to be ready to walk away or lose their investment when the situation calls for it.

5. For family offices that assign or hire family office personnel or a venture manager to oversee or work on direct investment or ventures, it is essential to hire high-quality talent, to compensate them well, and to expect and plan for possible turnover.

Perhaps above all, Babcock encourages investors to be flexible and take a long-term, patient view so that they are more inclined to do what is right. Although the direct investing process can be fun, investors should expect many ups and downs along the way.

Conclusion

The direct investment process is a rigorous process that may seem like a lot of unnecessary work for investors who believe they can quickly assess if an investment is a good fit. It is true that investors can create efficiencies over time, but rarely do the experienced investors circumvent their own carefully designed process. Through the phases and steps described in this chapter, the investment committee is able to create controls and accountabilities that help avert rash investment decisions. Some investors may have a more informal process, and cover the bulk of these steps; others will document and have a handbook outlining their process. Either way, adhering to a common set of rules and steps helps create a repeatable and more efficient approach to this bespoke area of investing.

Specifically, as part of Phase I, investors discover, initially review, and then thoroughly vet investment opportunities. In Phase II, the direct investment is deployed and relevant governance issues are addressed through activities such as preparing a formal offer and summary of terms. The conclusion of this phase is closing the transaction, which signals the start of the investor's ownership in the interest and partnership with the management team. The third and final phase of the direct investing process involves monitoring and providing oversight of the investment, exiting the company in an appropriate manner and at an appropriate time, and evaluating the successes and failures of the investment. Throughout the direct investing process, it is important to enlist the support of external advisors and consultants as needed to carry out the various steps.

As we have stated earlier in this book, direct investing is not suitable for every investor. However, the rigorous process introduced in this chapter provides a beginning roadmap for willing investors to follow as they explore the high-risk, high-reward world of direct investing.

Notes

1. Josh Lerner, Ann Leamon, and Felda Hardymon, *Venture Capital, Private Equity, and the Financing of Entrepreneurship*, Hoboken: John Wiley & Sons, 2012; Mahendra Ramsinghani, *The Business of Venture Capital*, Hoboken: John Wiley & Sons, 2014.
2. Tamarind Partners Direct Investment Survey, 2016, Question #9.
3. *EY Family Office Guide,* 2016.
4. Bonnie Collier, Tom DeMarco, Peter Fearey, "A Defined Process for Project Postmortem Review," *IEEE Software* (1996): 65–72.
5. Interview with Warner Babcock, chairman and CEO of AM Private Enterprises, October 10, 2016.

CHAPTER 6

Designing a Direct Investment Thesis

This chapter provides an overview of the process of designing a direct investment thesis. We begin by defining the direct investment thesis, illustrating how it relates to the broader investment thesis, and outlining some of the elements that are included in a direct investment thesis. The remainder of the chapter is dedicated to discussing the key considerations that influence the content of the thesis, including the family's desired asset mix, the family's pathway to direct investing, the barbell approach to direct investing, and the family's entrepreneurial orientation and desired style. Finally, a case study is provided to illustrate the concepts discussed in this chapter.

Defining the Direct Investment Thesis

A direct investment thesis refers to the statement of beliefs, criteria, and goals investors use to guide their decisions about investing in a business enterprise. This thesis helps investors decide what investments to purchase, what to sell, what other actions to take, as well as when and why they need to initiate these

115

activities. The thesis also outlines metrics that help investors determine when and to what extent they have achieved their goals.

Whereas the broader investment philosophy also outlines some of these same elements, an investor's overarching investment philosophy refers to the entire scope of investing activities, including goals and criteria for asset classes such as equities, fixed income securities, nontraditional investments, real estate, commodities, money market, and alternative funds. The direct investment thesis is narrower, addressing only the investor's activities related to investing in business ventures. For example, the direct investment thesis may outline such things as:

- Types of companies and sectors to invest in
- Schedule and timing of investments in a company
- Desired portfolio size and strategy
- How much to invest in any given company
- Acceptable levels of risks for any given investment
- Financial and nonfinancial (e.g., social or environmental impact) goals and objectives
- Knowledge, skills, and abilities available in-house and value you add as an investor
- Desired roles to play throughout the direct investment process
- Desired terms, such as capital commitments, operational controls, and minority or majority holdings
- Exclusion criteria (what factors would eliminate an investment opportunity from being considered)

In addition to these considerations, a repeated theme throughout this book is that a high percentage of investors—family offices included—tend to have one or more core holdings that drives broader growth or is the original wealth engine. Whether they are technology mavens, real estate moguls, or manufacturing enterprising families, these and other types of sector interests and domain expertise will shape their biases as it relates to sector, income distribution, time horizon, and risk tolerance for the investor.

A well-designed direct investment thesis helps investors rapidly identify the investing opportunities that are uniquely suitable and desirable for them, saving critical time and resources for the investor. Marketplace noise surrounding investment opportunities is abundant; therefore, having a clear and actionable direct investment thesis is essential for outlining the investor's unique capital deployment strategy. Without clearly defined investment parameters (reflected in the direct investment thesis), investors are subject to uncertainty, anxiety, and inaction on the one hand or a reliance on luck, gut instinct, and blind faith on the other. Both approaches can lead to missteps that potentially prevent investors from reaching their financial goals.

A direct investment thesis also helps investors clearly explain and justify their direct investment decisions and expectations. It is not uncommon for investors to publish their direct investment thesis (similar to company's publication of their mission statement) as a means for defining what investments they make and why. Additionally, although the direct investment thesis is specific only to investments in companies, care should be taken to assure that the direct investment thesis aligns with and supports the broader investment philosophy. The remainder of this chapter provides more details about constructing the thesis and, specifically, the key considerations that influence the content of the thesis.

Asset Mix and the Direct Investment Thesis

Asset mix refers to the overall percentage allocations of an investment portfolio into particular asset classes. Although investors may slightly vary in their classifications of possible assets, three major classes of assets are typically acknowledged: (1) cash and equivalents, (2) fixed income instruments (bonds, debenture, notes) and, (3) equity instruments (common stock or ordinary shares).

Determining and upholding a particular asset mix is intended to help the investor achieve desired returns while managing risk and volatility. Investors vary in their growth goals, desired timelines for returns, and tolerance for risk. Therefore, wealth management and investment advisors typically outline different investment strategies commensurate with these goals and objectives. Typical options include (1) conservative strategies, which seek to preserve capital, albeit with limited growth; (2) moderate strategies, which seek to balance preservation and growth goals; and (3) aggressive growth strategies, which seek to maximize growth, albeit with larger risk of loss and volatility.

Figures 6.1 through 6.3 present sample allocations for these three portfolio types. In the conservative portfolio allocation (see Figure 6.1), fixed income assets that generate regular income, reduce overall risk, and protect against volatility of a portfolio are favored, comprising 44 percent—nearly half—of the portfolio. In contrast, asset classes that are subject to higher volatility and

FIGURE 6.1   Sample Conservative Portfolio Allocations

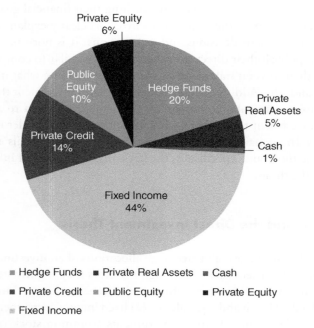

Source: Tamarind Partners Inc.

risk of loss comprise only a small portion of the portfolio—including private equity (6 percent), private real assets (5 percent), and cash (1 percent).

According to a moderate portfolio allocation (see Figure 6.2), investments in public equities that offer more favorable returns but also feature more risk comprise nearly a third of the overall portfolio (30 percent) and hedge funds comprise nearly another quarter (22 percent). In contrast, the more stable (and less lucrative) fixed income assets comprise only 18 percent of the portfolio.

The aggressive growth portfolio allocation (see Figure 6.3) shows a preference for even greater returns and volatility, with 50 percent of the portfolio dedicated to public equity, 20 percent of the portfolio dedicated to private equity, and a mere 5 percent allocated to fixed income assets.

As is common industry practice for any investor, it is important for family office investors to determine and adhere to their desired risk/return strategy when formulating their direct investment thesis.

FIGURE 6.2 Sample Moderate Portfolio Allocations

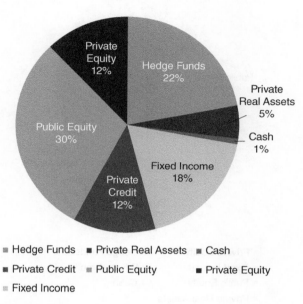

Moderate

■ Hedge Funds   ■ Private Real Assets   ■ Cash
■ Private Credit   ▨ Public Equity   ■ Private Equity
▨ Fixed Income

Source: Tamarind Partners Inc.

Family Pathways and the Direct Investment Thesis

The second key consideration for family office investors when composing a direct investment thesis is considering the specific enterprising pathway taken by the family. Roure et al. asserted that the pathway taken by a given family is determined by whether the family (1) still owns its main operating business and (2) has instituted a family office. These two dimensions give rise to four different enterprising pathways, as pictured in Figure 6.4. The four pathways are as follows:

> *Pathway 1: Family with an Operating Business.* This type of family retains ownership of its main operating business and has not instituted a family office. This means that most, if not all, of the family's wealth is tied to the operating business. Importantly, this family has no real need for broader exposure to direct investing, as its investments are already concentrated in this area through its main operating business

FIGURE 6.3   Sample Aggressive Growth Portfolio Allocations

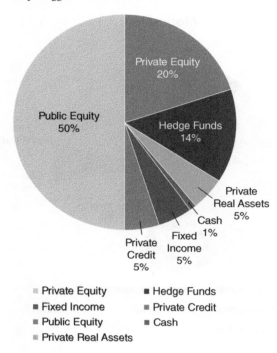

Source: Tamarind Partners Inc.

(and it may not have enough liquidity to invest beyond the main business).

Pathway 2: Enterprising Family. This type of family retains ownership of its main operating business but, unlike Pathway 1 families, has instituted a family office. This indicates that the core operating business is generating enough significant liquidity to enable the family to both redeploy capital into the main business and invest additional capital into other assets. As a result, these families may have an appetite for limited exposure to directs—whether simply to have additional interests or to hedge their core operating business position.

Pathway 3: Separated Approach. This type of family has sold its core operating business and has not opened a family office. This indicates that the family members have no desire to pool their investment capital and instead take their own individual paths. Individual family members may have an interest in direct investment, depending on their exposure and interest in operating a business.

FIGURE 6.4 Four Pathways of Enterprising Families

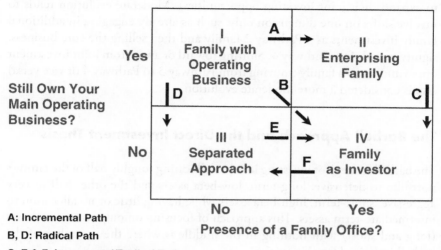

A: Incremental Path
B, D: Radical Path
C, E & F: Incremental/Radical Path

Source: J. Roure, J. L. Segurado, D. Welch, and K. Rosplock, *From the Family Business to the Family Office: Understanding the Development and Management of the Family's Other Investments, Ventures and Services FIVS*, IFERA Conference, Lancaster, England, July 2010

> *Pathway 4: Family as Investor.* This type of family has sold its core oper-
> ating business but has opened a family office, indicating the family
> members' continued desire to invest together—potentially including
> entrepreneurial opportunities for direct investment. It is understand-
> able that these families would indeed look to direct investing as a way
> to continue fulfilling their entrepreneurial orientation after exiting
> the core business. Pooling assets and having three or more investment
> vehicles also may allow non-accredited family member investors to
> take part, creating economies of scale for the broader family.

As described earlier, each pathway is associated with a different level of
interest in direct investment. Moreover, in these scenarios, families generally begin as Pathway 1 families, with ownership of their core business but
no family office. Their evolution toward direct investing may be incremental, moderate, or radical. Incremental evolution into direct investment would
occur as a shift to Pathway 2 as they increase their liquidity and expand into
other investments, signified by the opening of a family office. A more radical
evolution would involve moving from Pathway 1 by selling the core business
and shifting to either Pathway 3 (ceasing to pool their capital and engaging

in their own independent investments) or Pathway 4 (opening a family office to expand their joint investing opportunities). Moderate evolution tends to involve shifts on one dimension only, such as already engaging in additional family investments as a Pathway 2 family and then selling the core business, signifying a shift to Pathway 4. Shifting toward or away from joint investment opportunities as a family (moving from Pathway 3 to Pathway 4 or vice versa) also is considered a more moderate evolution.

The Barbell Approach and the Direct Investment Thesis

The barbell strategy of investing involves allocating roughly half of the family's portfolio to defensive, long-term, low-beta assets and the other half to very aggressive, short-term, high-beta assets while having little or no allocation to intermediate-term assets. This approach of focusing on only two asset classes (long and short) with nothing in the middle is where the metaphor of the barbell is derived (see Figure 6.5).

Families opt for a barbell strategy in order to diversify their portfolio and gain the benefits of both conservative, low-risk assets and aggressive, high-risk assets, in turn yielding better risk-adjusted returns. Implementing a barbell strategy requires active portfolio management to effectively monitor and exit short-term assets as they mature and adjust the allocations to long- and short-term assets as market conditions shift.

The metaphor of the barbell also is helpful for understanding the family office approach to direct investing. As mentioned previously, families generally begin as Pathway 1 families, where the initial focus is investment and ownership of a core operating business. This is where most of its wealth, strategic knowledge, and industry insight tend to be created, culminating in a bespoke facet of investing. J.P. Morgan and the World Economic Forum found in their survey of family offices that many of these have a significant concentration of family wealth held within their operating business and are not actively trying to diversify away from it.[1]

FIGURE 6.5   Barbell Approach

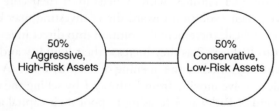

FIGURE 6.6 Barbell Approach to Family Office Direct Investing

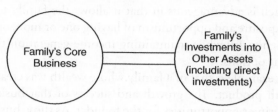

Despite this, tensions can emerge within these families as they increasingly desire to diversify through investments in safer, more liquid assets such as bonds or fixed income assets, or by shedding regular coupons. J.P. Morgan and the World Economic Forum found that 63 percent of family offices use more than one investment model to meet their objectives.[2]

As families evolve to add another form of investing, the family's core business becomes one side of the barbell, with the other side of the barbell emerging as the family's investments into other assets (made possible by the liquid wealth and cash flow generated from the core business), as shown in Figure 6.6. Thus, the barbell may be best demonstrated among enterprising families (see the discussion of Pathway 2 families in the previous section). Claude Kurzo, managing director and head of Strategy and Business Development at J.P. Morgan Asset Management, added that, in this regard, the family office can be a vehicle to diversify away from the exposure (and accordant risk) created by the family's core business. He explained a specific case example, "If you are a family that has a retail company that is mainly doing business in Europe, then you, the family, might want to diversify away from risk in retail and in Europe, like investing the family office outside of the geography and the sectors.[3]

Alternatively, a family's core business can be the inspiration for successive direct investments. Kurzo offered the example of a family who had a core business within the healthcare sector and developed extensive experience, key contacts, and in-depth industry insights about how healthcare would change over the years and what business opportunities would arise as a result. Therefore, after they sold the company, the focus of their direct investments was in a clearly defined healthcare space. Kurzo explained, "They do this because they say, 'Look, the reason why we can create value is because we have an advantage in that space. If I went to investment into basic materials, I wouldn't have that because I've never been in that space.'"[4] This family chose to specialize their direct investments in a way that leveraged the family's experience, knowledge, skills, and contacts.

Regardless of the specific focus of the family's direct investments, the barbell approach is advantageous in that it allows the family to continue to leverage the exposure and opportunism of having one or more operating businesses with higher risk while maintaining income generation through lower risk investment options.

One such example is that of a family whose wealth was created in a niche specialty health product. The growth and success of that business spawned several new business opportunities for the founder. As those businesses proliferated, so did the original core holding. Although some of the new businesses ultimately failed, the overall returns were enhanced, increasing liquidity for the other side of the barbell that was relatively conservatively invested as a hedge to the operating companies.

Entrepreneurial Orientation and the Direct Investment Thesis

Entrepreneurial orientation refers to the family's strategic orientation, strategy-making practices, managerial philosophies, and behaviors that are entrepreneurial in nature. General definitions of entrepreneurial orientation consider an organization's level of innovativeness (creating new combinations of resources), proactiveness (identifying and capitalizing on market opportunities), and risk-taking (dedicating scarce resources for the purpose of attaining a return) as a measure of its entrepreneurial orientation. External environmental conditions, such as industry restructuring, market and product fragmentation, increasing competition, and technological change also can spur entrepreneurism within the family firm.

Entrepreneurial orientation is believed to strongly predict organizational performance in general, particularly for those in turbulent environments. Specific to this book's audience, we assert that families in business have to be continuously entrepreneurial to adjust to ongoing marketplace changes and in turn create and sustain wealth for the long term across generations.[5] Moreover, the resulting increases in wealth "can be invested into new entrepreneurial ventures and investments, which can in turn sustain the growth of both the family and its businesses."[6]

Understanding and enhancing entrepreneurial orientation within a family business requires attention to family members' attitudes, perspectives and behaviors in successive generations, and the family's involvement in the core operating business. The family office also plays a central role in the entrepreneurism exercised by the family.

Family Member Attitudes

Zellweger, Nason, and Nordqvist added that in family businesses, the family members' attitudes and mindsets strongly influence the extent to which entrepreneurial behaviors and activities are exercised.[7] Stewardship perspectives, family firm culture, and members' desires for meaningful work all have been associated with entrepreneurial orientation.

Welsh et al. (2013) asserted that a stewardship perspective that involves holding family objectives of entrepreneurship higher than their own individual objectives is particularly instrumental for pursuing and capturing new entrepreneurial opportunities.[8] Such a perspective is important because family firms—particularly those later in the organizational lifecycle when members become increasingly focused on preserving rather than growing capital—often are believed to be risk averse and change resistant.

Family firm culture (including beliefs, values, and behaviors) as well as family members' perceptions of entrepreneurship help explain why and how family enterprises and their family offices grow and preserve wealth. For example, enterprising families that provide resources, mentoring and encouragement, and social capital that support entrepreneurial activities more often succeed in cultivating both entrepreneurism among next-generation family members and success in such endeavors. Roure et al. (2013) described such families as those who exhibit strong entrepreneurial behaviors for the purpose of deliberately identifying and exploiting opportunities to grow and protect shared wealth together through business value creation. Thus, they simultaneously capture economic value and build an enduring family legacy.[9]

Kurzo experienced that entrepreneurial drive is often associated with individuals' desires for purpose and meaningful professional achievement.[10] He explained that family members who are able to hold active roles in the core operating business often gain a sense of purpose that ignites and also satisfies their entrepreneurial passions. Successive generations who may not play a central role in the core business (either because it has been sold or because the key roles are filled) may turn to direct investing as a way to continue the entrepreneurial legacy and spirit of the family.

Perspectives and Behaviors within Successive Generations

Of particular importance in family businesses is how entrepreneurial orientation is sustained across generations.[11] Welsh et al. (2013) emphasized that each generation needs to see itself as a steward of the founding entrepreneur's business in order to generate feelings of responsibility for supporting future generations through continued entrepreneurial spirit and activities.[12] It is through this mechanism that an entrepreneurial mindset is cultivated across generations, leading to transgenerational wealth acceleration. Roure et al.'s (2013) study of 32 families indicated that development of a strong family entrepreneurial culture over generations was associated with the establishment of a systematic approach to pursue new opportunities in the family business.[13]

At the same time, to achieve success, subsequent generations not only need entrepreneurial drive; they also need to be developed through internal and external experiences to build the necessary knowledge, skills, and abilities to achieve entrepreneurial success. It is necessary to be particularly deliberate in these activities in later generations, as ownership becomes increasingly dispersed and fractionalized, and family members generally exhibit less stewardship, entrepreneurial drive, and risk tolerance while having more desire to conserve (rather than grow) family wealth created by previous generations. A study by Welsh et al. (2013) of 32 families indicated that founders had distinctly more comfort and confidence with taking risks with their wealth compared to successive generations. Additionally, senior generations more strongly asserted the importance of successive generations exhibiting entrepreneurial behavior for long-term wealth preservation and sustainability.

Involvement in Operating Business

Kurzo observed that family members' entrepreneurial orientation is influenced by the extent to which they are involved in the core operating business.[14] He explained that those individuals deeply involved in running the core business often simply do not have the time for direct investing. Conversely, once the core business is sold, the first generation that initially started the core business (and often the second generation) typically does go into direct investing as a continuation of their entrepreneurial drive and desire to grow wealth through investing.

Involvement and ongoing investment in the core operating business also can influence the family's appetite for risk. In a study by J.P. Morgan and the World Forum, more than 40 percent of families still have most of their wealth tied to an operating business, and these families report a slightly more conservative risk appetite than families without one (see Figure 6.7). This is because most of their wealth (and time) is already allocated, leaving little if any for directs.

FIGURE 6.7   Risk Appetite Based on Ownership of Operating Business

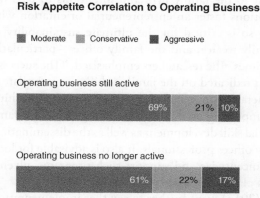

Risk Appetite Correlation to Operating Business

■ Moderate   ■ Conservative   ■ Aggressive

Operating business still active

| 69% | 21% | 10% |

Operating business no longer active

| 61% | 22% | 17% |

Source: J.P. Morgan and the World Economic Forum, *Inside the Single Family Investment Office Today,* 2016

FIGURE 6.8   Share of Family Net Worth Managed by Family Office

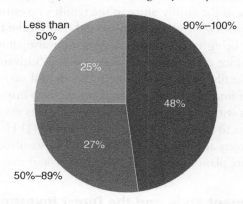

Less than 50%

90%–100%

25%

48%

27%

50%–89%

Source: J.P. Morgan and the World Economic Forum, *Inside the Single Family Investment Office Today,* 2016

Role of Family Office

The family office plays a critical role in the manner that wealth is organized, structured, and distributed across generations.[15] In a recent survey of family offices, 75 percent reported managing more than half of their family's net worth, with 33 percent managing all of the family's wealth (see Figure 6.8). This suggests that investment activities and the family office are inseparable.[16]

Welsh et al. concluded based on their study of 32 families that emotional attachment to the family firm and intentions to pass the firm on to successive generations foster an entrepreneurial orientation within the family office. Doing so is critical for the ultimate sustainability of the family business, the family wealth, and the family office—particularly during difficult economic times. The researchers emphasized, "The success of the family enterprise is also predicated on the family's ability to assimilate and acculturate its future generations to value and pursue entrepreneurship like the first generation."[17] Supporting mechanisms for doing so include family education and entrepreneurial skill development as well as the dissemination of academic research to family offices professionals. It also is advisable for local and federal governments to incentivize and support such programs, given the role that family businesses play in the national economy.

Roure et al. (2013) went further to say that implementation of the family office is itself an entrepreneurial process that draws on strategic management, entrepreneurial strategy, and financial management. They reasoned that creating a family office is an entrepreneurial action that strategically creates transgenerational wealth by the family shareholder group.[18]

Given the role of the family office in the family's investing activities, it is important to consider what implications would result if the family office was more focused on being entrepreneurial. Attention also should be given to how the family office could become an engine for cultivating and seeding new enterprise. Family office practitioners also should consider how direct investing might fit into the broader investment thesis to inspire a more entrepreneurial process within the family office. Practitioners may ask themselves three key questions to begin this process of reflection: (1) How much should be allocated to directs and why?; (2) Who should be involved and why?; and (3) What tax, estate planning, and investment oversight may be needed?

Family Investment Style and the Direct Investment Thesis

The final consideration discussed in this chapter that influences the direct investment thesis is the family's investing style with respect to preferred concentration, formality, and type of investing.

Preferred Concentration

As mentioned earlier in this chapter, the family's creation of a core business results in a deep expertise, strategic knowledge, and industry insight. Families vary in their preferences for staying close to this area of expertise versus diversifying away from it. Whereas some families prefer to "stick to their knitting," others may be more interested in taking a rifle shot at investing.

Kurzo noted that he has seen two primary types of families: one type that invests in sectors and geographies that they know well, and another type that uses the family office to diversify away.[19] In the former type of family, the members know a certain sector and region very well through their business. They also tend to be well connected in these areas, opening up many opportunities for direct investment into similar assets. J.P. Morgan and the World Economic Forum found in their survey of family offices that many of them are not actively trying to diversify away from the operating business.[20] In the latter type of family, which uses the family office to diversify away, less direct investing is typically done because the family lacks in-depth knowledge, insights, and contacts. Although this can produce a more balanced risk profile, returns also may be lower than for the first type of family. In another case, a founder left the investment banking realm after mastering the industry area as well as the structuring and preferences and understanding the opportunity set. He subsequently focused solely on direct investment opportunities and turned approximately $2 million into $250 million through methodical, rigorous, and careful investing. Today, the fledgling companies he invested in have grown into publicly traded companies in many of which he is a member of the board of directors.

Preferred Formality

Families vary in their approach toward direct investing, ranging from highly informal to highly formal.[21] Highly formal approaches are characterized by having investment committees; non-family member external professionals and other professional staff; and dedicated teams for sourcing, vetting and due diligence, structuring, monitoring, and exiting the investment. In such cases, the investment team conducts these various activities and prepares investment memos for the committee, outlining merits and risks and making recommendations to invest or divest. Kurzo estimated that roughly one-third of family businesses utilize structured approaches to investing with a formal investment committee.[22] Typically, the families that use formal procedures have large established family offices or have engaged in several direct investments and thus have formulated standard procedures and controls over the years. Formal procedures are particularly beneficial when the family extends beyond a single household or generation. In these cases, a more formalized governance model can help clarify decision-making authority and may circumvent conflict among family members.

FIGURE 6.9   Formality of Decision-Making Process

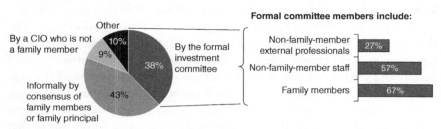

Source: J.P. Morgan and the World Economic Forum, *Inside the Single Family Investment Office Today*, 2016

Informal approaches are characterized by family members simply engaging in discussion and reaching informal consensus about whether to move forward on an investment. In such cases, the family members may want to remain loose and flexible, without codifying formal policies and procedures. Kurzo estimated that roughly two fifths of family businesses utilize informal approaches to direct investing.[23] J.P. Morgan and the World Economic Forum similarly found in their survey of family offices that 43 percent of families adopt an informal approach, where decisions are driven by a single-family member or consensus of multiple members (Figure 6.9). For example, one family office professional interviewed for this book shared that two brothers who were both in investment banking preferred to keep a relatively informal approach to their direct investing, as they had worked out an informal process of reviewing and assessing deal flow. One brother had industry expertise in healthcare, technology, and medical devices while the other had deep experience in real estate. Each brother was considered the lead in his own domains and would know the investors and subject matter experts to bring in to their respective deals. As a result, they did not feel the need for a formal board or investment committee, and they valued the flexibility this approach gave them.

Preferred Type of Investing

Given that family offices are often responsible for substantial portions of their family's sizeable wealth, how they put these assets to work is critical.[24] The basic investment activities include (1) selecting an appropriate mix of asset classes based on risk/return objectives, liquidity needs, and other constraints; (2) identifying, vetting, monitoring, and terminating third-party managers for traditional and alternative investments; and (3) buying and selling investments. Families enact these activities through four distinct investment styles:

1. *Outsourced:* The family office hires banks, external providers, asset managers, and consultants to conduct the activities. In this scenario one family office investment professional may focus on asset allocation while overseeing the external providers performing the other activities and then aggregating the results for reporting to the family. Only 11 percent use this style exclusively, while 23 percent use this in combination with other styles.

2. *Manager of managers:* The family office investment professionals determine asset allocations and then select managers for each asset class. Only 11 percent use this style exclusively, while 38 percent use this in combination with other styles.

3. *Direct private equity and real estate:* Family office professionals focus on illiquid assets, primarily equity stakes in private companies and real assets. Private equity funds, third-party managers, and personal contacts source the funds. Only 12 percent use this style exclusively, while 53 percent use this in combination with other styles.

4. *Direct active trading:* Family office professionals select securities with a hedge-fund-like operation focused on liquid markets. Only 1 percent use this style exclusively, while 33 percent use this in combination with other styles.

Notably, 63 percent of family offices utilize more than one investing model (see Figure 6.10), with 65 percent investing in direct private equity and real estate. This orientation reflects a strong entrepreneurial spirit.

FIGURE 6.10 Family Office Investment Models

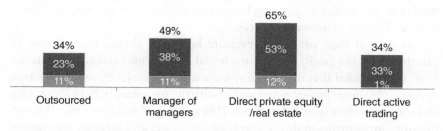

Source: J.P. Morgan and the World Economic Forum, *Inside the Single Family Investment Office Today,* 2016

Case Study

The Winchester Family historically was an enterprising family who had made significant wealth in manufacturing. The family had two main branches with four generations of family members still alive, including a total of 33 family members with over 70 accounts (see Table 6.1).

History/Background

In the early 1980s the family decided to sell their core operating business. The decision to sell was based on two primary factors: (1) The younger generations had not become involved in the business and with the older generations retiring there was little representation and involvement in the business by the family and (2) market conditions were favorable and the family was solicited by another company who they believed had a similar management style and culture so as to help protect their employees, some of which had been with the company for their entire careers. The sale netted the family over $400 million, which was split primarily among the second generation (40%) and the third generation (40%). The fourth and fifth generations also had some of the company stock (15% and 5%, respectively) in various generational skipping trusts, as an estate planning mechanism to get wealth down generations (see Table 6.2). The family always appreciated the money their niche manufacturing business provided, and after the sale, the family was interested in investing the proceeds of the sale of their company in ways that would continue to provide the family with both ongoing income as well as growth potential. They understood that traditional public market investment opportunities would not suffice. They believed strongly in allocating a portion of the family wealth to alternative investments. They also had a philosophy that in order to sustain the wealth for generations to come, investing not only in private equity funds but also in direct operating businesses needed to be an important piece to their ongoing investment strategy.

As part of their process to evaluate how they should best allocate to private equity, the family made some initial assumptions and considerations. First, they decided that they did not want to take a majority role in any core operating business, as they were familiar with the resources, both in knowledge and time, that were required to do so. They did, however, believe that through minority investments in direct operating businesses and through exposure to private equity funds they could synthetically mimic the return potential they had experienced from their former business. Second, they wanted to invest collectively as a family. They realized that only by taking advantage of the

TABLE 6.1 Family Ownership

Fac	Branch 1			
	Units	Members	Net Worth	# of Accounts
gen 2	1	2	40%	$88,000,000	5
gen 3	3	3	40%	$88,000,000	9
gen 4	2	11	15%	$33,000,000	22
gen 5	0	3	5%	$11,000,000	3
Total		19	100%	$220,000,000	39

Fac	Branch 2			
	Units	Members	Net Worth	# of Accounts	
gen 2	1	0	40%	3	$88,000,000
gen 3	2	4	40%	12	$88,000,000
gen 4	1	8	15%	16	$33,000,000
gen 5	0	2	5%	2	$11,000,000
Total		14		33	$220,000,000

Fac	Total				
	Units	Members	Net Worth	# of Accounts	Average Account Size
gen 2	2	2	$176,000,000	8	$22,000,000
gen 3	5	7	$176,000,000	21	$8,380,952
gen 4	3	19	$66,000,000	38	$1,736,842
gen 5	0	5	$22,000,000	5	$4,400,000
Total		33	$440,000,000	72	$6,111,111

Family sold operating company in 1980
Family net worth = $440,000,000
Branch 1 net worth = 50%
Branch 2 net worth = 50%
Allocation to private investments/alternatives = 30% ($132,000,000)
Percent of private investment allocation dedicated to private equity = 40% ($52,800,000)

buying power the family as a whole represented could they effectively build and maintain exposure to the alternative asset classes. This was the case because while the family had over $400 million in investible assets the money was split between generations and family members so that the largest single account within the second generation was approximately $55 million, the third

TABLE 6.2 Assumptions and Considerations for Investment Thesis to Direct Investments in Private Equity

Assumption/Consideration	Response
1. Lead Investor?	No—did not want to operate/manage businesses
2. Individual vs. Collective Investing	Collective—invest as a family unit for greater leverage and diversification
3. Exposure to Directs?	Yes—opportunity for "wealth engine" type returns from alternative and direct investing
4. Patient Capital and Liquidity Management	Yes—family had excess wealth and a long time horizon to warrant allocating to higher risk/reward illiquid investments

generation $30 million, and the fourth generation $4 million. The pooling of family assets also provides critical mass to build a properly diversified portfolio of private investments. Third, they believed that exposure to alternatives, particularly private equity, could be the "wealth engine" for their whole portfolio and, although it would increase their risk profile from an illiquid perspective, they believed it was well worth the opportunity for outsized returns. Fourth, they believed that they had patient capital to put to work, which meant they could be more opportunistic when putting their private capital to work.

Next, they began to answer a series of questions to operationalize how they would allocate to alternatives and directs. In order to understand how much, when, and how, the family walked through the following questions:

Direct Private Equity Investment Checklist

☐ Question 1: How much is my total net worth?
☐ Question 2: What is my current exposure to direct operating companies?
☐ Question 3: What is my target return profile?
☐ Question 4: What are my strategic reasons/purpose for investing in alternatives/directs? (staying rich vs. getting rich)
☐ Question 5: What are my liquidity constraints and time horizons? (5, 10, 15+ yr.)
☐ Question 6: What is the proper amount to allocate to alternatives?
☐ Question 7: What is the total amount of investable assets?
☐ Question 8: What is my target % allocation to alternatives?
☐ Question 9: What is my target % allocation to private equity?
☐ Question 10: What is my target % allocation to direct private equity?
☐ Question 11: What type of stake do I want to take? (minority, lead/sponsor)

□ Question 12: What are the sectors where I may want to invest? (sector options)
□ Question 13: In what stage of the company's lifecycle do I want to invest? (seed, venture, early, mid, late, etc.)
□ Question 14: What types of structures do I want to use to invest in private equity? (fund, direct, co-investment, combination)
□ Question 15: What size allocations should I make?
□ Question 16: Which criteria will I use to measure success? (return, current yield, tax efficiency, multi-gen dispersion, growth factor, etc.)

As they answered the questions to their checklist, the investment thesis for their alternatives began to take shape. See Table 6.3 for the data points to the questions posed in the checklist.

TABLE 6.3 Winchester Direct Investment Data Points

Direct Investment Data Points	Responses
Question 1: Net worth (including residences, collectibles, and art)	$540,000,000.00
Question 2: Current exposure to directs	5%
Question 3: Current allocation to alternatives (including directs)	15%
Question 4: Total amount of investable assets	$440,000,000.00
Question 5: Target % allocation to alternatives	40%
Question 6: Target % allocation to private equity	15%
Question 7: Strategic reasons/purpose for investing in alternatives/directs	Wealth creation; diversification
Question 8: Sectors where I want to invest (sector options)	Finance, Technology, and Healthcare
Question 9: Stage of the company to invest	Early/venture stage
Question 10: Types of structures	Combination (50% funds, 10% co-investments, 40% direct)
Question 11: Lead vs. minority stake	Minority
Question 12: Time horizon and liquidity constraints	10 years+
Question 13: Size of my allocations	Allocations from: $250k–$5M
Question 14: Return profile	20–25% IRR
Question 15: Success criteria	IRR; multi-gen wealth transfer

Of the $440 million of combined wealth, the Winchesters determined to allocate 35 percent ($132 million) toward alternatives with 40 percent of that or $52.8 million being specifically allocated to private equity. The Winchester family understood the importance of valuation and seeking investment opportunities when markets were depressed and underlying assets typically undervalued. Because of their patient capital approach, they were highly selective and erred more on the side of not making an investment than to jump into one. As such, they had a discerning and rigorous approach to their investing that aligned with their overall investment thesis. Figure 6.11 illustrates the Winchester family's overall target portfolio allocation.Similar to the endowment asset allocation model, the Winchesters believe that utilizing the full investment opportunity set at their disposal is prudent.

Alternatives to the Winchesters represent a source of enhanced return potential along with the opportunity for risk mitigation. Specifically, hedge funds provide access to nontraditional return drivers and uncorrelated sources of risk through sophisticated investment strategies not allowed in publicly traded investment formats. The inclusion of hedge funds allows the

FIGURE 6.11   Winchester Portfolio Allocation

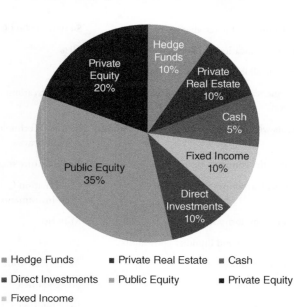

Winchester Portfolio Allocation

- ■ Hedge Funds   ■ Private Real Estate   ■ Cash
- ■ Direct Investments   ■ Public Equity   ■ Private Equity
- ▨ Fixed Income

Winchesters to create portfolios with better risk/return characteristics. Further, the Winchesters desire exposure to some of the greatest investment talent who are operating within top-quartile hedge funds. For the Winchesters, the opportunity to invest directly in operating companies provides a mechanism to participate in a wealth creation engine that has the potential to synthetically replicate the return potential of their former operating business without the same level of concentration.

The family also has a bias toward real estate and some real assets due to the finite supply of these sectors. Because of the increased demand, buying and holding select tracks of land and/or commercial properties that should appreciate over time is attractive.

In summary, the investment thesis when investing in private equity is to be able to do the following:

Winchesters' Direct Private Equity Investment Thesis

☐ Use the family's combined buying power
☐ Qualify all family members to invest in alternatives (including non-accredited)
☐ Find, due-diligence, and access top-tier managers and strategies (funds and directs)
☐ Gain critical mass to meet minimums and construct properly diversified portfolios of alternative asset classes
☐ Negotiate preferable terms with the manager
  ☐ Fees
  ☐ Liquidity
☐ Information rights

The key for the family was to understand what were the critical drivers and objectives for the broader portfolio, what part the direct private equity investment thesis played to achieve the long-range goals, and how this approach leveraged the collective family aspirations to continue to have an entrepreneurial orientation.

Conclusion

This chapter provided an overview of the process of designing a direct investment thesis. The direct investment thesis helps investors decide what investments to purchase, what to sell, what other actions to take, as well as when and why they need to initiate these activities. Several considerations need to be observed when designing the thesis, including the family's desired asset mix, the family's pathway to direct investing, the family's entrepreneurial orientation, and the family's desired style.

Asset mix refers to the overall percentage allocations of an investment portfolio into particular asset classes and whether the overall mix is designed to preserve wealth, aggressively grow wealth, or achieve a balance of both objectives. The family's pathway to direct investing is influenced by whether the family (1) still owns its main operating business and (2) has instituted a family office. These two dimensions give rise to four different enterprising pathways, which have strong implications for the family's ability and interest to engage in direct investing.

Understanding and enhancing entrepreneurial orientation within a family business requires attention to family members' attitudes, perspectives, and behaviors in successive generations, and the family's involvement in the core operating business. The family office also plays a central role in the entrepreneurism exercised by the family. Finally, the family's desired style refers to the family's preferred concentration, formality, and type of investing as it concerns direct investing.

All of these factors have implications for the direct investment thesis crafted by the family and the role the family office plays in it.

Notes

1. J.P. Morgan and the World Economic Forum, *Inside the Single Family Investment Office Today*, 2016.
2. Ibid.
3. Interview with Claude Kurzo, October, 2016.
4. Ibid.
5. Juan Roure, Juan Luis Segurado, Dianne H. B. Welsh, and Kirby Rosplock, "Toward a Conceptual Model of the Role of Entrepreneurship in the Family Office," *Journal of Applied Management and Entrepreneurship* 18(4), (2013): 42–63; Dianne H. B. Welsh, Esra Memili, Kirby Rosplock, Juan Roure, and Juan Luis Segurado, "Perceptions of Entrepreneurship Across Generations in Family Offices: A Stewardship Theory Perspective," *Journal of Family Business Strategy* 4 (2013): 213–226; J. J. Chrisman, J. H. Chua, and L. P. Steier, "An Introduction to Theories of Family Business," *Journal of Business Venturing* 18(4), (2003): 441–448; J. J. Chrisman, E. Memili, and K. Misra,

(2014). "Non-Family Managers, Family Firms, and the Winner's Curse: The Influence of Non-Economic Goals and Bounded Rationality," *Entrepreneurship Theory and Practice* 38 (2014).

6. Dianne H. B. Welsh, Esra Memili, Kirby Rosplock, Juan Roure, and Juan Luis Segurado, "Perceptions of Entrepreneurship across Generations in Family Offices: A Stewardship Theory Perspective," *Journal of Family Business Strategy* 4 (2013): 214.

7. T. M. Zellweger, R. S. Nason, and M. Nordqvist, "From Longevity of Firms to Transgenerational Entrepreneurship of Families: Introducing Family Entrepreneurial Orientation," *Family Business Review* 20(10), (2011): 1–20.

8. Dianne H.B. Welsh, Esra Memili, Kirby Rosplock, Juan Roure, and Juan Luis Segurado, Perceptions of Entrepreneurship across Generations in Family Offices: A Stewardship Theory Perspective," *Journal of Family Business Strategy* 4 (2013).

9. Juan Roure, Juan Luis Segurado, Dianne H. B. Welsh, and Kirby Rosplock, "Toward a Conceptual Model of the Role of Entrepreneurship in the Family Office," *Journal of Applied Management and Entrepreneurship* 18(4), (2013): 42–63.

10. Interview with Claude Kurzo, October 2016.

11. J. J. Chrisman, J. H. Chua, and L. P. Steier, "An Introduction to Theories of Family Business," *Journal of Business Venturing* 18(4), (2003): 441–448; J. J. Chrisman, E. Memili, and K. Misra, "Non-Family Managers, Family Firms, and the Winner's Curse: The Influence of Non-economic Goals and Bounded Rationality," *Entrepreneurship Theory and Practice* 38 (2014); Dianne H. B. Welsh, Esra Memili, Kirby Rosplock, Juan Roure, and Juan Luis Segurado, "Perceptions of Entrepreneurship across Generations in Family Offices: A Stewardship Theory Perspective, *Journal of Family Business Strategy* 4 (2013): 214.

12. Dianne H. B. Welsh, Esra Memili, Kirby Rosplock, Juan Roure, and Juan Luis Segurado. Perceptions of Entrepreneurship across Generations in Family Offices: A Stewardship Theory Perspective, *Journal of Family Business Strategy* 4 (2013).

13. Juan Roure, Juan Luis Segurado, Dianne H. B. Welsh, and Kirby Rosplock, "Toward a Conceptual Model of the Role of Entrepreneurship in the Family Office," *Journal of Applied Management and Entrepreneurship* 18(4), (2013): 42–63.

14. Interview with Claude Kurzo, October 2016.

15. Dianne H. B. Welsh, Esra Memili, Kirby Rosplock, Juan Roure, and Juan Luis Segurado, "Perceptions of Entrepreneurship across Generations in

Family Offices: A Stewardship Theory Perspective, *Journal of Family Business Strategy* 4 (2013).

16. J.P. Morgan and the World Economic Forum, *Inside the Single Family Investment Office Today*, 2016.

17. Dianne H. B. Welsh, Esra Memili, Kirby Rosplock, Juan Roure, and Juan Luis Segurado, "Perceptions of Entrepreneurship across Generations in Family Offices: A Stewardship Theory Perspective, *Journal of Family Business Strategy* 4 (2013): 222.

18. Juan Roure, Juan Luis Segurado, Dianne H. B. Welsh, and Kirby Rosplock, "Toward a Conceptual Model of the Role of Entrepreneurship in the Family Office," *Journal of Applied Management and Entrepreneurship* 18(4), (2013): 42–63.

19. Interview with Claude Kurzo, October 2016.

20. J.P. Morgan and the World Economic Forum, *Inside the Single Family Investment Office Today*, 2016.

21. Ibid.

22. Interview with Claude Kurzo, October 2016.

23. Ibid.

24. J.P. Morgan and the World Economic Forum, *Inside the Single Family Investment Office Today*, 2016.

CHAPTER 7

Sourcing, Deal Flow, Screening, and Deploying Direct Investments

Contributing Author: Euclid Walker

The purpose of this chapter is to provide a framework and action steps to sourcing deal flow, screening opportunities, and making direct investments. What is so critical about the sourcing, screening, and deploying steps of the investment process? This stage of the process is where investors are accessing hopefully the best-in-breed direct investment opportunities, screening for those that meet their unique investment criteria, and then efficiently and effectively deploying capital into these direct investments.

Equipped with an investment thesis as well as knowledge of the industry, the size and type of investments that an investor may be seeking may vary depending on the size of the investment, the relative risk, and its time horizon. Sourcing deal flow consists of assessing your network and determining who within it will be good potential sources of investment opportunities. Each of us has thousands of relationship possibilities from "friends and family" (i.e., people we grew up with, went to school with, play sports with, or have

FIGURE 7.1   Web of Direct Investment Deal Flow Relationships

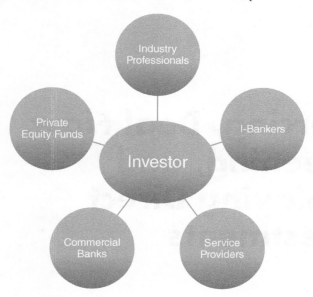

Source: Euclid Walker, 2016

a yoga class with) to people we've done business with. In a study on direct investment behavior, approximately 59 percent of the respondents indicated that they source direct deals from friends and family members.[1] The skill is in discerning which of these relationships are good potential sources of deal flow. This framework will help you focus on the categories of relationships that investment opportunities are most likely to come from. The most valuable component to sourcing deals is having a highly sophisticated, well-vetted, and trusted network of industry professionals, investment bankers, business brokers, service providers, commercial bankers, family offices, and business professionals. Figure 7.1 illustrates the web of key conduits to sourcing direct investment opportunities, which will be described in greater detail to follow.

Industry Professionals and Thought Leaders

If your thesis calls for investments in specific industries or sectors (technology, packaging, energy, aerospace, real estate, infrastructure, etc.), a very good source of deal flow can be through business executives in the specific industries. If you've worked in the industry, you can use your personal rolodex of colleagues, clients, and competitors. If you are new to the industry, attending industry conferences and networking with executives is a good strategy to develop relationships with industry executives, which will help with sourcing. The Association for Corporate Growth (ACG) can be a great resource for networking and expanding your relationships. ACG is a network for dealmakers and business leaders and has local meetings and events through 59 chapters and holds regional and global conferences focused on investing and growing businesses.

Personal relationships can also be a good source of deal flow if they know what types of opportunities fit your investment strategy. For these and other sources, marketing and communication are important. A firm overview provides a clear statement of the investment thesis and the types of companies being sought and is an important document to be developed and regularly updated as part of the deal flow development process. A great example of this is seasoned operator and manager Mike Green.[2] Mike ran a very successful packaging business, which he and his family sold to a private equity firm. Mike decided he wanted to use his expertise in packaging to make investments in the packaging and printing industries. He used his personal and professional rolodex to get the word out that he was looking to make investments in packaging businesses and provided his specific criteria (e.g., EBITDA slightly negative to $5 million, preference for businesses in the Midwest, control or co-investments). Within two months he was seeing good deal flow and within three months had made his first investment.

Investment Bankers/Business Brokers

Investment bankers and business brokers ("I-bankers" for simplicity) are in some ways the most obvious source of deal flow, because I-bankers are hired by a company to find an investor, partner, or buyer (depending on the situation). They often will seek to have a broad search and obtain as many offers for a company as possible. This can be both good and bad news for someone looking to source opportunities. It is good news because I-bankers are actively looking to form relationships with entities that have capital and are seeking to make investments in and/or buy companies. They will want to understand in great detail the types of opportunities that fit your investment thesis, so they know what types of opportunities to present. The bad news is I-bankers often want broad participation by both financial buyers (other family offices, private equity funds, and independent sponsors) and strategic buyers (operating companies seeking acquisitions or mergers in their industry or complementary industries) in processes they run; this means there will be significant competition for most opportunities from I-banks. Competition means you can get into a bidding war or the I-bank may run an auction process (where they require potential investors to submit bids, of which they will review and accept the highest offer). This type of process can often result in prices being driven up, and sometimes the company can become overvalued to the point where the winning bidder actually loses (because they've overpaid and made a bad investment).

Professional Service Providers

Professional service providers such as lawyers, accountants, and consultants often have close relationships with the companies they serve. A law firm may be asked to draft a new operating agreement if a partner is exiting or an accountant may be asked to explain the tax implications of selling shares. This often means service providers may know if their clients are considering selling the business or looking for an equity partner. Growing firms often discuss their cash needs and financial positions with their service providers, and those providers tend to suggest contact with providers of capital. Building relationships with service providers can prove to be an excellent source of leads for deal flow. Recently an attorney representing an entrepreneur we partnered with to make an acquisition called a few months after the closing with interest to share other investment opportunities. The attorney called to say she had a client who was in the early stages of considering expanding his business through a major acquisition. She was reaching out to us because, even though we were not her client, she got a sense of the types of investments we liked to make and thought this fit our criteria. This goes back to a point made earlier: It is critically important to take every opportunity to clearly articulate your investment thesis and criteria. We did not make this particular investment, but the law firm has presented three more opportunities since being introduced.

Commercial Banks

Companies of all sizes utilize commercial banking services, and the banks are incentivized for their clients to do well and grow. The banks win when their client's assets and business holdings appreciate and grow over time, as the bank may have other business and banking services it may offer the client.

For example, often commercial banks have clients that approach them seeking a loan, yet sometimes what the client would be better served to do is consider an equity infusion into the company. If the company's balance sheet is already overleveraged, additional debt may put the company at great risk particularly with maintaining its covenants. Developing relationships with commercial bankers can be a win-win, because the banker is able to refer the client to a source of capital that may meet their needs.

You should be aware, however, that commercial bankers are generally less proactive than the other sources of deal flow we are discussing here. It is even more important to schedule regular calls, meetings, and discussions with commercial bankers. Quite often opportunities only come from them when you initiate the dialogue and they have a live situation at that particular point in time that requires capital they cannot provide.

Private Equity Funds/Family Offices

Co-investment opportunities with private equity funds and/or family offices, covered in Chapter 3, are another very good source of deal flow. Almost 58 percent of the respondents to a 2016 direct investment survey indicated that they source investments from other family offices (see Figure 7.2). Deal flow from these sources can come in two forms: (1) deals that did not fit their criteria but may fit yours; and (2) co-investment opportunities. When private equity and family offices are well established they often get access to good investment opportunities that do not fit their criteria (e.g., wrong industry, too large, too small, wrong geography). If they understand your investment criteria, they may share opportunities that are interesting to you but may not fit their criteria.

They may also see opportunities that fit well for them but require more investment capital than they are willing to commit. In these instances, they may seek co-investors. Co-investment opportunities can provide the potential advantage of working with other smart investment professionals and sharing risk. Having two sets of investment professionals reviewing an investment and being involved in a company can provide more than a "second set of eyes." It can mean more smart people on the board of directors and having less of your precious capital allocated to a specific investment, allowing for a larger portfolio of investments and, theoretically, lower risk. Some of the best investment opportunities come from private equity fund and family office co-investments. We had an opportunity introduced by a private equity fund that was already an investor in the company (sometimes referred to as

FIGURE 7.2   Family Office Direct Investment Deal Sources

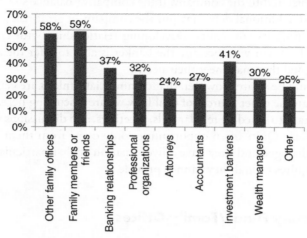

How do you source your direct investments?

■ How do you source your direct investments?

Source: Tamarind Partners Direct Investment Survey, 2016

a company in its portfolio or a portfolio company). The company was seeking additional capital to expand a factory and build a state-of-the-art piece of equipment that would lower their manufacturing cost and increase productivity. The fund had invested all of its capital and was in the process of marketing a new fund. (Private equity funds have finite capital and when the capital is depleted they can no longer invest from the fund; they can raise new funds, but the process may take several months to over a year.) They loved the investment opportunity but simply did not have the capital to invest. They knew we had a similar strategy and brought us into the opportunity. As a result, we were able to invest alongside another investment firm with industry expertise and history with the company.

Screening Process

Once the deal flow relationships have been established and the investor understands the types of investment opportunities they are most interested in, the amount of deal flow may be overwhelming. Omar Simmons is managing director of Exaltare Capital with over 20 years of experience investing in private companies. Omar shared, "Once things are up and running, quantity of deal flow is not the problem. Developing quality deal flow is the challenge and the key to that is the screening process."[3] In essence, if, for example, less than 5 percent of your pipeline of investment opportunities is high quality, then you are reviewing and vetting countless deals that you will likely never do. You may also miss great investment opportunities that either you don't vet in time or simply never get to. Improving your pipeline of deals to more like 20 to 30 percent high-quality deal flow only helps improve your odds.

Screening is simply the process of determining which of the opportunities sourced through the deal flow process fit well with your investment thesis and have the potential to be good investments. Omar believes, "Having a disciplined process of quickly getting to 'no' or 'maybe' is important for internally managing deal flow and improving the quality of future deal flow. I-bankers and companies really appreciate speed and providing a quick 'no' with the rationale why can help them provide higher quality opportunities in the future. But even more importantly, it helps manage internal resources."[4] These are important points, because most independent sponsors or family offices looking to do direct deals do not have the same resources as large private equity firms, so it is critical to make sure resources are not spending their time on opportunities that do not fit their investment criteria. The opportunity cost could be that you miss an exceptional opportunity while spinning your wheels on something that should have been a quick "no."

Screening should be at least a two-phase process, if not more (see Figure 7.3). Some use the terms *prescreening* and *screening* and others simply have *phase 1* and *phase 2*.

FIGURE 7.3 Sourcing through the Closing Process

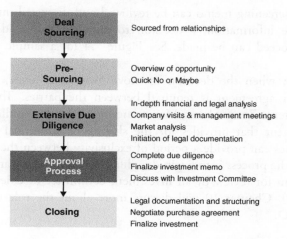

Deal Sourcing	Sourced from relationships
Pre-Sourcing	Overview of opportunity Quick No or Maybe
Extensive Due Diligence	In-depth financial and legal analysis Company visits & management meetings Market analysis Initiation of legal documentation
Approval Process	Complete due diligence Finalize investment memo Discuss with Investment Committee
Closing	Legal documentation and structuring Negotiate purchase agreement Finalize investment

Prescreening should consist of preparing a one- to two-page memorandum that can be easily reviewed internally for the purpose of determining if the opportunity should be analyzed further.

The memo should include the following four sections:

1. *Situation Overview:* Provide an overview of what is happening with the company and why there is an investment opportunity (e.g., founder retiring, expansion capital, etc.). Explain how the opportunity was sourced (e.g., direct relationship with the Company, I-Banker, etc.). Include a brief overview of the company (industry, size, locations, and so on) and the investment opportunity (e.g., $5 million equity investment).
2. *Investment Thesis:* Describe how the investment opportunity fits the investment thesis. Provide specifics of the rationale for investing in the opportunity and which criteria it meets within your thesis. Equally important is to identify if it does not meet certain criteria and what rationale to make an exception.
3. *Management Assessment:* Provide an overview of the management team and their positions with details (e.g., Is the founder/CEO retiring? Do they need management support? Does the business require new management or have a solid management succession plan if in transition?)
4. *Initial Financial Analysis:* Include historical, current, and projected financial information. Balance sheet and cash flow metrics along with key ratios are also important metrics. Potentially include screening financial return analysis. Sometimes outside audited reporting is also desired. Look at the industry benchmarks to understand whether this is a high-performing business.

This prescreening memo can be reviewed and discussed internally and, based on the information, a decision to move forward and learn more or to not proceed can be made. See Figure 7.4 for a sample prescreening memo.

Typically, when the decision to move forward is made, some documentation or agreement is required between the parties. This can be a Letter of Intent, Term Sheet, Memorandum of Understanding, or some other document that provides for the sharing of additional information and sometimes can provide a period of exclusivity between the parties. The next step in the process is to begin due diligence and prepare an Investment Memorandum for review by an investment committee or chief investment officer (CIO). Chapter 10 will discuss more about the role of the direct investing CIO.

FIGURE 7.4 Sample Prescreening Memo, p. 1

Sample Prescreening Memo – Page 1

Investment Screening Memo

ABC Corporation

Deal Team: _____ Date: _____

For Internal Use Only

Company Name	(Provide exchange and ticker, if public) **Website:** http://www.abccorp.com
Company Contact	
Phone /Fax/Email	**Phone:** (XXX) XXX-XXX Fax: (XXX) XXX-XXXX **Email:** Firstname.Lastname@ABC.com
Location	City, State, Country
Industry	Provide industry description and general overview (growth, economics, etc.). Competition, market share, barriers to entry.

Business Summary	• Describe business purpose and key products or technologies
	  List firm's lines of business and approximate contribution of each to total revenue. If an affiliate, determine the percentage that the firm contributes to the parent's total revenue
	• Discuss overall business objectives with respect to future growth over the next five years. Cover any present or planned areas of emphasis
	  Business execution strategy; patents, trademarks, intellectual property

Investment Rationale	• Investment is consistent with industry focus of the General Partner • Buy-and-build approach consistent with stated strategy
Exit Opportunities	• DEF Software with market cap of $20 billion actively acquiring technology firms
Performance Comments	• Company has exceeded original plans due to top-line revenue growth and improved operating margins. • Original equity has increased nearly three times due to ....

149

FIGURE 7.4 Sample Prescreening Memo, p. 2 (*Continued*)

Sample Prescreening Memo – Page 2

Sources and Uses

Sources	Uses

Management Assessment

- Comment on key management experience (industry and firm)
- Comment on key management's time together as a team
-

Financial Summary

	Year	Year+1	Year+2	Year+3
Sales	$			
Sales Growth	%			
Gross income				
Gross income margin				
EBITDA	$			
EBITDA margin	%			
EBIT	$			
EBIT Margin	%			
Net income	$			
Net income margin	%			
Cash flow	$			
Cash flow margin	%			

Current Capital Structure

Latest Valuation Date:	MM/DD/YY	Percent	Number of Security Holders
Total Credit Facility	$XX,XXX	X%	
Total Senior Debt	XX,XXX	X%	
Total Convertible Debt			
Senior Preferred			
Junior Preferred			
Common Equity			
Other (define)			
Total Value			

Due Diligence

Due diligence is the process of studying, evaluating, and investigating in detail a potential investment. This phase involves assessing the management team, products, customers, financials, and sales pipeline. The due diligence phase is critically important to the investment process, and even the most seasoned investors often utilize professional third-party experts to assist in various parts of the process. Seventy-four percent of them outsource due diligence to third-party experts.[5] Diligence always starts with a due diligence request list (see Appendix B at the end of the book for a sample request list), which is a comprehensive list of documents and information requested from the company. The company will often establish an electronic data room where the information will be compiled and can be electronically accessed and individual files can be downloaded and reviewed. Ahead we will discuss the key areas of due diligence and what is done to understand each area of the business.

Management

Management assessment is one of the most critical components of due diligence and the chief source of uncertainty in a direct investment. Understanding the capabilities, experience, and track record of the management team is vital because the decisions they make and the effort they put forward will determine if the investment is successful. Assessing the management team consists of:

- Background and reference checks (provided by firms like K2 Intelligence, Kroll, or Navigant)
- Meeting with and interviewing every member of the senior management team
- Reviewing employment history and track record with the company
- Conducting personality and/or leadership tests
- Understanding team dynamics (how well they work together, whether there are noticeable tensions)

The first step is to determine if the existing management team will remain in place or if the transaction is related to a change in management (founder selling).

If there will be management changes, determining the succession plan to replace management is paramount. If, for example, it is part of the investment thesis to provide management services in industries where there is expertise, the investment team's previous industry experience is an important benefit to the due diligence process. If this is not part of the strategy, a third-party industry expert consultant can be engaged to assist. These services should be factored into the overall cost of investment due diligence. We once made an investment into a company with a great product, a famous celebrity endorser, and demand for the product by major retailers like Target, Walmart, Costco, and Walgreens. Everything was lined up for success. Unfortunately, a rookie mistake was made and there was not enough attention focused on the management team. They were very creative and pulled everything together (the product, endorser, and product placement), but they had no experience or expertise running a business of this type. Unfortunately, it was not a successful investment. However, a valuable lesson was learned: If you don't have good management, even the best business idea will likely fail.

Market Overview

Understanding and analyzing the market/industry the company is working within is a key component to the due diligence process. The market overview section provides a quantitative and qualitative assessment of the market the company operates in, such as (1) growth rates including historical, current, and future, (2) market size, (3) potential and known threats to the market, and (4) position of the company.

Analyzing the overall market (is it growing, fragmented, consolidating) and the company's position within the market (are they a big fish in a small pond or a growing fish in a large pond) are important factors. There will also be an analysis of the end users of the product (consumers or companies). It is also important to understand the company's competitive position and what differentiates it. Are they the low-cost provider, the high-quality provider, or do they have a disruptive technology that creates an advantage?

A third-party industry expert also can be very helpful in assisting with the market assessment in industries where the core investment team does not have expertise. Many investors in the direct investment space may find themselves becoming generalist investors and relying on industry experts for industries where they have more limited domain expertise and experience. For example, a generalist investor made an investment in the waste removal, recycling, and waste management space and the industry expert was critical to understanding the industry and making the investment decision. The expert was a former executive in the industry and provided the key drivers for growth and a detailed competitive analysis, and even offered insights into the management team and market perception of the company being considered for investment.

Evaluating Risk and Suitability

Direct investors recognize that this type of investing is not suitable for all investors due to its having a high risk of failure. More transactions do not perform as expected compared with those that do, as noted in Chapter 4. This is due to general business risks, which can be managed, but ultimately unforeseen and unknown future occurrences can have a negative effect on any business. When investors decide on how to evaluate a company and place a value on the company, in the absence of an efficient public market, the investors are pricing the risk of the company in the present value of the target investment that they perceive.

Identification of opportunity-specific risks inherent to the company or target asset can be articulated and clarified up front in any process. Investors may ultimately accept the risks of the opportunity, so on a standalone basis the risks may not warrant declining the investment. Investors do, however, look for a risk-adjusted return, which means that the opportunity to extract value at some stage in the future is how the investor will outperform other investments through direct investing.

Therefore, accepting and pricing risk is a function of suitability with the investor. Does the investment align with the investment thesis? Does the investor have some inherent industry expertise or knowledge that will mitigate the risk profile of the company? Does the investor or investment office have certain capabilities that will mitigate risk?

An example of risk mitigation is the ability and willingness of the investor to make additional investments in the target company. Generally, growth-oriented companies perpetually struggle with financing new activities and CEOs and senior management will be perpetually raising capital. This is an operational risk in two factors: The management team is distracted with these activities on an ongoing basis, and the risk of not having the financing available to pursue a strategic opportunity that could bring significant value to the company cannot be secured. If an investor is willing to finance these types of strategic opportunities, that does not eliminate the risk, but it can change that risk parameter for the investor versus an investor who would not be willing or able to finance future transactions and therefore the risk remains in the company profile.

Financial and Valuation Analysis

The financial and valuation review and analysis of a company consists of understanding the historical and current financial performance of the business as well as determining the confidence you have in management's view of future performance and the value of the company. As it relates to historical performance, the previous three-to-five years of financial statements should be reviewed and analyzed (ideally the company will have audited or professionally reviewed financials). Engaging an accounting firm to review and perform a *quality of earnings* (QoE) should also be considered. The QoE provides analysis of the accuracy and sustainability of historical earnings and also provides:

- Breakdown of revenue by components
- Analysis of historic revenue trends
- Determination of onetime expenses versus recurring expenses (extraordinary items may be added back for valuation purposes)
- Determination of fixed versus variable costs
- Analysis of impact on both revenue and expenses due to management changes
- Analysis of assumptions used in cash flow projections and scenario analysis

In addition to the financial review, various valuation analysis will be used to test and justify the purchase price/investment value. Depending on the industry, a combination of intrinsic (e.g., discounted cash flow analysis) and market (e.g., comparable company, cash flow multiples) valuation analysis will be undertaken and various scenarios will be reviewed. Often there will be base, downside, optimistic, and management cases of the company's financial forecasts. The investment team will take the management team's financial forecasts and make changes to the assumptions to develop these cases. The legalities of structuring a deal and considering the proper terms will be explored in greater detail in Chapter 8.

Investment Memorandum

In parallel with completing due diligence, the team will develop the Investment Memorandum. The Investment Memorandum provides a detailed rationale for making the investment and provides information and analysis from the findings of the due diligence process. The decision-makers should be able to read the Investment Memorandum and have at their fingertips all the information required to make a final investment decision. The key sections of a high-quality Investment Memorandum include:

- *Background:* Information from the prescreening process (when was it pre-screened, how was the opportunity sourced, who is leading the internal review)
- *Situation Overview:* What is the investment opportunity?
- *Due Diligence Overview:* Key diligence conducted and highlights of findings
- *Company Description:* History, geography, and service/product
- *Industry Overview:* Industry trends, how the company is positioned in the industry, and competitive landscape
- *Investment Considerations:* Merits and risks
- *Financial Overview:* Historical and projected financials, year-to-date financial performance, audited financials, balance sheet, cash flow, ratio analysis, and capitalization table
- *Risk Factors:* Potential risks to the business (macro and micro) and key areas identified in due diligence
- *Investment Returns:* Base case and sensitivity analysis
- *Exit Strategy:* Timing and potential strategies for exiting the investment
- *Recommendation*

Investment Decision Process

Investment decisions can be made by committee or by a single decision-maker. It is more common to have an investment committee of at least three people; however, some entrepreneurial investors make the decisions themselves without the benefit of a committee. Investment committees are recommended for several reasons, including:

- Providing structure and consistency
- Checks, balances, and controls
- Benefits from different perspectives and skillsets

The investment committee should consist of representatives from the sources of capital (family members with decision-making authority) and trusted third parties with investment expertise. Including independent members of the investment committee provides different points of view, is good governance, and ensures processes are followed.

The role of the investment committee is to review and, from time-to-time, update the investment thesis and make investment decisions (based on the work of the investment team) in line with the investment thesis. Depending on the level of deal flow the investment committee can meet on a regular basis or as needed. The positive to meeting on a regular basis is that it allows for committee members to keep their schedules clear for set meetings and provides for a regular dialogue (even if there are not investments to review at every meeting). There are positives to meeting on an as-needed basis, as it provides the flexibility to move quickly if an investment decision is time sensitive or a competitive situation exists.

In situations where in presenting an opportunity to the investment committee the investment committee had questions that required additional due diligence or suggested changes to the transaction, the committee needs to be adaptable to convene on an impromptu basis. In these instances, a conditional investment approval may be made, which allows the diligencing partner to go back to the company and negotiate the changes knowing that, if successful, the investment could be made. Once the investment has received approval the next step is to finalize legal documentation and move toward closing.

Conclusion

This chapter provides the steps and a detailed overview of the critical processes of sourcing deal flow, screening, and analyzing opportunities and making the investment decision to deploy capital for direct investing. Each part of the process is equally important, and an investment cannot be successful without them. It all starts with having a quality pipeline from your sourcing network and determining which opportunities your team should spend time analyzing. The due diligence and investment decision process is the most time consuming and where most investors use third-party professional assistance. The next chapters will provide information on what is required after the decision to invest is made, from structuring and closing the investment to adding value once the investment is closed.

Notes

1. Tamarind Partners Direct Investment Survey, 2016.
2. A pseudonym for Mike's real name, as he prefers not to be identified.
3. Interview with Omar Simmons, August 2016.
4. Ibid.
5. Tamarind Partners Direct Investment Survey, 2016.

CHAPTER 8

Direct Investments: Deal Structures, Terms, and Portfolio Construction

Contributing Author: Jolyne Caruso

Direct investing into privately held companies requires significant upfront work that entails sourcing, understanding, and negotiating the structure of each investment. This chapter will cover alternative ways of structuring direct investments to achieve a target return and will examine terminology included in both equity and debt term sheets. When it comes to the many steps associated with the direct investment process, the importance of carefully structuring each investment cannot be overemphasized.

We will review the most common types of equity and debt investments associated with direct investing and the range of possible returns. We also discuss hybrid investments where both debt and equity are used in a single investment structure, such as mezzanine debt with warrants. Included is a case study of a hybrid investment in a privately held company that generated a venture capital return with a debt instrument. The chapter concludes with a Series A Preferred Stock sample term sheet. The term sheet defines commonly used terms associated with many typical direct investments and will provide a deeper understanding of the items that can be negotiated in any direct deal.

While individual investors should educate themselves on the terminology of direct investing, it is important to recognize that structuring is both art and science. Working with an experienced advisor or banker who can help structure and negotiate terms, co-investing and sharing diligence with a group of individuals in a club deal, or co-investing alongside a private equity firm will likely provide the best investment outcome. Alternatively, being part of a deal syndicate, which simply means investing with a group who act as one investor, often with an experienced investor acting in the lead role, allows for negotiating leverage with the underlying company. These are all ways to mitigate the numerous inherent challenges associated with direct investments.

How to Get Started

When constructing a portfolio of direct deals, as compared with investing in private equity funds, the first decision an investor needs to make is to determine where direct investments fit within the asset allocation of their investment portfolio. Within an asset allocation model, most investors include direct deals as part of their overall private equity allocation. According to a CampdenWealth/UBS 2016 Global Family Office report, family office allocations to private equity are forecasted to reach 22 percent, which is a 2.3 percent increase over 2015. Most of this increase is attributed to anticipated redemptions out of hedge funds. Within private equity, direct investments account for over half of the allocation. Campden qualifies directs as investments with either active or passive management roles into privately held companies of various stages. This allocation has gradually increased over the past five years as family offices seek greater alpha (investment performance due to active management rather than market-returns) in investment portfolios and look to mitigate fees, exert more control, and have greater transparency over underlying investments.

Once an allocation to direct investments is determined, an investor will need to identify a target rate of return, which will dictate the types of investments to source. Direct investments can include minority or control positions in privately held or public companies, as well as co-investments alongside traditional private equity funds. In this chapter, we focus specifically on direct investments into privately held companies where we see the greatest potential for family offices to customize a portfolio that aligns with their target rates of return. Many direct investments into privately held companies are structured as equity investments into a holding company. These types of investments, while able to potentially generate the greatest opportunity for returns, are often highly illiquid and require some kind of monetization in order for the investor to get his or her money returned. Investing in debt of a privately held company will usually result in lower returns than equity; however, an investor is senior in the company's capital structure, thereby having a higher probability of repayment. We will explore the benefits and risks to debt, equity, and hybrid structures.

Portfolio Construction

When it comes to direct investing, portfolio construction entails several steps, including determining the short- and long-term investment goals of the investor, his risk tolerance, and how direct investments fit within an overall asset allocation. For many investors, the most efficient way to structure a portfolio is to invest deal-by-deal in separate, discrete investments. For example, a pool of 10 to 15 investments can provide reasonable portfolio diversification, depending on the type of investment and the development stage of the portfolio company. An investor needs to determine what percentage of early stage, venture, and growth equity they wish to include in a portfolio, with early stage being the most risky and requiring strong portfolio diversification. Another important factor to consider in portfolio construction is liquidity. An investor who has a longer investment time horizon can afford to take more risk (and thereby expect a greater return) and may choose to invest in venture equity that will likely need several years to show value; a shorter time horizon necessitates safer investments such as debt instruments that provide periodic interest payments along the way (but often at the expense of return).

One option for an investor who is just beginning to invest in direct deals is to invest in a pledge fund. This structure allows an investor to customize a portfolio of individual direct deals while providing optionality and control over portfolio selection. Pledge funds are optimal for small-to-midsize family offices that do not have the staff to source, diligence, and perform the critical ongoing monitoring of each investment. A growing number of private equity funds are structured as pledge funds. In a pledge fund, an investor invests in a portfolio of direct deals, choosing to opt in or opt out on a deal-by-deal basis. A typical pledge fund allows an investor to pledge a specific amount of capital and, upon choosing to invest in the first deal, the capital is drawn, and a management fee is charged on that investment. The investment is usually held in a special-purpose vehicle (SPV) so there is no cross-contamination of deals. Each investment generates a separate return and an investor's capital account is calculated based on the performance of the collective SPVs in which they are invested. There are usually a limited number of times that an investor can opt out before losing the right to invest as part of the pledge fund. Investors can often increase their pro-rata allocation through co-investment rights, if the capacity of an investment is not satisfied by the existing limited partners (LPs) in the fund. In some cases, pledge funds offer a single K1 for each investor to simplify the tax reporting in any given year, an important consideration for families with large portfolios of direct investments.

The Capital Stack

Capital stack depicts the hierarchy of the total capital invested into a company and the relationship between each of these instruments to one another and the issuer. Understanding where an investment sits in the capital stack is an important factor in any transaction.

One of the most challenging moments for investors in direct deals is when they receive the deal documentation package including the term sheet and operating agreement. While the investor pitch-book may have made complete sense, the term sheet can seem like it is written in a foreign language. This is why investing with an experienced advisor or group of investors can be highly beneficial.

Among the first tasks to master in direct investing is to thoroughly understand the capital stack. An investor's position in the capital stack determines who gets paid first when something goes wrong and who is rewarded with the greatest upside if something goes right. It establishes who has the legal rights to specific assets and income, who receives priority of payment in the event of a default, and the order in which each party may be repaid following the liquidation of assets in the event of a bankruptcy or sale. Here, we will discuss the capital stack, and the prioritization of an investor's rights based on his or her investment in a company. Further, we outline the advantages and disadvantages of the three most common structures of direct investments: (1) equity, (2) debt, and (3) hybrid investments, or investments that combine both equity and debt structures.

Figure 8.1 illustrates the capital stack structure. At the top is senior secured debt, which has the lowest risk and potentially lowest return, but the highest claim for repayment. At the bottom of the stack sits equity or

FIGURE 8.1   Capital Stack Structure

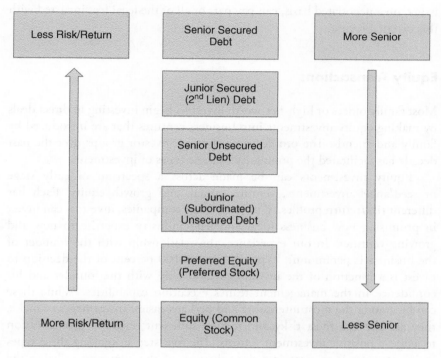

common stock that has the highest potential return, but with the highest risk in the event of a default. In a bankruptcy of a company, after taxes and employee wages are paid, the waterfall of repayment is as follows: Senior secured bondholders are paid followed by junior secured and then unsecured bondholders. Preferred and equity holders are typically *impaired*, meaning that they get less than their stated claim. In some instances, an investor holding a senior secured position may still lose money depending on the difference between the value of the assets securing the debt and the amount of capital originally invested in that debt. Therefore, a senior secured position does not always guarantee safety of principal.

Investors must clearly understand their position in the capital stack and the value of the collateral backing the investment, if any. When investing in debt instruments, one should always rely on the experience of an advisor or attorney to ensure the safety of the investment and to review the legal documentation that governs the investment. In fact, it is common practice and highly recommended that the investor group retain independent legal counsel to review all documents on behalf of the investor class. In some instances, the issuer, on a negotiated basis, can pay part or all of the legal fees incurred with this external review.

Equity Transactions

Most family offices or high-net-worth investors begin investing in direct deals by making equity investments into business ventures that are introduced by family and friends. The proliferation of angel investor groups over the past decade has facilitated the popularity of these types of investments.

Equity investments can be made across a spectrum of early stage or seed/angel investments, venture capital, and growth equity. Each has different risk/return profiles. With early stage companies, investors can invest in promising new business ideas and lend industry expertise to new and growing ventures. In our experience, the relationship with the founder of the business is paramount. Typically, almost 100 percent of the decision to invest is a function of the investor's relationship with the founder and his confidence in the management team's execution capabilities. While these can be among the most interesting and perhaps easiest investments to make, they are also the most risky and require sufficient portfolio diversification to achieve positive investment returns. The first step in making these types of investments is to negotiate the valuation of the company utilizing the company's financial projections and the projected value of the company at exit. Valuation methods include transactional value, market value, and the return as a multiple of investment. In an early-stage company, investors can own anywhere between 20 and 50 percent of a company with pre-money valuations averaging under $5 million. Valuations of early-stage companies are often highly negotiated and a lead investor has significant leverage in driving the valuation.

When investing in early- or seed-stage companies, it is important to size the investment properly, which means that an investor needs to consider the initial investment relative to the total dollar amount he or she is willing to commit to the company. It is wise to keep the initial investment small in dollar terms and reserve additional capital, or "dry powder," for future capital rounds. The majority of early-stage companies require additional capital rounds that can be potentially dilutive to existing investors. Investors also need to take into account the industry dynamics. For example, biotechnology or consumer product businesses typically require substantial additional capital rounds to get to market or to achieve profitability. Understanding the future capital requirements and keeping dry powder for additional rounds must be considered at the outset of any investment. Investors who don't appropriately assess the initial investment may find that the risk premium ratchets up considerably if multiple follow-on commitments are required and were not considered at the outset. Finally, and probably most importantly, an investor needs to conduct extensive diligence on the founding management team, including their previous experience and track record, since the team's ability to execute a business plan and drive the company to profitability is the most critical factor in the success of any new business. Due diligence was covered more extensively in Chapter 7.

Types of Equity Securities

Common Stock

Many early-stage investments are structured as common stock of a holding company. As such, investors are entitled to own one vote per share as well as any future dividend payments as determined by the management and board of the company. Common stock is typically owned by the founders, management, employees, and early investors of a company. If the company fails, the claims of secured and unsecured creditors, bondholders, and preferred stockholders are senior to the common stockholders. As mentioned in the capital stack discussion, an equity investment carries the highest risk and highest return potential but has the least liquidity, since a monetization is required either through a sale or public listing. Negotiating the proper valuation is paramount to any equity transaction with a goal of establishing a low initial valuation that can increase over time as the company achieves specific milestones and raises additional capital rounds.

Preferred Stock

Preferred stock is frequently issued to early-stage investors, including angel and venture capital firms. Institutional investors such as venture capital firms prefer preferred stock over common stock for the additional return and protection features described ahead. Preferred stock can be classified as straight, participating, or convertible preferred. Preferred stock typically pays a dividend that can be paid in cash or paid-in-kind (PIK). Preferred stock has a favorable position to common stock if a company goes bankrupt or liquidates. In this instance, preferred holders have priority in repayment of invested capital, along with any unpaid dividends (known as a preferred return), before the common stockholders receive any distributions. This important feature, known as a liquidation preference, is often highly negotiated in the term sheet. If investors own participating preferred, they will be repaid their original investment plus any unpaid dividends upon liquidation, and then share in the company as if it were common stock. Participating preferred stockholders could earn a return, even if common stockholders receive nothing.

Convertible preferred stock is convertible into common stock at the option of the holder and can be converted into either a fixed number of shares or a specific percentage of common stock outstanding. When structuring a deal with convertible preferred, an investor often sets terms without having to agree to a valuation on the company, negotiating only the conversion discount to the valuation of the next capital round.

Advantages of Equity Securities

- Ability to learn about new technologies, business models, transformational ideas
- Opportunity for investors to use their experience and skills to help an entrepreneur grow a business
- Ability to secure a board seat or observer rights
- Potential for investment returns of 25–50 percent IRR

Challenges

- Bottom of the capital stack
- In early stage investments, chance of business failure is high
- Investment is often highly illiquid and duration can be 7–10+ years
- Dilution risk is high since most early stage companies will require additional capital to grow
- Requires diligent monitoring and oversight
- Monetization requires a sale of the company to a strategic investor, private equity fund, or a public listing

What Investors Can Do to Protect Their Investment

One mechanism to consider is to structure a preferred or convertible note. With these types of structures an investor can achieve the following objectives:

- Seniority in the capital stack
- Coupon or preferential return with upside of common stock
- Ability to invest in a future round at a discount valuation
- Option to secure one or more board seats
- Ability to assert covenants or veto and blocking rights

Additionally, investors can negotiate anti-dilution protection, which will protect their percentage ownership in the company in the case of a down round, defined as a capital round that is priced at a lower valuation than the last round.

Another way to mitigate the risk of equity investments is to invest in more-mature companies in later stage financings. Growth equity financings are investments in a Series B or later round in profitable companies with at least $5 million of net income, or EBITDA. By investing in growth equity rounds, an investor will often invest at a higher valuation, which can result in lower returns, but can achieve the following objectives:

- Proven product or business model with more seasoned management
- Usually last step prior to a sale to a PE fund or strategic buyer
- Valuations are typically higher than earlier stage investments
- Investor has less ability to impact the business but has less risk

Equities are the most common vehicle for investors considering a portfolio of direct deals. While they are often easier to understand and have the greatest potential for high returns, they also carry a considerable amount of risk. It is advisable to also include debt instruments in a diversified portfolio of direct deals. To follow is a broader discussion of debt structures as an alternative to equity investments.

Types of Debt Instruments

When assembling a portfolio of direct deals, an investor who requires short-term liquidity or cash flow should consider diversifying the portfolio to include debt instruments. While there are numerous debt instruments to consider, including senior and junior secured and unsecured debt that vary in structure and duration, we outline two of the most common debt structures associated with direct investments in privately held companies. It is important to note that no matter where you are in the capital structure, repayment is not assured even when your investment is in company debt.

Convertible Notes

Convertible notes are typically issued in the form of a promissory note and offer holders the right to convert to equity upon the occurrence of specified events or to hold the note to maturity for repayment. The conversion rate is either fixed or variable and can increase over time or under certain conditions. The conversion is often triggered upon a "qualified financing," which can be defined as a minimum dollar amount to be raised in a future capital round or another defined event. The note will convert at a discount to the price of the next round (usually 20% but can be between 15 and 50%) and will often include additional warrants. This discount and/or warrant coverage gives early investors additional ownership for taking on increased risk. The interest also converts along with the principal. The notes can be secured or unsecured and the maturity date should be sufficiently long to allow the company to achieve the next milestone in their growth trajectory.

Convertible notes are frequently used in early-stage angel financings where the business is too young in its lifecycle to assign a valuation. The convertible note benefits the investor by deferring valuation until the company is more seasoned while providing certain advantages to compensate for the risk. While a convertible note is senior to equity, investors must take into account the fact that many early-stage businesses fail without ever reaching a valuation event.

Advantages of Convertible Notes
- Seniority in the capital stack
- Provide all the advantages of both equity and debt
- Simpler and usually faster to negotiate and execute versus a stock financing and there is no valuation debate
- Although typically unsecured, it can be secured by assets of the company

Challenges
- No board seat or voting rights—less control
- No economic rights such as liquidation preference
- If there is no loan extension or repayment, there are no assets to recover from the borrower
- Frequently seen in angel investments where risk of business failure is high

Mezzanine Debt

When assembling a portfolio of direct deals, mezzanine debt can be an attractive alternative to equity or straight debt instruments and should be considered. In a normal economic cycle, senior secured debt is not a common direct investment for family offices. Commercial banks, specialty lenders, and other institutional lenders typically provide abundant low-cost capital to borrowers. Mezzanine debt is a layer of financing that is below senior debt but above equity in the capital stack. It is most often used in companies that are cash flow positive and can be in the form of subordinated debt. It is frequently structured with warrants or preferred equity, which enhances the return of the instrument. The debt is typically issued with cash coupon interest but can also be PIK, which increases the principal amount of the security by the amount of the interest. The coupon frequently ranges between 12 and 18 percent with an average maturity of 5 to 7 years, with permitted early repayment. Mezzanine debt total returns are in the range of 15 to 25 percent due to the value of the warrants or equity attached to the debt.

With all debt, it is important to understand whether the financing is at the operating company or holding company level. Investments at the operating company are usually preferable to those at a holding company since the operating companies have assets and businesses to directly support the debt obligation. Holding company debt is reliant on what the operating companies dividend to it. Even if debt is offered at the operating company, an investor must determine if the cash flows are sufficient to repay the debt and if there is adequate collateral that may be used to repay the debt if there are cash flow shortfalls. As a result, a senior secured investor at a holding company (usually secured only by operating company stock) may be worse off than an unsecured investor at the operating company because cash flow must be up-streamed to service the holding company debt. With an investment that is highly structured, like mezzanine debt, it is critical to work with an experienced banker or lead investor to ensure a thorough understanding of the investment. Often, the type of investment can be more difficult to understand than the company you invest in.

In conclusion, when approaching investing in direct deals, an investor needs to start by outlining the investment parameters, including total dollar amount allocated to direct deals, a target return for the overall portfolio, and the associated risk he or she is willing to take. Most importantly, less sophisticated investors should spend a considerable amount of time finding the right advisor or group to invest alongside as they build their knowledge of the underlying investments and gain confidence in the direct investing process. Virtually no direct investment is the same and each one has a bespoke set of circumstances.

In the next section, we introduce a case study of an investment in an early-stage solar energy finance company. This actual deal is an example of a hybrid investment and is included to provide the reader with insights into the numerous steps required to ensure what ultimately resulted in a highly successful direct investment.

Case Study: Early-Stage Solar Energy Finance Company

Case Background

This deal was an actual investment into an early-stage solar energy company. The lead investor was able to negotiate a transaction that resulted in equity-like returns utilizing a debt structure. It is informative to review the progression of the deal beginning with the initial offer by the company and the analysis that influenced the final structure of the term sheet. The transaction is included as an example of a highly negotiated and creatively structured deal that resulted in a 37 percent annualized return in less than two years.

The lead investor in the transaction was an experienced chief investment officer (CIO) who worked with family offices, identifying and structuring direct investments. In this case, the CIO was brought a transaction by a group of bankers who were specialists in the energy/power industry. The energy bankers contacted the CIO in the early stages of discussion with their client regarding the financing, which enabled the CIO to influence its structure.

The company's main business was to finance small-scale solar projects that were installed on rooftops of municipalities and school districts. The projects were to be systematically rolled out across the United States, utilizing the same financial contract for each project. The company's management team, who were experienced structured finance professionals, developed a financing vehicle that was attractive to utility companies interested in investing in one- to five-megawatt solar projects in a highly scalable structure. With the help of their investment banker, the company was able to secure a financing commitment from two major public utilities that provided the capital to roll out the solar program. Once the utility financing was secured, however, the company needed additional working capital to build its team and scale the operations. The company initially contemplated an equity investment in its holding company at a pre-money valuation of $40 million. The lead investor determined that the valuation was too high for the nascent stage of the company's operations. Rather than engaging in a protracted negotiation over what was considered a rich valuation, the lead investor determined that the future cash flows of the company, resulting from the rapid deployment of the solar projects, could likely support a debt transaction. He then worked with the banking team and company's CEO to structure a debt deal.

Structure

The investment was ultimately structured as a five-year senior unsecured loan with an initial coupon of 10 percent (PIK) that increased by 1 percent per quarter once the note was outstanding for 18 months. The lead investor also negotiated the inclusion of warrants totaling 3.3 percent that increased to 4.66 percent once the note was outstanding for 24 months. Finally, there was an additional repayment fee equal to 25 percent of the investment that increased to 35 percent after 12 months. The investor structured a transaction that made it increasingly costly and restrictive to the company with each year that the note remained outstanding. If the note was outstanding for more than two years, there were additional limitations placed on the management team's compensation, along with other restrictions. Since the cash flows supported early repayment, these considerations were acceptable to the company and finalized in the term sheet. From the company management team's perspective, they were able to retain 100 percent of their equity and they avoided taking on bank debt that required personal guarantees. Therefore, the structure made sense from an economic standpoint and the term sheet was finalized.

After the first 12 months that the note was outstanding, the company successfully rolled out multiple solar projects and the business plan was on track. In the second year of operation, the company was successfully sold to a public utility that was not one of the original utilities providing the early financing. As part of the total consideration of the buyout, the unsecured loan was repaid and the warrants were exercised. This resulted in a 37 percent IRR or a 1.75 multiple of cash invested. While typical mezzanine investments return 15 to 25 percent, this investment resulted in a higher return due to the sale of the company, which resulted in a repayment of the debt and the upside from the value of the warrants.

This deal is an example of a uniquely structured investment that combined both equity and debt components that produced an outstanding risk-adjusted return. The key takeaway for the reader, however, is to understand that the success of this transaction was a result of the lead investor's strong background in structuring mezzanine investments. Deals utilizing hybrid structures must be done with an experienced advisor or lead investor who understands the capital stack and can implement protective features for the noteholder. While this deal structure could be utilized in other direct investments, the unique characteristics of the underlying company made this type of structure possible. The debt component ensured repayment to the investor while the restrictive covenants made it increasingly costly for the management team each year the note was outstanding. By including warrants, the investor was able to secure additional upside from the sale of the company.

A short summary of the case study illustrates the history and terms in the direct investment. (see Figure 8.2)

FIGURE 8.2   Early Stage Energy Deal Summary

Early Stage Energy Deal Case Study

Investment : Early stage Solar finance company
Investment Date: July 2011
Monetization Date: May 2013
Investment Type: 5-year senior loan

Coupon: 10.0% initially; increasing by 1% per quarter after 18 months
Warrants: 3.3% initially; increasing to 4.66% after 24 months
Repayment Fees: 25%, increasing to 35% after 12 months
IRR: 37% gross
Multiple: 1.75x

Business and Transaction Summary

- Company was founded for the purpose of financing and developing renewable energy projects with an emphasis on commercial and industrial scale solar projects. Company management had been senior structured finance executives and were able to use their financing background to develop a proprietary financing structure for small scale solar projects. Investment banking team met company at inception and introduced them to major utility company who formed a first-of-kind project financing program for small scale solar projects.
- Company approached investor group for a working capital line that would allow it to purchase and install solar panels while it waited to collect on its accounts receivable from the program. Company initially wanted to sell equity but after modeling cash flows and determining repayment, investor group negotiated a 5 year loan with warrants.

Investment Thesis

- Since investors affiliated investment banking principals had helped structure the financing program, and had worked with the utility company for several years, investor group was able to rely on banker's technical industry expertise and client relationship knowledge to provide a loan to help advance the program.

- Investor group negotiated to be senior in capital structure due to the start-up nature of the business and put in place management and financial controls to protect its investment.

Post-Investment Developments & Performance

- Banking team sold Company to another major utility
- Investment was monetized in fewer than 2 years when Company was sold, triggering a mandatory repayment.
- Investment achieved 37% IRR/ 1.75x in 22 months

A Primer on Important Term Sheet Items

Before concluding the chapter, we thought it would be useful to include a sample term sheet for a typical Series A Preferred Stock investment. As mentioned earlier, the term sheet can be intimidating but investors who do not understand its components may miss an opportunity to negotiate important deal terms and investor rights. While not exhaustive, the term sheet provided here is meant to be a useful guide for investors and outlines the most common terms that one will see when investing in privately held companies.

This term sheet outlines standard offering terms for a preferred stock investment. When structuring any investment, an investor needs to carefully review each item in the term sheet, paying attention not only to the details of the financing but also to the investor rights, which are often highly negotiated. Among the other important items to pay particular attention to are the information rights. One of the challenges of direct investments is the ability to receive timely updates and information on the underlying company. Typically, the lead investor will ask for representation on the board, either as a director, advisor, or observer. Once a term sheet is agreed upon, it is important to have independent counsel review it on behalf of the investor group. This fee is often paid by the issuer and should be negotiated upfront.

TERM SHEET GUIDE

FOR SERIES [A] PREFERRED STOCK FINANCING OF NEWCO INC.

The Term Sheet summarizes the principal terms of the Series A Preferred Stock Financing of Newco Inc. It will clearly state it is intended to be nonbinding and conditional upon due diligence and documentation, except for certain specified provisions such as No Shop/ Confidentiality and Expenses. Binding provisions will be governed by a governing law clause, frequently California, Delaware, or New York.

Offering Terms (*describes the basic terms of the financing*)

Closing Date: Describes the proposed closing date of the financing and can provide for multiple closings, if applicable.

Securities: Identifies the securities being offered. In addition to Preferred Stock, commonly offered securities include warrants, convertible debt, or securities combining one or more instruments such as units.

Investor: Identifies the Lead Investor and can include other Investors mutually agreed upon by the Lead Investor and the Company.

Amount Raised: Identifies the maximum amount of the proposed financing. Can be structured in multiple tranches contingent upon the achievement of certain milestones by the Company. Staged closings contingent on milestones are less common than an unconditional closing.

Price per Share: Identifies the price per share, based on the capitalization of the Company. Also referred to as the "Original Purchase Price."

Capitalization: Describes in tabular format the Company's capital structure before and after the Closing. Can be set forth on Exhibit A.

Charter (*a document filed with the secretary of state of the state in which the Company is incorporated that establishes the rights, preferences, privileges, and restrictions of the Preferred Stock*)

Dividends: When a Company makes a profit, it can pay part of these profits to its shareholders as cash, additional shares, or other assets. Such payments are known as dividends.

Dividends can be noncumulative or cumulative. With a noncumulative dividend, if the Company's board fails to declare the dividend in any fiscal year, the right to receive the dividend will be extinguished, but no

(Continued)

junior class of stock will receive a dividend, either. With a cumulative dividend, the dividend is calculated each year and the right to receive the dividend is carried forward until it is either paid or the right is terminated in some way.

Dividends may be participating or nonparticipating. After preferred preferential dividends, new preferred may participate in further dividends, may not participate, or may participate up to a cap or based on an agreed-upon formula.

Liquidation Preference: Liquidation preferences establish pre-negotiated returns to Investors in the event of the liquidation or acquisition of the Company. Investors in the event of the liquidation are non-participating, fully participating, or an intermediate between the two, where the Preferred Stock will be paid first on a liquidation event, then participate with the common stock up to an agreed-upon cap. Thereafter, any remaining liquidation proceeds will be distributed only to the holders of the Common Stock.

Voting Rights: Preferred Stock typically votes with the common stock on an as-converted basis, except for specific voting rights given to the Preferred Stock, such as the ability to elect certain directors to the Board.

Protective Provisions: As long as shares of an agreed-upon percentage of Preferred Stock are outstanding, the preferred holders will vote as a separate class to approve various material corporate actions, such as the creation of new classes of securities or creating indebtedness.

Optional Conversion: Optional conversion allows the preferred holder to convert its Preferred Stock to Common Stock at any time. The most likely situation in which a holder of Preferred Stock will elect to convert is where the holder determines upon a liquidation event that conversion to Common Stock would result in a higher return to the holder than accepting the liquidation preference and participating amount granted to the holder with respect to the Preferred Stock.

Anti-dilution Provisions: Provisions that protect the Investor's investment from dilution as the result of new shares issued in the future at a lower price than the Investor paid by adjusting the option price, conversion ratio, or issuing new shares. A broad-based weighted-average formula is the most commonly used formula and is less favorable to Investors because it takes into account unexercised options and outstanding convertible notes and warrants. The effect of the issuance of shares in a "down round" is diluted or spread over a broader base. A narrow-based formula includes only Common Stock issuable upon conversion of a particular series of shares of Preferred Stock outstanding, and not any shares issuable upon exercise of outstanding options or warrants. There are variations on the foregoing.

Full-ratchet anti-dilution is quite draconian to the Company's existing holders of Common Stock and is not typical. It provides that upon a dilutive financing the conversion price of the diluted shares will be adjusted downward to the issuance price of the newly issued shares, regardless of how many of the new shares are actually issued.

Mandatory Conversion: Investors will frequently be required to convert all of their shares into common stock prior to a qualified IPO (initial public offering). Investors will only want this conversion mechanism to work where an IPO is likely to provide a sufficient opportunity for them to dispose of their shares after the expiration of the lockup period. Investors will therefore want to define criteria in advance that must be met for an IPO to trigger automatic conversion such as minimum gross proceeds, and so forth.

Redemption Rights: The right of redemption is the right to demand under certain conditions that the Company buys back its own shares from its Investors at a fixed price. This may be included to require the Company to buy back its shares if there has not been an exit within a predetermined period.

Stock Purchase Agreement *(sets out the terms upon which an Investor will purchase shares in the Company)*

Representations; Warranties: Terms in the stock purchase agreement whereby the founders and key managers of the Company present information with respect to the past and present operating condition of the Company. Breach of a warranty gives the Investor the right to claim damages and, if significant, may enable the Investors to terminate the contract.

Closing Conditions: Contains conditions that must be satisfied prior to the closing of the financing, including satisfactory completion of financial and legal due diligence, qualification of the shares under applicable Blue Sky laws, the filing of a Certificate of Incorporation, and an opinion of counsel to the Company.

Counsel/Expenses: This provision sets forth the party responsible for drafting the financing documents and typically obligates the Company to reimburse the Investor for legal expenses up to an agreed-upon dollar amount.

Investors' Rights Agreement *(sets out the rights of Investors)*

Registration Rights: The contractual right of Investors to participate in the registration of the Company's stock for sale in the public market. Investors will have demand rights, which require the Company to file a registration statement to register the holder's class of securities so that the holder may sell them in the public market, and "piggyback" rights, which provide them

(Continued)

with rights to have their holdings included in a registration statement if and when the issuer files one.

Expenses: Typically borne by the Company, including fees for one independent counsel to represent all the participating stockholders, capped at an agreed-upon amount.

Lockup: In an IPO, a 180-day lockup period is customary so that existing "insider" shareholders do not also sell into the market while the company itself is attempting to raise capital.

Information Rights: Investors will want to receive quarterly and annual financial statements and an annual operating budget within 45 to 60 days after each quarter and fiscal year-end.

Right to Participate: Pro rata right to participate in subsequent issuances of equity securities of the Company (excluding certain agreed-upon exceptions).

Non-Competition and Non-Solicitation Agreements: Some Investors require Founders and key employees to enter into such agreements. Some will not require them for fear that employees will request additional consideration. Non-competes are not allowed in certain states like California except in connection with the sale of a business or are narrowly construed in others.

Non-Disclosure Agreement: Requires each Founder, employee, and consultant with access to confidential information or trade secrets to enter into a nondisclosure and proprietary rights assignment agreement.

Board Matters: Requires D&O insurance in an amount and with a carrier satisfactory to the Board. Investors sometimes require that Board approval of certain corporate actions must include one or more of the Investor directors. If Investor directors control the Board following the financing, these covenants would be superfluous.

Key Person Insurance: Requires the Company to acquire life insurance for certain key employees/founders with proceeds payable to the Company.

Right of First Refusal/Right of Co-Sale (Tag-along): Right of First Refusal consists of the right of the Company/Investor to purchase shares by other shareholders before such shares may be sold to a third party. Right of Co-Sale allows the Founder or Investor to participate in the sale by the other shareholder. Typically, subject to agreed-upon exceptions such as charitable donations or for estate planning purposes.

Drag-Along: A mechanism ensuring that if a specified percentage of shareholders agree to sell their shares, they can compel the others to sell, ensuring that a prospective purchaser can acquire 100 percent of the Company.

Voting Agreement

Board of Directors: Describes the composition of the Board. The Lead Investor will typically require the right to choose at least one director or observer seat.

Other Matters

No Shop/Confidentiality: Investors may want the Company and its Founders to agree to a no-shop provision for a period of time before they commit time and resources to a potential financing. The Investor will also want the Company to maintain confidentiality regarding the proposed transaction.

Conclusion

The growing interest in direct investments by family offices will likely be a continuing trend that will have profound future implications for the private equity industry. In this chapter, we hope you gained a greater understanding of how to approach constructing and structuring a portfolio of direct deals. As mentioned numerous times throughout the text, with any direct investment, the key to a successful outcome is to find a trusted, experienced advisor or to align with an investment group who can help source, perform due diligence, structure, and monitor the underlying deals. While many investors can get caught up in the excitement and activity of the deal, the follow-up is as important as the term sheet structure and must be done to ensure a successful exit.

As described in the case study, once the solar energy deal was executed, the lead investor met regularly with the company management team to ensure that the rollout of solar projects was on track and the company was operating within its projected budget. This monitoring was particularly critical since the company had to meet specific milestones or it would be subject to financial and other penalties. Even in equity deals, every investment should be constructed with clear milestones and deliverables for the company's management team. Investors should require written quarterly updates, including financials, which are included in the investor rights section of the term sheet.

In the current low-yielding investing environment, direct investments can be an important contribution to the overall return of a portfolio. A diversified and well-constructed portfolio of direct deals can provide uncorrelated incremental alpha to traditional stock and bond investments. Additionally, direct investments can offer the investor an opportunity to learn about and participate in exciting new business ventures and to lend their expertise and influence to the companies. When structured and executed correctly, investing in direct deals can be highly rewarding and financially lucrative.

CHAPTER 9

Investment Monitoring, Exit Strategies, and Harvesting Returns

Contributing Author: Adam Goodfriend

Introduction

There is increasing emphasis by individual investors on augmenting their private equity fund portfolios with self-directed private investments as a way to increase control, tailor their investments to specific objectives, and enhance returns by reducing fees. The sections that follow discuss (1) certain considerations of monitoring and oversight of direct investments as a minority stakeholder, (2) different ways of engineering returns from privately held businesses or assets, and (3) how to plan and time a sale to maximize the results of your investment objectives, including return on investment. As part of this discussion, the sections not only focus on some of the tools used to execute a successful private investment, but also illustrate that having an exit strategy, even as early as at the time of investment, is critical to maximizing return.

Alignment of Objectives

A fundamental requirement in considering exit strategies and the harvesting of returns in direct investing is to make sure that at the outset there is clear alignment of objectives and interests among the minority stakeholders, majority stakeholders, and management, especially with regard to interim cash distributions and investment exit (monetization) time frame. If investors seek cash flows by means of interim distributions, they should not look to invest in an early-growth-stage company since those companies likely need to reinvest all of their generated cash in their daily operations and growth. Similarly, investors seeking to exit within a certain time frame should be sure that the management team shares this goal and possibly choose to avoid closely held family businesses that may provide interim cash flows but have no clear path to monetization.

In private transactions, it is advisable to work as closely as possible with the management team ahead of finalizing an investment in order to develop a detailed and agreed-upon operating plan and general strategy. These plans may be noted in writing within the closing documents or as an agreed-upon business plan that includes exit objectives and outlines how both the investors and the management team foresee the company developing over time. In addition, and as discussed later in this chapter, investors should try to negotiate favorable and flexible terms to allow them to sell their positions to third parties in the event they want to liquidate their holdings and, if their investment is sizeable, perhaps negotiate a position on the company's board of directors so that they can influence the management of the company and the timing and process of a future sale. In short, planning an *entry* in an investment is usually more important than planning an *exit* since, as a likely minority stakeholder, you can negotiate how you can make the investment, but have only limited ability to influence future decisions and strategies including when to sell the company for an exit.

Monitoring Direct Investments as a Minority Stake Owner

Monitoring a public company investment as a small shareholder is a relatively easy task given the information disclosure requirements of virtually all publicly listed companies. Financial information is reported at least quarterly (including annual audits) and material changes and news items are disseminated via press releases. Additionally, depending on the size of the company there may be research and other third-party reports published. In contrast, monitoring an investment in a private company is a more difficult and complicated task. Without the legal requirements of a public company, private issuers and their investors must negotiate the type and timing of information that is provided. These negotiations are often part of the term sheet and investment documents and are known as *information rights*. Information rights should provide a balance. On the one hand, investors should receive the necessary information for them to be informed about the status and prospects of their investment while, on the other hand, such requirements should not be overly burdensome to the issuing company. Typical information rights include the rights for investors to receive quarterly updates (including financial information), access to management for periodic questions, and possibly reports of certain board actions. However, it is important to note that having the information in and of itself does not provide any other protections or alternatives. In other words, just because you know of something doesn't mean you can act on it or force others to act—such as being able to sell (or even add to) your investment or compelling management to act in a certain way. As a general rule, a larger investment usually allows a greater level of negotiation to get the information rights you feel you need—including board observation rights (the right to attend board meetings as a nonvoting participant) or full board rights as a representative of a stakeholder class.

Why Timing of an Investment Exit and Not Just the Investment Return Is Critical

> *"Only buy something you'd be perfectly happy to hold if the market shut down for 10 years."*[1]
> —Words of wisdom from the Oracle of Omaha, Warren Buffett

Most minority stake direct investors do not make an investment with an "infinite" timeline. There is usually an exit expectation at the outset. Not only is this a visceral desire, it is also an economically smart one. There are several common measures that direct investors can utilize to monitor and review their investment performance. Of these, two popular measures are return on investment (ROI) and internal rate of return (IRR). ROI measures how much you receive from the investment above the cost of the investment itself—similar to an "investment profit." It is often calculated as:

Expected Gains from Investment – Cost of Investment / Cost of Investment

IRR, on the other hand, measures how well an investment does *over time* and factors in the concept that the longer it takes an investment to generate a return, the less valuable is the return (the technical definition is that IRR is the interest rate that makes the cash outflows of an investment equal to the inflows over time).

Putting this into perspective, Figure 9.1 shows a straightforward calculation of a five-year investment. In this example, the investor made an investment of $1 million in year 1 in exchange for 29.5 percent of the company. Over the next five years, the company grew such that the business was sold, or *monetized,* in year 5 for $15 million. This represents a $4.4 million valuation of the investor's 29.5 percent stake, or 4.4× the initial investment. Given the amount and timing of the exit, this investment produced a 45 percent IRR.

While Figure 9.1 does indeed present a significant return, what may be missed is how dependent the IRR is on the timing, or *harvesting,* of the sale. For instance, if the monetization were to take place in year 6, assuming the valuation of the company remains constant, the IRR would decline

FIGURE 9.1   Five-Year Return Calculations

Transaction Parameters					
Investment Amount	$1,000,000				
Post-Investment Ownership	29.5%				
Liquidation Event					
Company Valuation	$15,000,000				
Investor Proceeds	$4,425,000				
Investment Return (5 Year Exit)	**Year 1**	**Year 2**	**Year 3**	**Year 4**	**Year 5**
Investment	$ (1,000,000)				
Liquidation Proceeds					$ 4,425,000
Total Proceeds	**$ (1,000,000)**	**$—**	**$—**	**$—**	**$4,425,000**
IRR Calculation	45%				
Investment Return Multiple	4.425				

Notes:
[1] Does not calculate any tax liabilities which will vary from structure to structure and investor to investor.
[2] Terms and structures such as multiple classes of equity or exercised employee option plans may further dilute the shareholding of the company.
[3] Assumes that company is debt free and that no further dilution to the investor over the five year period, including classes of shares or other securities, occurs.

from 45 percent to 35 percent due to the extra year required to generate the same dollar return. If the monetization occurred in year 10, the IRR would drop to 18 percent. In each case, the ROI is constant, but the IRR changes significantly, as it takes more time to generate the same level of return. See Figure 9.2.

Since IRR is dependent on the timing of an exit, many longer-term investments are not desired by institutional investors whose return and liquidity requirements drive exits/monetizations usually to a 5- to 7-year period. However, private investors may choose to extend this time frame for as long as desired or to pass investments down through generations, often without regard for monetization or exit potential.

In longer-term investments, even without a complete exit, investors may want to receive some interim distributions such as dividends or partial returns of principal so that the entire return is not predicated on the sale of the investment. The businesses that provide these are oftentimes more mature companies with predictable, but perhaps slower growing, profits and earnings streams. This preference highlights a key difference between institutional and private investors. Without high growth, institutional investors are unlikely to be able to generate sufficient returns on the sale of the company. To private investors, a consistent and predictable earnings stream may offer enough of a return to provide for an attractive investment. Thus, in some cases, there is no direct exit strategy considered at the outset of the investment because the annual income and dividends are enough to fulfill the investor's risk-adjusted return expectation.

While it is easy to appreciate that different companies have different growth and payout potentials, it is interesting to consider that an individual company will likely change its growth and payout potentials as it goes through its own corporate lifecycle and that, depending on where it is in its lifecycle, it may hold more or less appeal to different investor constituencies.

Importance of Company Lifecycles with Respect to Timing and Harvesting Returns

As was introduced in Chapter 4, when planning a private equity investment strategy, it is essential to understand at which stage in its *lifecycle* is the target company. Depending on the stage, there will be a different level of risk and return potential. Additionally, certain exit strategies are more applicable to certain lifecycle stages, since depending on the maturity of the company, it may be more or less appealing to certain investor constituencies. Many private

FIGURE 9.2 Six- and Ten-Year Return Calculations

Transaction Parameters										
Investment Amount	$1,000,000									
Post-Investment Ownership	29.5%									
Liquidation Event										
Company Valuation	$15,000,000									
Investor Proceeds	$4,425,000									
Investment Return (6 Year Exit)	Year 1	Year 2	Year 3	Year 4	Year 5	Year 6				
Investment	$(1,000,000)									
Liquidation Proceeds						$4,425,000				
Total Proceeds	**$(1,000,000)**	**$—**	**$—**	**$—**	**$—**	**$4,425,000**				
IRR Calculation	35%									
Investment Return Multiple	4.425									
Investment Return (10 Year Exit)	Year 1	Year 2	Year 3	Year 4	Year 5	Year 6	Year 7	Year 8	Year 9	Year 10
Investment	$(1,000,000)									
Liquidation Proceeds										$4,425,000
Total Proceeds	**$(1,000,000)**	**$—**	**$—**	**$—**	**$—**	**$—**	**$—**	**$—**	**$—**	**$4,425,000**
IRR Calculation	18%									
Investment Return Multiple	4.425									

[1] Does not calculate any tax liabilities which will vary from structure to structure and investor to investor.

[2] Terms and structures such as multiple classes of equity or exercised employee option plans may further dilute the shareholding of the company.

[3] Assumes that company is debt free and that no further dilution to the investor over the six- or ten-year period, including classes of shares or other securities, occurs.

investors are active in early-stage *seed* or *angel* investments. These are investments in companies in the earliest stages and although they typically offer higher returns, they also are the riskiest and the least likely to generate interim cash flows. During the seed and development stages, companies usually reinvest any excess cash flow to grow the business and enhance their long-term prospects instead of paying dividends or making distributions to investors. Investors in the seed stage must be prepared to forgo interim distributions and a timely monetization for the hope of a higher payoff later.

Figure 9.3 shows the relationship between risk (as illustrated by company development stage) and valuation/reward as a company matures from an early-stage startup to a mature company ready for monetization.

The example shown in Figure 9.3 is based on a high-growth company with a likelihood of expansion through each of the charted lifecycle phases. The investment curve illustrates a business that will consume cash up front before sales are generated as it is establishing itself and building out its operating platform. At this riskier phase, funding is usually provided by angel and seed investors. As the company begins to move toward the more profitable expansionary/growth stages, the trend is for venture capital to fund the

FIGURE 9.3 Company Lifecycle

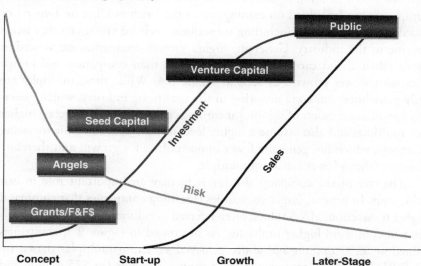

Source: The Company Financing Lifecycle—Primaxis Technology Ventures (www.marsdd .com/mars-library/angel-investors-seed-or-venture-capital-investors-that-depends-on-your-stage-of-company-development/)

company and provide the expertise to drive value and growth toward an exit. In later-stage companies, once growth has become more stable and risk is reduced, the company may be monetized either by selling to another company or by listing it in the public market.

As such, it is not unusual for seed and angel investors who finance the earliest and riskiest rounds of capital to be bought out by venture groups (or, if not bought out, having venture groups provide several interim rounds of financing) who will grow the company to a point where it is ready for a complete sale or public listing once it has matured.

Exit Valuations and Multiples

In addition to the timing of the monetization, returns are also driven by exit valuations. These are often calculated using multiples, a method in which buyers determine the price they are willing to pay for a company by picking a common measurement of company value, such as earnings, and applying a multiple to those earnings—such as price to earnings (P/E—how much in price you have to pay for a given amount of earnings). Multiples vary by industry and many other factors with higher growth industries (higher "E" potential) commanding higher prices for their shares. Where there is no "E," companies can be valued on earnings potential (such as Uber or Twitter) or based on other metrics, including subscribers, website visits, or other items specific to the industry. Generally, higher growth companies are viewed as more valuable and carry higher exit multiples than companies and industries with slower growth, as seen in Figure 9.4. While these multiples are only guidelines, someone investing in the healthcare industry, which generally has an expectation of significant earnings growth, should expect a higher exit multiple, and also assume a higher level of risk, than someone investing in energy, which has generally fewer opportunities for growth and therefore usually carries a lower valuation multiple.

The size of the company also tends to play an important role in exit valuations. In general, larger companies (meaning companies that command higher transaction/M&A values, often referred to as Enterprise Value or "EV") tend to command higher multiples. As illustrated in Figure 9.5, companies valued at $250 million and above achieved valuation multiples (based on EV/EBITDA) that were twice those of companies valued at $25 million and below. This is likely fueled by a number of factors, including the assumption that larger companies are less prone to "startup risk" and they may be more attractive to big private equity investors and institutions looking to put large

FIGURE 9.4 Multiples by Industry, 2015

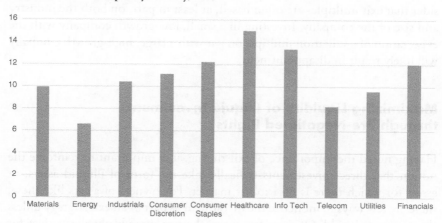

Source: Cognient Investment Bank, June 2015 Industry Valuation Multiples Report

FIGURE 9.5 Direct Correlation between Enterprise Value and Exit Multiples

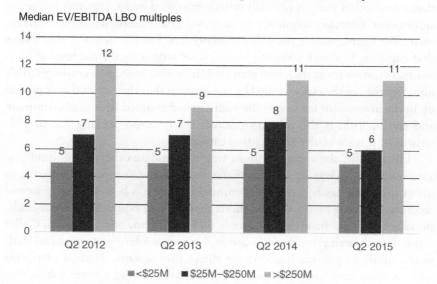

Source: 2016 1Q US PE Breakdown, Pitchbook

sums of capital to work. Irrespective of the reasoning, an investor should consider that exit multiples are often based, at least in part, on both the industry and size of the company. Investing in a small, low-growth company with the expectation of a valuation multiple on par with a large, high-growth company will likely result in disappointment.

Maximizing Liquidity of Illiquid Investments through Pre-Negotiated Rights

Having noted the importance of exit timing, it is important to reinforce the notion that direct investments typically take the form of illiquid assets, or assets for which there is no explicit market. For owners of assets like these, there are few ways to monetize the investment as part of an exit strategy unless the company is sold. Of these few ways, the two most likely alternatives for investors seeking monetization are selling shares back to the company or to another individual investor through a secondary transaction.

The process of selling shares back to the issuing company is often a complex, difficult-to-execute transaction that rarely results in any return on investment since the investment is usually sold back at a discount. The selling of shares to another party is typically strictly governed by a company's operating agreements, normally requiring the approval of any combination of management, the board, and/or the other shareholders. For the investor, this means that engaging in direct investing likely comes with a significant level of illiquidity. Investors must therefore plan their investing strategy accordingly. This liquidity risk, or the risk assumed by the investor that their capital may be tied up in the investment for longer than anticipated coupled with small-company and startup risk, is the primary tradeoff for investors seeking the sizeable returns of private equity and venture capital.

Historically, the most common way to liquidate otherwise-illiquid private investments was to sell the shares back to the company. However, as direct investing has become more common, there has been an emergence of secondary trading platforms and funds that provide liquidity for these traditionally less liquid investments. Funds such as Ardian, Saints Capital, Coller Capital, and Lexington Partners are building secondary platforms and dedicated funds to provide liquidity for direct investments. Trading platforms such as these have grown in popularity and are creating a more robust secondary market. According to one industry participant, $16.2 billion of private equity secondary "trades" occurred in the first half of 2015 and $5.5 billion of face value direct investment (not fund) holdings were purchased in the same period.[2]

Even though a new market is developing to provide liquidity to private investors, it is crucial that investors negotiate investment documents to allow for maximum flexibility. When an investor agrees to make a direct investment, that investor will likely be party to a subscription agreement and other documents that govern certain actions and afford specific rights, some of which include:[3]

- *Tagalong Rights:* One of the most commonly negotiated rights is the right to tag along. A tagalong right gives the minority investor the right to participate in a sale orchestrated by, and on the same terms as, the majority shareholder. Tagalongs effectively oblige the majority shareholder to include minority holders in the negotiations and preclude a majority holder from "doing a deal away" from other shareholders and leaving them with a new majority holder. This right helps minority shareholders even when there is no public sale, as it allows them to participate in the transactions normally arranged by the majority. As with most rights, minority shareholders have the option, but not the obligation, to participate.
- *Drag-Along Rights:* Investors will also likely be subject to drag-along rights—rights that obligate the minority shareholders to go along with a sale on the same terms as the majority holder. This allows a third party to negotiate a transaction with the majority holder and force the minority holders to sell, at the same terms, in order to facilitate the acquisition of the entire company. This right may actually benefit minority holders by making the company in which they invest more attractive to a potential purchaser. Such purchaser would know that if he negotiated a deal with a majority holder, no minority stakeholder could refuse to sell and therefore thwart the transaction.
- *Registration Rights:* In addition to the tagalong and drag-along provisions, investors may, depending on the specifics of the investment, negotiate registration rights as a way to enhance their liquidity position. Generally, these rights are important to investors, as they provide them with a contractual right to demand that the company register their shares with the U.S. Securities and Exchange Commission (SEC)—a necessity for selling the shares publicly. The basis for this right stems from the U.S. securities laws that permit the company, but not the shareholder, to register the company's securities.[4] Registration rights can help investors who hold private shares gain access to the public market (creating liquidity) by requiring the

issuing company to go through the IPO process, a process the issuer might not otherwise undertake given the time and expense required. Often registration rights do not take effect immediately, allowing the issuer time to mature and stabilize before being forced to IPO.

In summary, maximizing liquidity of an investment is not only a function of the underlying company in which the investment is made (such as size, industry, and point in lifecycle) but also of the negotiated terms agreed to as part of the investment process. In negotiation of these rights, an investor will gain valuable insight to management's and the majority stakeholder's view on monetization timing and other objectives.

Exit Value Drivers

Having noted the importance of valuation metrics for making both an entry and exit decision for an investment, the question becomes on which metrics should a direct investor focus, especially since there is likely little if any public information available on the target company and certainly no Wall Street research on the specific investment.

As previously noted, in public companies, investors have many valuation metrics from which to choose and a history of operations and results by which to judge opportunities. Alternatively, private companies often provide substantially less information, financial or otherwise. Even when these companies do provide the necessary information, it is not typically regulated in the same way as audited financials required of publicly traded companies, and as just discussed, if the wrong decision is made in a private investment, the path to liquidity is much less certain than selling a publicly traded security. Differences like these make investing in private companies more complex than other investment strategies.

Still, there are some basic value drivers that every investor should review as part of the due diligence process. Many of the factors found in Table 9.1 are common points evaluated by investors to see whether an investment meets their requirements.

With a background knowledge of the features and drivers of direct investments and their exits, what remains are questions regarding the process itself: How are these companies sold? When is the best time to sell? What types of transactions yield the best results? As with all the nuances of direct investing, the answer to all these questions is, "It depends." However, there are several structures and strategies that are relatively common.

TABLE 9.1 Sample Value Drivers

Financial	
Revenue	Amount of revenue and whether this revenue is stable, growing, and/or predictable.
EBITDA	Earnings before taxes, depreciation, and amortization—a surrogate for profitability.
Assets	Book value of assets, equipment, or hardware has value to the buyer.
Management	Buyer looking to acquire talent and wants management to remain post-transaction.
Intellectual property	Defensible science, technology, or patents that the buyer can get access to via a transaction.
Market position	Competitors or market share consolidation through a transaction.
Tax benefits	Carried-over tax credits from which an acquirer can benefit.
Users or customers	Acquiring customers through an acquisition is cost effective for buyers.

Common Exit Strategies

As widely expected, maximizing return on investment is the objective of most investors. So far, we have discussed (1) the role that is played by the timing and value of an exit; (2) how to negotiate rights to ensure that a minority investor is not especially disadvantaged when the company is sold and to make sure that even as a minority there are information rights that help in monitoring the investment; and (3) certain value drivers on which management can focus to prepare the company for sale.

While taking a company public by means of an initial public offering is often the most-thought-of exit strategy, it is much less common than many realize. In order to go public, companies need to have the necessary size to attract public capital and comply with numerous regulatory requirements, which are both onerous and costly. Therefore, the majority of investors plan their exit strategies around having their company bought. There are two principal types of buyers of nonpublic companies, (1) strategic buyers and (2) financial buyers, with the difference between the two based on their investing approach and expectations.

A strategic buyer is an entity that sees an opportunity to strengthen its core business by acquiring another company, usually in a related business line. The purpose is to grow either more rapidly or in a new direction with a buy-rather-than-build strategy. The acquirer can often afford to pay a premium (an amount above an expected purchase price) because it believes that the sum of the parts is greater than the individual pieces due to synergies. *Synergies* refers to the operational leverage between two previously independent companies. Such leverage may include reducing redundant headcount in divisions with overlapping responsibilities (such as accounting or marketing) and even some senior management positions such as CFO and CEO roles. By reducing redundancies, earnings are increased and a strategic buyer can therefore afford to pay more than a financial buyer who is simply acquiring a company and keeping it and its cost structure intact.

There have been several examples of strongly synergistic mergers with strategic buyers. A high-profile current example is the $107 billion AB InBev acquisition and merger with SABMiller. This transaction is expected to generate over $1.4 billion in annual synergistic savings (an amount equal to 9 percent of SABMiller's sales). These synergies are expected to be comprised of savings related to: 20 percent from Procurement & Engineering (raw materials sourcing and packaging); 25 percent from Brewery Efficiencies (bottling, shipping, and distribution optimizations); 20 percent from Best Practices (cost management, efficiencies, and administrative costs); and 35 percent from corporate/personnel rationalization.[5] InBev has a good track record achieving synergies as evidenced by realized cost savings representing about 18 percent of sales when it bought Anheuser-Busch Cos. in 2008 and synergies representing 21 percent of sales of Mexico's Modelo in 2013.[6] Without these synergies, AB InBev would likely not be offering to pay as much as it is for SABMiller.

On the other hand, a financial buyer is an investor or group that buys companies based principally on financial performance and that assesses the value of a business largely based on its assets and financial condition using metrics such as revenues, cash flows, EBITDA, and gross margins. The typical model for this type of buyer is to value an outright acquisition of the business and then implement financial controls and mechanisms to support continued revenue growth. In private equity, the standard model is to finance a portion of the acquisition price with equity and then secure leverage through sizeable loans that can be serviced through cash flows. The view is to control as much as you can with as little equity as possible so that the return to the equity is highest. This strategy is usually referred to as a leveraged buyout (LBO).

Arguably the most famous of all LBOs was the 1989 LBO of RJR Nabisco for more than $25 billion by Kohlberg Kravis Roberts & Co (KKR). RJR had a low debt level before the transaction, allowing KKR and its lenders to finance more than $19 billion of the acquisition price with KKR investing only

$4 billion in preferred and $1.5 billion in common equity.[7] KKR's plan was to sell underperforming assets and shed personnel while using the company's relatively stable cash flows to service its debt. Ultimately, the transaction suffered under its huge debt burden and investors in KKR's fund did not achieve the advertised returns. However, perhaps the most leveraged of LBOs was the 1982 acquisition of Gibson Greetings by former Treasury Secretary William Simon. Simon and his group invested $1 million of their own money and borrowed $79 million to buy Gibson. Eighteen months later, the company was sold for $290 million.[8] The debt was repaid and the equity holders received greater than $200 million on their $1 million investment.

Many private equity firms combine the traits of strategic and financial buyers by first buying a platform company in an industry and then adding onto that company with subsequent acquisitions designed to provide synergies. In these ways, they increase profitability as well as subsequent transaction size, each a value driver to the investor.

As illustrated in Figure 9.6, add-ons are an increasingly important tool to financial buyers, and as such, an important exit route for smaller private companies.

FIGURE 9.6 Add-ons as a Percent of Buyouts

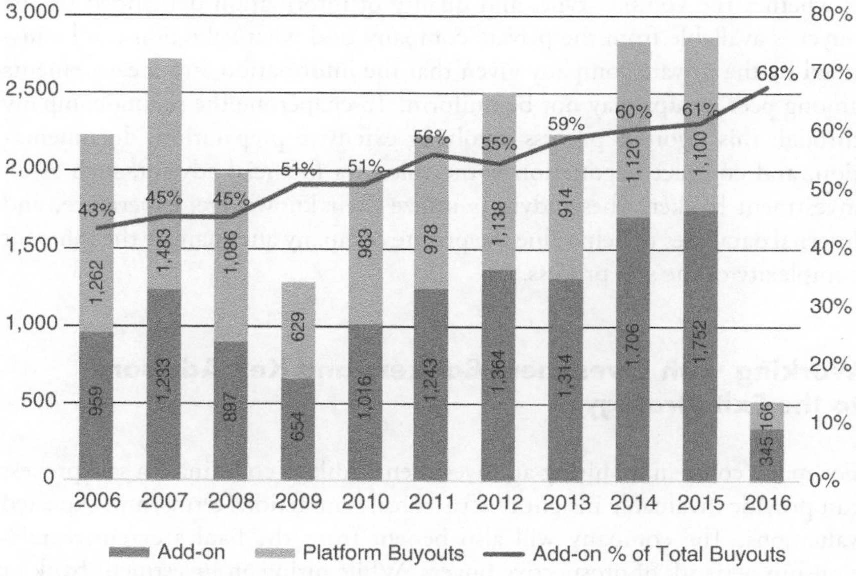

Source: 2016 1Q US PE Breakdown, Pitchbook

Mergers and Acquisitions

Since both financial and strategic buyers are more common avenues to liquidity for private direct investors than a public exit via an IPO, an understanding of the process that a company will go through in its sale to either of these two types of buyers—namely a merger or acquisition (M&A)—is worthwhile. M&A transactions consist of a process in which the invested-in (target) company is sold to, or merged with, an entirely separate entity.

M&A transactions can take many forms, with the majority of deals being structured as one of the following:

- *Joint Ventures and Strategic Alliances:* The creation of a partnership between two independent companies whereby each company contributes assets or equity in order to establish a mutual initiative
- *Mergers:* The combination of the assets and equity of two independent companies to form and operate as one single entity
- *Acquisitions:* The outright purchase of an independent company by another independent company whereby the acquirer ends up owning all or a portion of the assets of the acquired company

Again, a problem with these transactions involving private companies is whether the volume, type, and quality of information demanded by the buyer is available from the private company, and what valuation can be justified by the private company given that the information and measurements among peer groups may not be uniform. To chaperone the selling company through this rigorous process involving extensive preparation, documentation, and contract negotiation is the role of a financial advisor, such as an investment banker. These advisors utilize their knowledge, experience, and internal databases to help value the private company and manage the inherent complexity of the sale process.

Working with Investment Bankers and Key Advisors to the Exit Strategy

For many companies, hiring an investment bank to coordinate a sale process can provide invaluable insight to structures, transactions terms, and expected valuations. The company will also benefit from the bank's extensive relationship network of prospective buyers. While hiring an investment bank or advisory group can take several months, an informed decision based on the advisor's reputation, relevant transaction experience, knowledge of potential buyers, and, of course, fees, is essential. Once hired, an advisor will follow a number of typical steps, including:

1. Identifying potential buyers.
2. Preparing a short teaser or summary of the company and its earnings and growth profile.
3. Drafting a confidentiality agreement (CA) or nondisclosure agreement (NDA) to be included with the teaser; if a potential buyer is interested in learning more information, the buyer will sign and return the CA or NDA.
4. Preparing a more detailed description of the company, including financial projections, in a document often called a private information memo (PIM) or confidential information memo (CIM), to be made available to those potential buyers who return the CA or NDA.
5. Collecting and evaluating nonbinding indications of interest from buyers interested in pursuing a transaction after reviewing the CIM. These indications will have general pricing, financing, and management terms. If the advisor judges the buyer to be credible, the advisor will invite the buyer into the confidential data room, which will have generally undisclosed information about all aspects of the company, including business, financial, tax, legal, environmental, management, and personnel information. While the advisor will help the company compile this information, it generally comes from the books and records of the company and can take quite a while to accumulate.
6. Coordinating with interested buyers as they review the data room information, schedule meetings with management, and perform many aspects of due diligence, hopefully culminating in an acceptable offer that will likely lead to a share purchase agreement.

These steps should not be taken lightly and they can strain management's resources and divert attention away from running the business. Having a professional help in the sale process and preparation is essential, especially since it is likely that the buyer will have his own team of advisors. But this advice does not come cheap. On smaller M&A transactions (enterprise values below $50 to $75 million), expect the banker to charge the selling company (sell-side mandates) up to 2 to 3 percent of the value of the transaction and, on capital raises, expect the fees to range between 4 and 8 percent of the funds being raised. These fees, while seemingly high, better ensure a level of professionalism and access that the company is unlikely to have developed on its own, which should translate to better deal terms and higher valuations. From a minority investor's point of view, a banker will add discipline to the process and help ensure that all constituents (such as smaller stakeholders) are treated fairly.

Conclusion

In conclusion, this chapter reinforces to the reader that an important part of a successful minority stake private investment strategy is the upfront thought given to monitoring, oversight, and exit strategies. This chapter reviews many of the significant upfront considerations that direct investors need to weigh in order to maximize their likelihood of achieving a desired exit. Particularly, for minority investors, making sure there is an alignment of interests between management, majority stakeholders, and the minority investors is critical with respect to the adoption of an exit strategy and the harvesting of the investment. Further, negotiating for information rights and transaction rights is essential and is best accomplished as part of the initial investment, not after it. Minority investors should not necessarily rely on the efforts of the majority investor since different investor classes may be afforded different rights as part of their investment negotiations.

The chapter also notes that the amount of return only tells a portion of the story, and that looking at the timing of the return sheds greater light on the true success of the investment. Certain metrics such as return on investment (ROI) and internal rate of return (IRR) provide two measurements as to the success of the harvesting of return. The chapter continues by demonstrating that harvesting returns is closely related to the lifecycle of the underlying company and that, depending at which point in the company lifecycle the investment is made, the investor should expect differing levels of risk, return, and time to harvest. Additionally, depending on the lifecycle stage, the investment may be more appropriate to differing constituencies, which may also drive an exit strategy.

Understanding the risk/return profile and the associated exit strategy helps identify the harvesting opportunity. Differing exit valuations and multiples result as a function of the lifecycle of the investment, segment, and leadership capabilities. In this regard, investors should consider various exit value drivers such as EBITDA, book value of assets, strength of the management team, defensibility of the intellectual property, the firm's market position, and the tax ramifications in the exit phase.

Finally, the chapter discusses several common exit strategies for direct investments, including taking a company public, and compares certain considerations of a sale of a company to a strategic versus a financial buyer specifically with regard to creating synergistic value. The chapter concludes with a brief discussion of the complexities of the company sale process and the role and importance of advisors such as investment bankers to the exit strategy. The following section provides some unique perspectives on direct investing in terms of the perspective of the direct investing CIO, direct investing and the next generation, and international direct investing.

Notes

1. www.forbes.com/sites/agoodman/2013/09/25/the-top-40-buffettisms
   -inspiration-to-become-a-better-investor/#55d24fff250d.
2. Setter Capital Secondary Market Volume Report, FY 2015, www
   .secondarylink.com/static/files/1a74e00f-a900-4ca5-b26f-8795cedbc5c8/
   LG/52/0ebfe56a41c311e5bcbb274af6f918ee_Setter_Capital_Volume_
   Report_H1_2015.pdf.
3. As discussed early in this chapter, minority investors should also carefully negotiate other rights, including "Information Rights" to make sure that necessary financial and other information is provided on a timely basis. Since private companies generally do not have reporting obligations except as directly negotiated with investors, this may be the only way to ensure the receipt of periodic updates.
4. Venture Capitalist Term Sheet, Eric Koester, 2009.
5. www.abinbev.com/content/dam/universaltemplate/abinbev/pdf/
   investors/11November2015/Investor%20Presentation%20-%20Building
   %20the%20First%20Truly%20Global%20Beer%20Company.pdf.
6. www.bloomberg.com/news/articles/2015-11-11/ab-inbev-to-buy
   -sabmiller-for-107-billion-as-u-s-deal-agreed.
7. www.jstor.org/stable/4479468?seq=5#page_scan_tab_contents.
8. www.nytimes.com/1990/01/21/books/the-granddaddy-of-all-takeovers
   .html?pagewanted=all.

PART III

Direct Investing Perspectives

CHAPTER 10

The CIO Perspective

Contributing Author: Robert G. Blabey

The chief investment officer (CIO) perspective of a *direct investing*–style family office is a very special breed of investment leader, one who typically has deep operating expertise and/or C-level experience in one or more companies. This chapter delves into their unique perspective, qualifications, education, and experience and the importance of compensation and interest alignment. It further demonstrates the importance of how to consider "success" standards for the CIO differently perhaps than a traditional CIO. Further, the chapter outlines the different qualities between direct investments from an SFO (single-family office) and an institutional investor. The chapter details anonymous real-life case studies and debriefs on the key lessons learned. It concludes with the key criteria when searching and selecting a direct investment CIO and pitfalls to avoid.

Implementation of a direct investing plan requires appropriate consideration as to the personnel and resources required; the timeline for all aspects of sourcing, negotiating, performing due diligence, and consummating the transaction; and the capital. This chapter homes in on the CIO perspective, qualifications, types of experiences, and lessons learned the hard way. It provides in-depth case studies that open a window into the senior leadership who execute on behalf of family owners and wealth holders and the unusual breed and pedigree many of these top senior leaders have as compared to the traditional private equity investors or investment bankers found on Wall Street. History offers many examples of SFOs that embraced the direct investing opportunity without fully understanding the many facets required when it comes to talent management.

Sourcing Top CIOs to Oversee Direct Investing in the SFO

Perhaps one of the primary mitigants for any SFO considering direct investments is sourcing a qualified CIO who can manage the pre- and post-investment strategy and execution. While SFOs may dislike the fixed and performance-based fees charged by outside investment firms, these firms do, generally, use their fee revenue to hire investment teams with specialized backgrounds. SFOs, therefore, should not overlook the necessary skillsets and backgrounds of investment personnel capable of working in this space. A qualified candidate for CIO will have a combination of business and investment skills along with an ability to communicate and assess risk factors that are unique to direct investing. Should the SFO require broader portfolio investment management, the CIO will be required to balance the needs of illiquid and liquid investment exposures. Additionally, it's always beneficial if the CIO has experience with legal contracts and agreements and a background dealing with relationships and communication pre-/post-investment and inside/outside the SFO. A CIO who manages a collection of public investments and tradable assets/fund managers can often be more research oriented in her approach to investment management and risk management; in contrast, the direct investing CIO will, in most instances, be involved with constituent groups outside of the SFO that have direct influence on the direct investment holdings/investment process. Strong leadership, organizational, and time-management skills are critical for any qualified CIO to possess, and, as this chapter will demonstrate, can often be a primary determinant in the success of the direct investment.

A typical job description would look like the following:

Sample Job Description for CIO with Direct Investing Capabilities

Depending on the intended focus or parameters of the direct investing the SFO chooses to pursue, a successful CIO candidate may have some of the following characteristics and background experiences:

- Direct operating or business-building experience
  - Turnaround or management consulting experience

- Transaction structuring and negotiating experience
  - Legal background, accounting background, M&A banking background, real estate investing, loan origination/structuring/loan book management
- Leadership roles
  - Prior roles as C-level executive in business development, corporate M&A, product development/engineering
- Securities specialist
  - Credit and equity analyst, public security pricing/risk management
- Principal investing experience
  - Historical experience investing and managing principal capital

The direct investing vertical can be professionally and financially rewarding, but the SFO and CIO must have a balanced appreciation going into the process that initial timelines and expectations will likely be adjusted many times during the course of the investment. If both parties are not properly aligned, then seemingly small day 1 issues have the potential of creating internal friction within the SFO and may have amplified influences on the investments. Even minor misalignments can have magnified and unintended consequences when applied to the typical long-term horizon common to direct investing.

Mini-Case Example of Compensation Misalignment

An SFO wanted to build an internal direct investing team in order to build out a direct investing division within the SFO to fulfill the family's portfolio diversification goals. The SFO went about hiring a team and tasking them with sourcing and executing on transactions. The SFO structured a below-market compensation package for the team but offered the investment team the opportunity to structure a current compensation catchup provision in the employment agreements. The basic construct allowed for a fixed percentage of the income stream earned on the direct investments to be added to the current compensation packages, essentially making up for the initial salary discounts the team was offered. In fact, if the team deployed enough capital, the agreements presented the opportunity for the team to make above current market compensation—a potentially dangerous incentive. This structure was intended to allow the SFO to get in the business on the cheap while incenting the team to source and invest in value-oriented transactions with characteristics that allowed for reasonable current income back to the investment team and the SFO. The family viewed value investing and current income as providing additional layers of protection and overall risk mitigation. From the outset, the SFO expected this investment book to be value oriented, high yielding, illiquid, but in the middle of the risk spectrum curve. In reality, the compensation dynamic encouraged the investment team, who had no capital at risk, to pursue direct lending transactions with warrants. This form of quasi-debt/equity is not uncommon in the direct investing/private finance markets, but the sector is notorious for its hidden risks and market traps. If the transaction worked, the SFO had the chance to get paid well above the risk-free rate with the future option of generating significant equity gains through the warrant participation. This space is also prone to larger *tail risk*, meaning that when problems do occur they are apt to occur in the outer years after the investment has performed for some period of time. At the extreme, this construct creates a dynamic whereby the direct investing team earns short-term compensation off of the SFO's investment capital, with the SFO receiving the bulk of its investment return during the higher tail-risk period of the transaction. What do you think happened?

The team executed on a number of transactions with success, but in their reach for yield and short-term gain the investment team also originated or participated in some loans that experienced defaults or went nonperforming in the outer years. The consequent loss of investment principal on this small percentage of transactions more than offset the gains earned on the winners. As their prospect for income evaporated, the investment team left the SFO and the SFO's administrative staff was left to clean up the problem investments. Were the investment team to have a more balanced compensation/incentive structure these problem investments might have never been made. Furthermore, any problems that did arise may have been managed/handled differently by a team that is incentivized to rework/restructure the investments. Ultimately, all parties would have benefited from this balanced approach.

The primary takeaways are: (1) have market rate compensation for the investment team, (2) require some form of, even minor, co-investment from the team, and (3) promote a balanced payout structure that includes a multi-year lock with graduated performance pay based on the health and stability of the entire direct investment portfolio along with a philosophy of total return and absolute return. This case demonstrates what can happen when misalignment occurs and the unintended consequences faced by the SFO.

What's the Edge?

Most institutional investors market around having an "edge" to the market, or a strategic advantage, or what has been described in Chapter 1 as an "unfair advantage." Maybe it's relationships, industry knowledge, or structuring expertise. It can be helpful for an SFO and CIO to have a similar plan when approaching direct investing. Private markets tend to be relatively efficient, and most experienced CIOs have an edge (even though they may not always know it). Even seemingly minor advantages, such as familiarity with a specific geography or personal relationships, can have immense positive influence on the pre- and post-investment process. In Chapter 13, on direct investing globally, this is certainly the case.

SFOs tend to have many built-in advantages when compared to the institutional competitive-set. These include:

- Flexible investment timelines
- Speed of execution
- Lack of bureaucracy
- Domain/industry expertise
- Family history/reputation
- Competitive insight
- Associated holdings
- Relationships
- Infrastructure
- Surety of close/dependability
- Future plans for investment

The SFO and CIO should consider each of the items on this list, as they can often have significant influence on the outcome and success of direct investing scenarios. Many direct investing specialists consider the initial point of investment (time, price, and structure) as consistently the most influential aspect of the average direct investment and a consistent predictor/determinant of future success. Therefore, the CIO should leverage his edge and any edge the SFO possesses to maximize the influence these factors may have on the investment from the earliest stage possible.

What Defines Success for the CIO?

As the CIO considers success, it's important to consider how best to define success within the confines of the SFO.

- Does the SFO simply want to control the destiny of their investment process?
- Is the initiative built around an expectation that superior returns can be achieved?

- How does legacy factor into the discussion, and, if a direct investing program promotes more active involvement from family members, does that influence the plan?

These are only a small subset of considerations, but as an extension to the prior discussion on alignment, families may view success as broader than simply investment returns.

The CIO should be operating under investment guidelines and risk management directives from the SFO. A sophisticated CIO will manage the SFO's direct investments with an emphasis on absolute returns and generating growth/profits in excess of public market indexes and inflation over an extended period of time. For any SFO to accept the prospect of illiquidity and often ambiguous short-term valuation estimates (common to many direct investments), the SFO must expect that their investment will outperform the traditional public market comparables over a multiyear period. Valuing and measuring the growth of most illiquid investments can be challenging, and, consequently, developing a transparent methodology to accomplish this goal should be a priority for the CIO. Because there can often be some "art" to what many valuation experts view as typically more scientific, the CIO should maintain a healthy degree of rigor and consistency to whatever methodology is predetermined. Elements to consider when developing this methodology may include: the growth rate and/or stability of any current yield the investment may be generating; general investment return volatility/stability; competitor or industry comps; external lending institution valuations; return over the assigned "cost of capital" or risk free rate; external market influences to valuation (examples may include commodity price influences, interest rate sensitivity, or foreign currency impacts, to name a few). An experienced CIO should document and communicate the valuation parameters and metrics to the SFO, and engaging in open dialog and debate on this matter can beneficially influence the process. Lastly, the CIO should be expert at detailing how the SFO's direct investment(s) have performed against broadly reported indexes of alternative market returns. (Examples may include the HFR index or broadly reported private equity indexes from groups like Cambridge Associates.) The common theme is that a skilled CIO is resourceful, creative, and adept at managing not only the selection and implementation of the direct investment portfolio but also the benchmarking, tracking, and post-investment management. As you will read in the next case study, the CIO utilized his structuring and business/investment acumen to create substantial long-term value for the SFO employer while marshaling resources and creativity around an investment project that required many of the skills detailed above to realize maximum value.

Smith Family Case Study

The Smith family owned a sizeable tract of land that was being underutilized. In coordination with the CIO, the family formulated a plan to develop this property for commercial use. The SFO did not wish to burden the investment project with substantial debt, but the total development costs were substantial, requiring the family to source outside equity capital. The family also wished to utilize the direct investment opportunity as a means to engage their oldest son in the development as project manager/developer and post-construction operator/owner. The son's resume and past work experience supported this role/involvement, so nepotism was not an issue. The CIO hired an outside advisory firm to assist with sourcing the additional required equity, valuing the transaction, and structuring a tiered investment structure that guaranteed that the Smith family maintained control of the project and majority ownership upon completion of the project. Because of the Smith family's industry expertise, the strength of the development plan, and family reputation, the CIO was able to raise the required debt and equity to accomplish the objective. An outside SFO was identified as co-investment capital partner and invested senior equity with a deferred dividend/pay-in-kind. Once the project was operating and had stabilized revenue, the advisory firm working with the Smiths' CIO was retained again to assist with refinancing the development debt and equity. The outside SFO remains a minority co-investor today, and the Smiths' SFO has created a valuable asset their son can operate and grow for many years. Additionally, the Smiths leveraged their family legacy, the low-cost basis they held in the project, and managed to avoid punitive tax consequences.

This case exemplifies how a CIO with direct investing expertise can help maximize the value of a static asset on the SFO's balance sheet while creating a future income stream and expanding the career opportunities for one of the dependents. Multiple levels of success were achieved for all participants, but of critical importance to consider is the fact that the family took a reasonable amount of financing and execution risk on an asset that held considerable value even in its undeveloped stage. It's only because of careful planning, expectation setting/management, capital structuring, and full alignment for all participants that this project achieved its level of success. The Smith family gained added name recognition and notoriety, and are well positioned to execute on future transactions with similar constructs.

The CIO who managed this direct investment project for the Smith family distinguished himself in a number of capacities.

- The CIO enabled substantial value to be created for the Smith family.
- A next-generation family member moved into an active role in advancing the family's legacy and reputation.
- The CIO proved to be an objective participant in a complex process between multiple SFOs, outside advisors, large sums of investment capital, long investment timelines, and personal land-holdings that had sentimental value to the operating family.
- The CIO sourced and hired outside advisors to add depth of experience, specialized perspective, and market credibility to a complex long-dated project.
  - This focus on building an institutional quality offering added value to the project during the initial planning/investment stage, which translated to a higher long-term value for all participants.

SFOs often pursue internal direct investing platforms as a way of avoiding the costs and complexities of investing through more traditional institutional direct investing funds/programs, but the CIO for the Smith family added value to this investment process by bringing in the appropriate amount of external advisors and institutional process/procedure. The CIO understood that the external participants would mitigate the Smith family's project risk while also adding an appropriate level of institutional quality and credibility. This was all achieved with the appreciation that the Smith family wished to execute on the project plan with flexibility and minimal external constraints. The SFO co-investor providing the senior equity capital, meanwhile, gained access to a unique investment that benefited from a passionate and heavily invested operating family partner and institutional-quality underpinnings from valuation metrics, legal protections, and balanced structure/accountability and risk. The Smiths' CIO certainly earned his compensation and orchestrated a balanced transaction template that the family can implement in the future. The CIO had the foresight and acumen to tap into the emerging space of family-to-family investment partnerships that have existed for generations but are becoming more popular because of scenarios like the Smith family case. Had the Smith family not hired a CIO with this level of direct investment experience and awareness, the results might have been very different and potentially impactful on both the SFO and the Smiths' son's career. The CIO proved to be a good fit for the SFO and the transaction.

The CIO Fit

A CIO's background does not necessarily have to be in the financial/investing markets. In fact, there are many examples of CIOs who have expertise operating and managing companies or projects and may have limited formal investment experience, but who have detailed knowledge of how to manage capital exposure from an operational perspective. Conversely, a more classically trained investment CIO who has some operational experience can be an excellent candidate for direct investing success. Often SFOs focus predominantly on investment backgrounds. Making the investment and allocating the capital are often the easiest part of the transaction, and CIOs who have a demonstrated record of managing post-investment exposure have unique perspective that can only be learned through experience and time. A CIO who has direct investing awareness/exposure and can manage communications and relationships up to the family principals or board of directors and down to the execution personnel is critical. Team building, leadership/consensus building, and resource management are all qualities of successful CIOs. In order to handle all of the intricacies and potential requirements, a CIO should also have experience in managing employees; managing internal and external resources; competitive awareness; budgeting, P&L management, forecasting, cash flow management, and valuation analysis; and fundraising. Additional background experience working with detailed legal agreements, product development, corporate development, or conflict resolution can be valuable to any direct investing initiative. It's not necessarily practical to expect that the CIO will have expertise across all categories, so focusing on someone who can work with the resident resources available and source outside resources when required to accomplish these goals is essential.

A CIO who has significant direct investing expertise should be relatively easy to evaluate and benchmark. Along with a customary review of results, the CIO should be able to speak to past transactions in detail and offer references to past involvement and contribution. Understanding how the CIO managed past transaction challenges and opportunities is critical while appreciating where in the cycle or trend the CIO invested will help to quantify the CIO's investment acumen and validity of performance. When doing so, the SFO should consider the appropriate measurement and segmentation of these relevant skill sets.

Specifically:

- Has the CIO transacted more in the private or public space?
- What types of securities, and have transactions tended to be control or minority?
- Is there a bias toward distressed or performing and have transactions been domestic or international?
- Has there been diversity of exposure to early and later stage, and has the CIO worked within the confines of an established institution with a formal structure or in a more entrepreneurial setting?

Often the type of training, past business exposure, or institutional structure in which the CIO trained may have as much influence on the potential success or "fit" the CIO is likely to have within any given SFO structure as the CIO's past successes or investing experience. Evaluating the CIO's complete background is paramount in avoiding a scenario such as the Jones family faced.

The Jones Family Case Study

The Jones family engaged in a comprehensive search for an experienced CIO to launch the family's direct investing initiative. The CIO the Joneses hired had multiple years of direct investing experience with another large SFO, excellent market/analytical credentials, and a stellar reputation within the market. It didn't work.

The CIO the Joneses selected was experienced at investing in marketed transactions represented through the broker channel. The Jones family was entrepreneurial and wanted proprietary deal flow or internally generated investment ideas. The CIO was accustomed to transacting with large institutions sometimes as a lead but in many instances as a co-investor. The SFO had a desire to lead and control a majority of their transactions, and this required significant internal due diligence, forecasting/analytics, and business development. The Jones family wanted to create an investment company platform that offered uniqueness and individuality, while the CIO had experience working as a participant in a broader investment structure with diversified institutional partners all acting as support and contributing to the process. Over multiple years of engagement not one transaction was completed and both parties ultimately left the relationship frustrated.

The Jones family approached the process in an appropriate manner, and the CIO embraced the initial opportunity to enter a new office with a large uninvested balance sheet and mandate to invest across a broad spectrum. Neither party is at fault; it was simply a misalignment of skillsets and expectations. The CIO would have been better served to consider that the very fact the Jones family sought to avoid the institutional market was not consistent with his exclusive background of only working in the very structured and regimented world of institutional transactions presented, prepared, marketed, and managed through a formal sales process by institutional firms. The Jones family failed to appreciate that their entrepreneurial tendencies and desire for individuality and creativity throughout the direct investing process was a significant departure from the more formal and structured world of institutional investing. Given these distinct viewpoints, the family would have been better served had they hired a CIO with a more diverse investment background. In hindsight this seems obvious, but the allure for a CIO to enter a new SFO with unencumbered capital and a clean-slate investment book presents a powerful combination. He may have believed he could adjust to this new culture, but the example helps to demonstrate that the intangibles of the investment process and way in which direct investments are sourced and constructed can have significant influence on the process and presentability to a family that "knows what it wants and knows what it doesn't want."

Risk Management at the Investment Level and Portfolio Level

Because direct investments can often take years to mature and achieve a liquidity event, it is important for the CIO to understand investment-level risk management and portfolio-level risk management. Many families become emotionally attached to direct investments and are passionate supporters of their investments. While often highly beneficial to determining the outcome, families can be less inclined to objectively assess risk management tactics or implement hedging/risk-mitigation strategies across the portfolio. Empowering the CIO to develop strategies for risk management and hedging can alleviate stress during market fluctuations.

The success the Smith family enjoyed, in the example previously detailed, demonstrates the importance of communication and interpretation between the SFO and its CIO. Clear communication and expectation management are critical elements of the SFO and CIO relationship. Given the extended horizon common to the direct investment vertical, a CIO who can understand the communication styles and preferences of the family is particularly important. Communicating investment-level progress and how this progress may be influenced by the broader macro-trends can be challenging. Investment confidence and resolve can be tested when capital market volatility increases, and a highly-qualified CIO will have the foresight and conviction to overlay a concise market analysis with the potential impact on the direct investment and broader investment portfolio. A current example might be a family with direct investment exposure to the oil and gas industry, which is typically cost intensive and long dated in nature, having offset exposure to the transportation index, which likely will benefit from lower costs on the primary input: fuel.

Although hedging and risk management are often difficult to size and implement, a CIO who can identify correlations between direct investment-level and portfolio-level exposures and regularly track and manage this exposure with an emphasis on communication and expectation management with the family is critical. Often this management can occur in the background, but it is during periods of elevated market volatility that families may be the most distracted by external influences. Furthermore, periods of volatility often present investors with extreme pricing/valuation fluctuations, offering the possibility for opportunistic off-market valuations. If the CIO has not previously communicated a plan or managed expectations, then any benefit that market volatility may offer can be lost. Worse still, the CIO should avoid scenarios where external volatility forces change to the portfolio or direct investment holdings that are executed at inopportune times, as this will likely be detrimental to the performance.

The Clark Family Case Study

A scenario that played out for the Clark family could have been managed and avoided had there been better initial communication and expectation management. The SFO still might have suffered significantly from the broader market volatility, but there would have been a greater level of awareness and accountability measurement.

The Clark family built its fortune over decades in the construction industry and had a successful operating business with multiple family members involved in senior management positions. The SFO developed a plan to expand beyond their broad public market exposure and into the direct investment space. The SFO formed a plan to invest in operating companies and originate direct loans to companies that serviced and worked in the construction industry vertical. The family's CIO implemented their plan and began an active investment process in 2005. As the market turned in 2007, many problems emerged within the direct investment portfolio. These challenges occurred simultaneously with the severe stress the family faced at its core operating business. The correlations between the Clarks' primary company and direct investment portfolio were largely matched. The CIO had not adjusted the SFO's public market allocations so the upshot of the situation was that the family's intent to leverage off their sector expertise, while valid, had driven the investment portfolio into a more concentrated bet on a single industry vertical at a cyclical peak. While it is always easy to draw clarity from events in the past, the CIO should have insisted that the now-smaller public market portfolio be more conservatively invested with specific emphasis on allocating away from sectors, industries, and securities that were closely correlated to the construction/real estate industry and perhaps even into sectors that would benefit from weakness in the construction/real estate vertical.

In retrospect, it is easy to detail missteps and assign blame, but the true measure of a qualified CIO is helping families focus on questions and issues that may not be obvious or even popular to consider. Starting with communication and expectation management, families can at least be made aware of hidden correlations and potential portfolio exposures that may offer a hedge. A CIO should run analytics and provide data that assigns probabilities and correlation overlaps across the family's portfolio. The SFO must challenge the CIO to not be complacent but prepare and plan for portfolio stress and hidden correlation overlaps. Understanding how the CIO has handled adversity in the past, whether business/investment or personal/academic, can be a good predictor on the CIO's preparedness and problem-solving abilities. The fact that many family office fortunes have been earned during periods of market volatility is reason enough to "hope for the best but prepare for the worst." Therefore, a qualified CIO should not only have a cogent defensive plan in place but a plan for taking advantage of market dislocations.

CIO Compensation

Much of this chapter has discussed what a family should consider when choosing a CIO and how to best evaluate and analyze the needs of the family and attributes of a successful CIO candidate. Of primary importance in this process is the element of CIO compensation and alignment of interests. Once the direct investment mandate has been established and the family has made the internal commitment to pursue this investment strategy, the family should utilize a goals-based approach when designing its compensation plan. Specific to this plan is expectation setting, goal measurement, and developing a balance between market-based current compensation and results-oriented participation compensation. This approach should influence the right type of candidate and bind the parties around the common core goal of direct investing and portfolio management.

A compensation plan that coordinates current compensation, taking into account the CIO's background and expertise and resume of accomplishment, with a longer-term compensation structure, should produce mutually beneficial results. Effectively presented and communicated, this plan can be a strong recruitment tool.

Specific compensation components may include:

- *Annual Base Compensation:* Market rates for base salary will range from $250,000 to $1,000,000(+) depending on a number of factors including: geographic location, size of office/assets under management, CIO background/knowledge, and breadth of investment responsibilities. In addition, the SFO should be prepared to provide comprehensive benefits.
- *Annual Bonus Compensation:* Bonus structures vary depending on multiple factors, but typically, there is an element of subjectivity (has the CIO performed well in relation to the assignment, such as team building, sourcing, risk management, communication, and infrastructure oversight) and objectivity (how have the investments performed and what are the financial consequences associated with the CIO's involvement). The subjective-versus-objective/formulaic bonus can vary substantially, but common target ranges are from 50 percent of annual base compensation to many multiples of annual base compensation.
- *Long-Term Compensation:* Long-term compensation plans range from highly formulaic (CIO paid X percent of net returns after Y percent cost of capital hurdle) to more subjective (CIO paid based on combination of factors and results custom to the SFO's individual expectations; examples may include: CIO involved multiple generations in the investment or sourced investment partners for the opportunity, thereby reducing the costs/risks of the SFO). Long-term compensation may also include SFO-sponsored leverage for the CIO (examples of this include: CIO personally invests $100,000 into the direct investment but has economic exposure to $500,000 based on leverage from the SFO's position). This final example provides closely aligned incentives for both parties and may be structured to minimize the risk that the CIO resigns prematurely or promotes transactions that have an unbalanced risk/reward ratio.

Beyond a competitive compensation structure, an SFO that can leverage its family history, pedigree, and track record of success can be a powerful recruitment tool and intangible form of compensation. The allure of direct investing by family offices often comes from the opinion that a successful family has what it takes to replicate its prior success on a direct investment basis and not only can maintain more control over its investments but can do so with lower absolute costs. As previously detailed, short-term cost savings can ultimately lead to misalignment and avoidable investment losses, so designing a thoughtful and comprehensive compensation plan for the CIO should provide long-term benefits for all participants. Some of the most successful single-family offices have been built around world-class investment professionals and institutional-quality infrastructure that has been built to outlive the current family generation and that in some cases become self-sustaining independent investment companies. In many instances, this success has evolved from a structure that encouraged entrepreneurial thinking, active communication, balanced compensation, and hiring seasoned investment professionals with a long-term stake in the success of the institution and corresponding growth of the family's wealth.

As there are many different types of strategies, another way for SFOs to consider CIO compensation and investment operating costs is to build a budget based on the assets under management (AUM). This example will focus on goal setting, measurement, and compensation development for a single-family office of up to $1 billion in AUM. Using these criteria, were a family to treat its AUM as a generic alternative investment fund, the annual fee stream (operating budget) would equate to $20 million per year on total committed capital of $1 billion at the rate of 2 percent. This $20 million should be sufficient to support the current compensation requirements of a qualified CIO, office staff, office operating costs, legal, advisors, and travel/diligence costs. Along with developing a budget, the SFO and CIO should share a common view and expectation around the anticipated timelines for sourcing and implementation of the direct investment strategy along with a broader analysis of post-investment goals and responsibilities. While the SFO may consider $20 million annually as well in excess of what actual costs may be, there is a real potential that any direct investment may require years of "seasoning" prior to either generating current yield or achieving a liquidity event. The CIO and SFO may pursue multiple transactions, so developing a realistic operating budget that takes into account full diligence costs, plus the potential for broken deal costs, is a complex undertaking.

Additional budget/compensation considerations will likely be influenced by the style of direct investing the family pursues. Does the family wish to acquire/invest and own/operate/manage the investment for generations, or is the investment strategy more oriented toward investing with a view toward financial improvement and more immediate profit realization? Each case dictates a very different style of CIO and has a direct impact on the compensation structure. A shorter-horizon investment strategy based on set investment goals is likely to appeal to a different style of CIO who may have a background oriented in capital markets, private equity, or alternative investing (a financial engineer CIO). An SFO that intends to acquire, operate, and hold their portfolio companies may want a CIO with more direct operating expertise or business-building skillsets (an operating or consultative CIO). Either way, the CIO should be financially invested in the opportunity. Many SFOs offer co-investment rights with imbedded leverage, allowing for the CIO to participate significantly in the upside performance of the investment. Specific examples include CIOs receiving from 2× to 10× leverage on any dollars invested along with "granted" economics based on a more traditional bonus or carried interest model. Together, the CIO can earn returns well in excess of their annual "current" compensation and more akin to senior-level private equity or hedge fund professionals. The SFO should appreciate that qualified CIO candidates need visibility to total compensation that is commensurate with competing institutional or corporate competitors. Given the potential upside rewards offset by the potential downside risks (in time and capital) that are present in the direct investing vertical, SFOs are well advised to approach the compensation process just as an institution would, which is to say that an AUM-based budget build offers a good starting point.

When assessing the value a prospective CIO can bring, it's critical for the family to honestly determine their own commitment and time allocation to the direct investing initiative. Once capital is committed, talent and infrastructure can be stressed and tested. Family members may overlook the institutional support they benefited from in prior transactions and may underestimate the benefits they received from prior in-place infrastructure.

The Miller Family Case Study

The Miller family made its fortune in the consumer products vertical, and ultimately sold their company and formed an SFO to support the comprehensive needs of G1 and G2. Mr. Miller assumed the family office title of CEO, but he hired a CIO to actively manage the investment portfolio and assist him with sourcing direct investments in the consumer products vertical. The SFO made a number of control and non-control direct investments in the consumer products space, but Mr. Miller failed to appreciate that his particular operating and investment oversight style was not highly scalable. The CIO was well suited to carry some of the load, but the diversity of the

investment book and the basic requirements of the direct investments created significant strain on the SFO and negatively impacted the product it was
designed to offer the family. The direct investment companies required constant monitoring, board participation, information management, and management team building and support. The investments performed well, and
the CIO's capabilities matched well with that of the family, Mr. Miller, and
the underlying management teams. What happened is the classic scenario that
even non-control investments require substantial time, attention, and maintenance. Mr. Miller gained access to some of the investments specifically because
of who he was and what he had accomplished previously, which had limited scalability. While the CIO had a complementary background, it became
a story of two individuals attempting to scale themselves to the benefit of
multiple businesses. Even minor tasks involving scheduling, administrative
matters, and human resource issues created complications and inefficiencies.
Mr. Miller intended to utilize his SFO to grow his general/passive financial
portfolio and manage his family's personal affairs, but what he ended up creating, unintentionally, was another business, the SFO, which required more
of his time than he had spent at the company he founded that created the
wealth. Breadth of holdings and the sheer number of responsibilities, all of
which were performing well, created an environment that was overburdened
and physically and mentally draining. In actuality, the SFO's direct investment portfolio could have grown more quickly and produced greater levels of
success had the various companies had less internal competition for attention
within the SFO.

This example underscores not only the potential time commitments
required to properly mentor and support underlying direct company investments, but also the capacity constraints that even skilled CIOs will face when
tasked with managing a broad portfolio of investments in direct and portfolio
investments. Many families underestimate the imbedded resources they
benefited from in their legacy company, and once they are in an independent
family office environment the small things can add up. The CIO can enhance
the situation, as he did for the Miller family, but ultimately, the scalability of
a small team of people can quickly be overwhelmed. Finding a solution can
be a delicate proposition for the CIO and the family. Many entrepreneurial
families approach situations such as this with the view that simply a bit
more work, focus, and time can rectify the situation. Ultimately, it's the
CIO's responsibility to tactfully make the family aware of the potential and
actual costs associated with pursuing an investment program with limited
scalability/resources. Had market volatility created additional complications,
the overall results might have suffered dramatic losses.

Conclusion

The CIO role at an SFO focused on direct investments can offer a rewarding career path and dynamic work schedule. Few careers provide the opportunity and challenge to make a potentially dramatic impact on multiple generations of a family while offering the chance to receive competitive compensation in a quickly evolving business sector. If the SFO and CIO are on the same page, a lifelong bond and atmosphere of trust and shared success can be created and perpetuated for many years. It is not uncommon for families to view their CIO as a true part of the family group and for these relationships to last well past the professional working years of the CIO.

In response to the 2008–09 financial crisis many SFOs were either established or strengthened as a reaction to the instability of the banking sector and multiple conflicts of interest that came to light between institutions and their clients (examples include: auction rate securities, hedge fund gates, and assets seizures/freezing by institutions and regulators). Following this period, many families adjusted their external advisor relationships to assert more control over their own finances/investments. This trend offers CIOs greater opportunities to manage and direct SFO capital. Furthermore, many institutions now view the SFO sector as an area of distinct capital growth. Even firms like BlackRock, KKR, and Blackstone, which have historically focused on targeting institutional capital sources, have established specialized groups tasked with specifically addressing the SFO market with products designed to address SFO desires (examples include: lower fee specialized/customized products, SFO controlled investment offerings where the institution is the silent or minority partner, and one-off co-investment products built around exclusivity and confidentiality). Expect this trend to continue as SFOs, while typically difficult to "sell," can prove to be loyal clients with an aversion to switching institutional relationships.

For the CIO who understands this changing investment landscape and how to access/utilize it, the combination of these trends along with the increased pool of investment options/resources presents institutional price competition and access to sophisticated investment products that even 5 to 10 years ago were not available to SFOs. Expect the market to continue this path of evolution; for sophisticated institutions, which understand how to work with SFOs and efficiently address their needs, there is an opportunity to develop long-term relationships with SFOs and the CIOs that guide the capital. Given the fact that many SFOs are institutional in AUM size, it will be more critical than ever for the CIO to have the awareness and sophistication to utilize resources outside of the SFO to minimize costs and in-house

SFO infrastructure needs while taking advantage of the immense resources (examples: financing, analytics/computing, research, hedging) available in the institutional market. A CIO who can harness this pool of external financial and research capabilities will offer the SFO world-class investment tools previously used only by the largest global financial institutions. For families, it will continue to be important to stay current on these evolving trends and to measure the CIO based on where the broader marketplace is going versus where it has been in the past.

Properly managed and implemented, the SFO should expect that the right CIO will develop an internal culture of professionalism while implementing procedures and processes to improve transparency, facilitate communication, and allow the SFO to have investment practices that are first rate. The direct investments and broader investment portfolio should provide the SFO with better long-term returns, lower volatility, easier benchmarking/results measurement, and expanded opportunities for hedging and risk-mitigation strategies. With a secure business foundation supporting the SFO's investment activities, a good CIO will ensure there are personnel and systems-based redundancies in place. Stability, transparency, and defined goals should translate into an office culture that also represents consistency and longevity for the SFO and the professionals who work there. Done correctly, this will not only reduce long-term operating costs but generate superior returns for the family and maximize the opportunity that the SFO outlives the current generations it serves today. The CIO should build investment infrastructure that promotes generational investment process continuity and supports the family's legacy of investment success for future generations. In certain circumstances, the CIO has integrated his or her own wealth within the SFO, thereby binding the CIO's family with that of the founding family. These rare examples create the purest form of alignment between the primary participants and often lead to powerful combinations of wealth and prowess that truly set the standard that others seek to emulate.

CHAPTER 11

The Millennials and Direct Investing: A Look at Impact Investing

Contributing Author: Temple Fennell

This chapter covers the direct investment interests and objectives of the next-generation or Millennial family members (Millennials), who were born between 1981 and 1997, as well as addresses how a family can engage them in the direct investment process. The chapter will also focus on Millennials' specific interest in social and environmental challenges with market-based solutions, also known as *impact investing*.[1] Interest in impact investing is not the sole providence of Millennials and often spans multiple generations in a family. Engaging a broad base of family members in an impact investment development process may generate valuable intangible benefits, labeled here as *experiential returns*, for the family, including strength of family unity, growth of human assets, and expansion of the family's "circle of competence."

Millennials have been extensively studied over recent years, researching who they are, what they want, how they are engaged, as well as how they are similar and different from previous generations. Engaging Millennials in the development of an impact investment strategy may help families reach the proverbial brass ring of training the next generation of family members to be valuable contributors in the family's investment decision process.

The chapter also addresses the challenges and barriers impact investing may cause for a family's existing asset allocation model and investment process. It concludes with an introduction to Harvard Business School professor Hirotaka Takeuchi's work on "knowledge creation" within an organization and MIT Sloan School of Management professor Peter Senge's work on creating a "learning organization" and how this work can be applied to family offices.

Who Are the Millennials and What Do They Care About?

The 75 million Millennials in the United States are now the largest living generation.[2] In 2012, Deloitte surveyed 5,000 Millennials with an advanced degree and who were employed full-time to choose what they believed to be the primary purpose of business. The survey revealed that Millennials ranked "to improve society" as the number-one priority of businesses, with "generate profit" a closely following second priority.[3] Millennials want to see the impact of their financial and human capital and want to be involved in creating impact. They are also creative and tactical in the use of their capital and willing to use any strategies, assets, and tools necessary to create positive impact.[4]

Millennials' investment perspectives have been largely shaped by a bombardment of information regarding climate change, social unrest, terrorism, economic inequality, worldwide recession, distrust of financial markets and institutions, scarcity of natural resources, and other global issues. Millennials are not motivated solely by the "feel-good factor" of impact investing; they are responding responsibly to large secular shifts in the global economy and seeking accountability, and long-term returns, as well investments that are measurable and sustainable.[5]

Millennials associate the financial markets with capital destruction and believe that the capital markets alone will not be enough to sustain family wealth, or the planet for that matter. Many Millennials are skeptical of modern portfolio theory and do not believe the pubic markets are fair and efficient. According to a 2014 Morgan Stanley/Campden Wealth report, many Millennials believe capital markets are synonymous with volatility, historically low interest rates and their associated bond yields, and moderate long-term equity performance.[6] Even after the 2015 bull market, only 26 percent of the Millennials had a "bullish outlook" versus 45 percent of all high-net-worth investors who were optimistic about the public markets.[7]

The values and impact filters that Millennials want to apply to their asset allocation are often not well supported by their advisors or the senior generations. In the 2015 OppenheimerFunds/Campden Wealth Study, 80 percent of the Millennials surveyed indicated that they want their portfolios to incorporate values in the decision-making process and to increase allocations in impact investing, microfinance, Sustainable and Responsible Investing (SRI) filters, and venture philanthropy.[8] Millennials often connect with diverse groups of peers and influencers to source and process investment ideas. Investment information is often gathered through networking, online research, social media, and other idiosyncratic sources. These dynamics provide greater awareness of knowledge and opportunities that requires proper filtering, focusing, and processing frameworks that the senior generations can help Millennials develop.

Millennials' Respect for the Senior Generation

Millennials hold sincere and authentic respect for the values and ideals of the senior generation. They are mindful of the privilege and stewardship of the legacy assets, and like their parents and grandparents, many Millennials consider "themselves stewards charged with sustaining the family wealth for future generations and embrace the responsibility to support and promote causes that speak to their family values."[9] One study reported that 64 percent of Millennials and Generation X members believe their values are highly aligned with the senior generations.[10] A 2015 OppenheimerFund/Campden Wealth study asked Millennials' to select the responsibilities they believed were most important with regard to the family assets; 94 percent selected stewardship of the family legacy, 88 percent viewed preservation of capital, and 89 percent perceived wealth growth as very important or important.[11]

Although the Millennials and senior generations may share concerns regarding global issues, family values, importance of legacy, and stewardship of assets, they often differ with regard to how to use family capital to achieve these objectives. Specifically, the rising generation differs from the senior generation in three distinct ways: (1) mandate to be actively engaged in entities they fund, (2) desire to learn and employ new tools to create impact, and (3) the importance to create immediate and measurable impact.[12] These differences are noteworthy, as they illustrate the Millennials' natural gravitation toward applying innovative models and solutions, and the desire to see true impact with their investment, not simply financial returns.

The Millennials tend to be problem- and solution-focused at the company or organizational level, whereas the senior generations have been historically more focused at the institutional level. The senior generation tends to invest in *established* organizations, whereas the Millennials want to *help establish* organizations. The senior generation tends to deploy impact investment capital as relatively passive grants, whereas the Millennials want to deploy capital as active investments. This is a subtle but significant difference from the perspectives of risk-return objectives, use of assets, experience, and investment management.

Millennials' interest in investing in solutions to solve global problems coexists with a deep concern for financial security and stewardship of assets. Several studies revealed that Millennials are financially more conservative than the older generations. One study revealed that 60 percent more Millennials were determined to transfer wealth to their families than Baby Boomers or Generation X cohorts.[13] Additional studies reported that 30 percent of Millennials were more concerned about financial security than any other age group,[14] 39 percent more Millennials identified themselves as "conservative" versus Baby Boomers, and 21 percent more Millennials "seek comfort and predictability" than Baby Boomers.[15]

Many Millennials are seeking guidance from senior generations and advisors to build the knowledge and skills with training that reflects their individual interests and aptitudes. Millennials express a deep desire to learn from the tacit knowledge (i.e., experience, values, and legacy) and the explicit knowledge (i.e., investment skills, policies, and processes) of their parents and grandparents.[16] The OppenheimerFunds/Campden Wealth study reported that nine out of ten Millennials valued wealth transfer as important or very important and look for advisors to guide them. The report advocates advisors to work with Millennials to develop structure to help them engage.

What does all this research reveal? The bottom line is Millennials are aligned with their senior generation's values, views on legacy and stewardship, and are committed to passing on wealth to heirs, but have underlying concerns of secular, global issues that may impact financial security. To fully participate with the Millennials, advisors and senior generations need to engage with the Millennials and to help them build an impact investing strategy, establish policies and procedures that allow Millennials to make informed investment decisions, and build out investment options.[17] It is essential for the senior generations to devote time and resources to understand the interests, needs, and requirements of the Next Generation.

Growing Interest in Impact Investing

There is an ever-growing interest in impact investing, likely driven by the heightened awareness of climate change, health issues, social inequality, war, and global economics. Proprietary research conducted by MIT Sloan School of Management of 40 ultra-high-net-worth families and advisors (median net worth of $500 million) revealed that close to 90 percent wanted advice on delivering greater societal impact.[18] Similarly, in a 2015 study of 1,800 participants by Barclays, 66 percent of the high-net-worth respondents expressed interest in exploring impact investment[19] and 62 percent of the respondents in another study agreed that "it is possible to achieve market-rate returns investing in companies based on their social or environmental impact."[20]

Research into the areas where Millennials are most interested in investing include education, water, the environment, gender equality, and economic justice, and involvement with their parents in impact investing is key.[21] During the Paris COP21 meetings in 2015, Georg Kell, founder and former executive director of the United Nations Global Compact, coined the term "Generation S" as a generation of all ages that "share one vision: combining economic value creation with environmental stewardship, social inclusion, and sound ethics. They are collectively the custodians of tomorrow—as we all are—who understand the power of sustainability to create positive change." Kell expresses the view that Generation S is not generation specific and that people from all walks of life share "a binding passion for entrepreneurship based on values that deliver the solutions our resource-constrained and unequal world so desperately needs. They know that old models of classic industrialization have to give way to cleaner and smarter forms of value generation."[22] Despite the incredible growth in mainstream interest in impact investing, it is not translating to comparable growth in investment activity. According to Barclays' research, only 9 percent of the survey respondents had actively engaged in impact investing.[23]

Making the Case for Impact Investing

In spite of the sluggish flow of capital to impact investing, there are a number of reports that support the urgency for long-term investors to refocus asset allocation toward managing future risk from climate change. One recent report from Cambridge Associates asserts that "considering climate factor is an economic risk management and opportunity capitalization issue core to prudent investing for the long term."[24] The report further expresses the view that negative impact on assets will not be isolated to fossil fuel companies, but will also affect real property, supply chains, and possibly financial markets due to increased uncertainty and risk aversion. Cambridge Associates recommends that long-term investors need to stay ahead of the climate risk curve both defensively by preserving wealth in their portfolios, and offensively with proactive, solution-oriented strategies to capitalize on opportunities in technological advances, business model innovation, and policy evolution. The report identified five climate change investment themes: renewable infrastructure, clean transportation, smart energy, building energy efficiency, and water and agriculture efficiency.

Families that do not begin to expand their investing circle of competency and wealth creation into new sectors and asset classes may find their wealth permanently impaired by climate-related factors. Many family office investment portfolios are long-term biased with investments intended to be held for several years. The investment decision analysis conducted by many family offices does not consider the negative impact on their portfolios of company assets that can become impaired or stranded. A *stranded asset* is any asset that loses value or becomes a liability before the end of the asset's expected economic life. There is a good deal of publicly available information projecting oil and gas discoveries as unburnable in order to prevent global temperatures from rising by more than the 2°C target set at the Paris COP21 conference. Several reports recommend that existing oil and gas reserves should be written down as stranded assets.

The consequence of carbon emission on rising global temperatures is considered a negative "externality" and historically has not been priced into the use of fossil fuels as an energy source.[25] The external side effects or consequences of burning fossil fuels are being priced into economies with taxes on carbon emissions, carbon emissions limits and credits, and other regulatory mechanisms. According to the World Bank, at the time of the COP21 conference, 39 countries and 23 subnational jurisdictions, including the EU, China, Japan, and several of the United States and Canadian Provinces, have implemented or are in the process of implementing carbon pricing.

Carbon emissions are not the only *externalities* that have negative side effects with unintended consequences that may cause assets to be stranded. Other externalities include air pollution, lack of freshwater for basic needs, and degraded human health from high-sugar, low-nutrition diets, to name a few. The cost of water for commercial use in food production, raw-material production, and product manufacturing and processing may also increase as freshwater is regulated and reserved for basic human needs. Even seemingly unrelated industries such as consumer retail apparel can be negatively impacted; current cotton production practices have a high dependency on large volumes of freshwater, pesticides, and other agrochemicals. Regulation of the marginal costs of inputs within supply chains can cause manufacturing plants, production practices, and processing methods to no longer operate competitively and therefore become stranded assets.

Stranded assets may not just be hard assets and supply chains. They can also be soft assets such as brands, business knowledge, and skills.[26] Future regulations may prevent or impede consumer package food companies from marketing and distributing high-caloric, low-nutrition foods, causing highly profitable brands to be stranded assets. Childhood obesity rates in the United States have more than tripled since the 1960s and are linked to chronic conditions such as diabetes, heart disease, hypertension, and other health illnesses.[27] The economic impact of these chronic conditions is significant. The total cost of the U.S. population reporting diabetes rose from $17.0 billion to $271 billion between 1998 and 2003.[28]

Family office investment professionals may take false comfort in knowing that their publicly traded securities that may have stranded-asset risk are in relatively liquid markets and that they can always sell the security. Divesting out of all public securities that have potential stranded assets is challenging. How does a family office identify what sectors and companies will suffer from stranded assets and when? How do they time the market trade to prevent loss of dividends or incurring early capital gain taxes? How do they construct a cost-effective hedge or find a counterbalancing public security?

It may not be enough to just reduce risk by divesting out of the potential stranded assets of public securities. It may be equally important to play offense and proactively counterbalance the family offices portfolio by investing in private companies that generate net-positive *externalities*—companies that clean up industrial water or produce healthy snacks for children. Family offices can also play offense by investing in companies that benefit from the "disruptive creation" caused by innovation and shifting business environments, antibiotic-free protein sources, non–fossil fuel based transportation fuels, microbial soil enhancements, precision irrigation, graphene based water filtration, and others.[29]

Conducting business in a smart, ecofriendly fashion is just logical and a natural progression of business ethics and philosophy. Regardless of whether the family's current portfolio contains companies that are specifically impact focused, there is considerable scope for operational performance across the portfolio of both public and private investments. For families that invest in later-stage companies, engaging directly with those companies to improve their sustainability practices can deliver impact on a company's profitability.

One report reviewed 190 studies of sustainability and its correlation to corporate performance and determined that 90 percent of the studies concluded that sustainability standards decreased the cost of capital of companies, 88 percent of the research showed that solid environment, social, and governance (ESG) practices resulted in better operational performance, and 80 percent of studies showed that stock performance is positively influenced by good sustainability practices.[30]

As compelling, or alarming, depending on one's perspective, as the above research is, it is often difficult to engage asset managers, both internally and externally, to take action. This can be particularly true for Millennials who are marginalized from the investment decision-making process. Millennials often struggle to have the CIOs of the family office engage meaningfully in conversations regarding portfolio exposure to climate change.

For many seasoned investment professionals, the labels of *impact investing* or *sustainable* imply below-market risk-adjusted returns. An obstinate mental model of many investment professionals is that financial returns must be conceded in order to achieve returns that benefit the social good. It is often more effective for Millennials not to use the terms *sustainable, climate, impact, equality,* or *clean* when making a case for impact-related investment. It is more effective to discuss the risk a portfolio may be exposed to if externalities are priced in. Investment professionals of long-term investors such as family offices, need to assess the probabilities of potential stranded-asset risk and the concomitant loss of portfolio value.

At the 2015 "Impact Investing Strategy for the Next Generation" education module, Rebecca Henderson, John and Natty McArthur University Professor at Harvard University, presented a scenario analysis tool to help Millennials initiate the conversation with their family's CIO and advisors.[31] Professor Henderson presented two questions for Millennials to ask CIOs:

Renewable Energy Investments

- What do you believe is the probability carbon emissions *will not* be a cost of goods in the United States in the next seven years?
- What is the probability that natural gas *will not* lose significant market share to renewable power generation in the next seven years?

Given the political climate in the U.S. in 2017, a CIO may believe that there is a 90 percent probability that carbon emission will not be priced into the U.S. economy through regulation or legislation. Given the 2015–2016 price of oil, a CIO may believe there is an 80 percent probability that renewable fuels will be more expensive than fossil fuel–based energy for the next 5 years (see Figure 11.1).

FIGURE 11.1   Scenario Analysis

RENEWABLE ENERGY INVESTMENTS				
Analyze the risk of your fossil fuel exposure.				
Enter your probabilty estimates in the **LIGHT** green boxes				

	90%	Probability Carbon Emissions **WILL NOT** be a Cost of Goods (COG) in U.S. in next 10 years.
11% 10%	80%	
		89%
Probability that Renewable & Storage **WILL** surpass Natural Gas & Coal in next 10 years. 1%	9%	Probability that Renewables & Storage **WILL NOT** surpass Natural Gas & Coal as base load feedstock in next 10 years.
Probability Carbon Emissions **WILL** be a Cost of Goods (COG) in US in next 10 years.	10%	

According to your estimates, the portfolio assets are managed with   80%   certainty that carbon emission will not be a COG? How do you balance for the   20%   uncertainty?

Source: Rebecca Henderson, Harvard University

The scenario matrix reveals that the CIO's portfolio has a 28 percent risk due to the CIO's self-acknowledged uncertainty to carbon emission being priced into the economy and that fossil fuels will remain at the 2015 price relative to renewable energy and fuels. Scenarios can be developed for other potential stranded-asset sectors such as the risk from water scarcity and food regulation.

Water Scarcity Investments

- What do you believe is the probability that the price of water for industrial and commercial use *will not* significantly increase in water-stressed areas of the U.S. in the next five years?
- What is the probability that freshwater regulation *will not* be introduced to reserve water for basic human needs vs. commercial use?

Healthy, Sustainable Food Investments

- What do you believe is the probability that food production prices *will not* be impacted by regulation of pesticides, herbicides, and fertilizer?
- What do you believe is the probability that new regulations *will not* regulate sugar and mandate healthy, sustainably produced food?

Tools such as Henderson's scenario analysis may not provide solutions, but they can start the conversation for researching ways to play offense in managing the risk of climate change and other externalities being priced in. The pricing in of externalities causes both risk (beta) and returns (alpha). Investing in emerging sectors such as clean energy, sustainable food production and water are alpha seeking strategies that benefit from the pricing in of externalities. One first step that active impact investing families engage in is to invest in fund managers that specialize in direct shareholder engagement of public equities. This type of direct engagement is beyond the scope of this chapter, but may be worth exploring within the family portfolio.[32]

How to Source Impact Investments

Engaging and activating the family in the development of an impact investment strategy requires patience, open-mindedness, and willingness to seek advice from new sources of expertise. Chapter 12 presents a framework, *SCIE (Sustainable Cycle of Investing Engagement)*, to help families engage in a process to guide the family through the development of an impact investment strategy. The SCIE framework recommends that the family clarify *why* the family is willing to risk capital, time, and energy in an impact investing strategy and *what* resources they have and are willing to commit to the strategy, *what* risks they are willing to take, and *what* they expect to achieve with the investment. Thoughtfully working through the SCIE *why* and *what* processes helps filter *how* the family will invest by defining what problem is meaningful to the family, what amount of capital the family is willing to risk, who will be involved in the process, and what the family expects to get out of an impact investing strategy.

Impact investing offers investors a broad range of asset classes and risk-adjusted returns that can be included in a family's asset allocation model. The Monitor Institute segments impact investments based on an investor's primary objectives:

> *Financial First* investments for investors who seek to optimize financial returns with a floor for social or environmental impact and typically commercial investors who seek out investments that offer market-rate returns while creating social or environmental impact.
>
> *Impact First* investments for investors who seek to optimize social or environmental impact with a risk-adjusted return that may be considered below market. This risk-return concession may include a high financial return that is not commensurate with the high perceived risk. Most impact first investors expect at least a return of the principal investment.[33]

By most definitions, an impact-related company or fund must be intentionally delivering a product or service that provides positive social and environmental impact. Investments may create social and environmental impact in a number of different ways. Some investments have product-based impact, such as clean energy technologies that reduce overall greenhouse gas emissions; other investments have process-based impact, such as the creation of sustainable and fair-practice supply chains, or the production of organic foods. Other investments may have people-based impact strategies, focused on at-risk or underserved populations in sectors such as education for at-risk students, empowerment of women and girls, or small farmers in emerging markets. Impact investments can also have place-based impact, focused on affordable housing, job creation, or access to clean water and health services within a specific community or region.[34]

In Table 11.1 a framework is presented that can be worked through from left to right to help families filter investment opportunities based on their risk tolerance, financial objectives, and impact expectations.

For a family's first impact-related direct investment, it is recommended that the family choose an asset class and sector that are similar to or adjacent to its current business or investments. The three primary direct impact investment asset classes are real assets, early-stage or venture investment, and private equity or growth investments. Impact-related real assets cover a broad range of cash flow producing assets, including sustainably managed farmland, renewable power generation plants, affordable housing, green buildings, sustainable fisheries, mining operations, timberland, and others. A family with commercial real estate experience can choose an adjacent sector such as financing of affordable housing (real asset) or a new energy efficiency technology for office buildings (early stage). If a family has retail product experience, it may choose a growth investment in a similar consumer-facing business such as an organic food brand (growth stage) that is highly dependent on production costs and sales from effective marketing and distribution.

It is essential for the family to assess its capacity to source, diligence, and manage investments in an impact-related asset class or sector. The family's impact investing capacity, and likelihood of success, can grow over time through a reinforcing process of three key capacity elements: network of likeminded families and advisors, relationships with fund managers that provide co-investment rights, and an internal team working together to create new knowledge and experience. There are several impact-related conferences that family members can attend to start to build their network of likeminded investors, including SOCAP, Nexus Youth Global Summit, Conscious

TABLE 11.1 Categories Table for Impact Investments

Asset Class	Sector	Geography	Impact Strategy	Return Profile
Public Equity	Education	Sub-Saharan Africa	Product-Based	Market-Rate
Fixed Income	Environmental Conservation	Middle East & North Africa	People-Based	Concessionary
Private Equity	Sustainable Consumer Products	Central & South America	Place-Based	Off-Market
Venture Capital			Process-Based	
Real Assets			Behavior-Based	
Hedge Funds	Housing & Community Development	Asia & Oceania	Model-Based	
Social Impact Bonds		Eastern Europe & Russia	ESG-Screened	
Cash	Agriculture & Food	Western Europe	SRI-Screened	
	Energy & Resource Efficiency	North America Emerging Markets		
	Safety & Security	Developed Markets		
	Healthcare & Wellness	Global		
	Access to Finance			
	Employment & Empowerment			
	Base of Pyramid Services			
	Sustainable Infrastructure			
	Sustainable Banking			

Source: TheImPact.org. The attributes listed for each category are intended to be illustrative, not definitive nor comprehensive.

Capitalism, Impact Capitalism Summit, Ceres Conference, Sustainatopia, Impact Investing Conference, Net Impact Conference, and others.

Sourcing deals to develop an initial pipeline of high-quality deals can be challenging for families as they initiate their impact investing strategy. A good place to start is with some of the most active groups of impact investors and online resources, such as The ImPact, CREO Syndicate, Impact Assets 50, ImpactBase, Circle Up, Toniic, Mission Investor Exchange, Omidyar Network, pymwymic.com, Tiger 21, Aspen Network of Development Entrepreneurs, and Global Impact Investing Network.

One way to begin to develop capacity is to invest in emerging managers of relatively small funds that have traditional fund management experience, provide true transparency to their investment process, and give limited partners full co-investment opportunities. A recent study reported that impact investment funds launched between 1998 and 2004 outperformed conventional private investment funds, 8.1 percent versus 6.9 percent, respectively. Furthermore, impact investment funds that raised less than $100 million, many of which were first vintage funds, outperformed similar-size private funds by more than two times, 9.5 percent versus 4.5 percent, respectively.[35]

In the due diligence process of selecting an emerging manager, it is essential that the family is comfortable that the manager will provide the transparency to the sector, market, and investment process such that the family can build its internal expertise. Families that build close relationships with emerging managers are able to leverage the fund managers to provide deal flow and due diligence as well as greater transparency of the investment process to support the family objective of new knowledge creation.

Selecting a fund manager and your relationship with the emerging fund managers should be considered an active, not a passive, relationship. It is important to request past quarterly newsletters, speak to limited partners who have invested with the manager before, contact funds that intend to address the same market, and reach out to both current portfolio companies and target companies. Investors should require the fund manager to establish a limited partner advisory committee (LPAC) with transparency to the operations and decision-making process of the fund. The fund manager should establish a reporting and co-investment process that provides the family sector, market, and company insights that allow the family to learn without being overly burdensome to the manager. In an ideal situation, the family would have the right to co-invest in all deals the fund invests in; however, this is often not practical. Limited partners that are offered co-investment rights need to be careful that they are not offered only deals that the fund manager believes are too risky or require too much capital.

The family needs to commit the time and human resources required to learn from their experience investing in an emerging manager. A thorough due diligence process of a fund may involve 20 or more reference calls to "trust but verify" the information provided by the fund manager. There are idiosyncrasies and unique dynamics in impact investments within asset classes and sectors. The family should verify from outside sources the market assumptions of the manager, quantity and quality of deal flow, and demand for the type of financing offered by the fund. The SCIE framework of Chapter 12 guides family work through the time and resources it has to devote to impact investing.

It may be helpful to work with a financial advisor that has a robust database of impact-focused funds. There are several financial advisors that have begun to develop the team, network, and expertise to source and diligence impact-related funds for their clients. Some of the leading advisors that actively source and diligence emerging fund managers include Cambridge Associates, Athena Capital, Arabella Advisors, Brown Advisory, Imprint Capital (acquired by Goldman Sachs), The Caprock Group, and Veris Wealth Partners, to name a few.

The immense scope of impact investing opportunities often causes decision-making paralysis even for families with the most ardent intent. A careful and thoughtful development process of a long-term investment strategy can also deliver returns (i.e., *experiential returns*) to the family that may be as or more valuable than the financial returns.

Experiential Returns: Intangible Benefits of Impact Investing

Former Harvard Business School professor John Davis defines three key ingredients for family success: growth of family assets, family unity, and family talent. Davis describes preservation and growth of family assets, both financial and human, as the Holy Grail of many family offices. The nonfinancial returns that build the human assets, family unity, and the knowledge base of the family, but cannot be measured with the precision of financial asset metrics, are labeled as *experiential returns*. Each family will have different experiential returns that are bespoke to the interests and structure of each family.

Potential Experiential Returns

- Investment knowledge and expertise transfer from the senior generations to the Millennials during rigorous investment analysis
- Thoughtful and structured process to build Millennial investment experience and skills
- Engagement of family members who do not have strong interest in financial or investment decisions
- Expansion of a family's "circle of competency" to include new domain expertise
- Deeper and broader agreement of the family's legacy and collective sense of family purpose

- Participation of family members not in investment decision-making roles
- Richer communication and understanding of the diverse interests and priorities of family members

The SCIE framework proposes a process to help families identify experiential returns and create clear actionable objectives to realize the returns, which is covered in Chapter 12. In spite of the research that supports impact investing and the intangible benefits that can accrue to a family, there are several barriers that impede families from deploying capital in impact-related sectors.

Common Challenges and Barriers to Impact Investing

Millennials often have little influence or access to the investment decisions of their families and struggle to have their investment perspectives heard. Their efforts are often impeded by entrenched structural barriers and control of assets that reside solely with the senior generations. Most families are idiosyncratic, political, and complex organizations of diverse stakeholders. The challenges the Millennials face can be categorized under at least one of three organizational perspectives, or lenses: strategic design, political challenges, and cultural challenges.

How investment decisions are made within a family is primarily viewed through the lens of the family's *strategic design*, that is, the formal structures and systems designed to achieve investment goals. The challenges and barriers that often are not fully understood or acknowledged can cause decision-making conflict or paralysis when a family is considering impact investing. Millennials can develop a deeper sense of their family dynamics with two coexisting lenses that describe the internal power structure: the political and cultural perspectives. The following has been adapted from the *Three Lenses on Organizational Analysis and Action* model and applied to the unique challenges of family offices.[36] The obstacles are presented vis-à-vis the three lenses.

Strategic Design Challenges

The family office investment team is often structured with clear performance metrics providing financial incentives and rewards. Investment objectives and decision-making processes are established based on an allocation of human and financial resources. The investment team is recruited, trained, tracked, and rewarded accordingly. The available time, energy, and knowledge of the investment is a constrained resource.

Impact investment may introduce fundamental challenges to the limited human capacity of the family office to source and filter investment opportunities in new sectors (e.g., sustainable agriculture, clean energy, microfinance, etc.). Most professional investors come from investment environments where liquidity options and timeframes are reasonably understood. Many impact-related investments have uncertain liquidity timeframes in sectors with limited mergers and acquisitions and few initial public offerings. Furthermore, the team's investment analysis framework may be not suited to properly diligence investments of funds or companies with limited track records, market information, and third-party advisors.

A key structural issue is passive or active resistance from family office investment executives who receive bonus compensation based on portfolio performance. Resistance may occur from family office investment executives who do not want to compromise their compensation by devoting financial or human capital to anything other than financial returns. To ask an investment team to devote financial or human capital to anything other than financial returns is essentially asking them to make decisions against their financial best interests.

Another structural design challenge experienced by many families is the lack of coordination between the philanthropic team and the investment teams. Investment opportunities that promote impact as well as financial returns can ping-pong back and forth between investment and philanthropy teams, with neither taking ownership nor working together.

Political Challenges

Investment decision-making authority usually resides with an entrenched subset of stakeholders, typically the senior generations, with low transparency and few opportunities for input from other family stakeholders. Political challenges arise when there is an overemphasis on strategic design without a balancing consideration of the political power of family stakeholders who are not part of the strategic design.

Inter- and intra-family challenges occur when investment decisions have become entrenched with a small group of decision makers, disenfranchising many other family stakeholders. The marginalized stakeholders may be accepting of this dynamic when they have little emotional connection to the investments, but may be less accepting with regard to impact investing.

As the stakeholders become more personally connected to the investments, they may push for greater transparency in the decision-making process, more opportunities for input, and a clear process to communicate the status of the investments.

Families often do not devote the time and energy to identify and understand the key internal and external stakeholders and learn their stake in what the family does. Asymmetry of information can create a chasm between the family members who are sourcing impact investing knowledge and opportunities and the family office investment professionals and advisors. It is particularly important to discover the latent interests that individuals may not be aware of or that may not be a priority such as training the Millennials.

As discussed earlier, external financial advisors may not be incentivized by their firms to help families develop and execute an impact investing strategy. The interests of other stakeholders, such as lawyers, accountants, and financial advisors, may also cause passive resistance when they are engaged to process investments outside of their domain expertise. Internal and external stakeholders may fear a loss of power, diminishment of value to the family, concern that new skills need to be acquired, and expectation of more work that will tax an already resource-stressed environment.

Cultural Challenges

A family's culture is a set of basic assumptions, both acknowledged and hidden, that drive what the family pays attention to, what the family values are, and what actions and decisions take place in the constantly changing environment. The assumptions, also labeled *mental models*, usually emerge from past problem solving that has been relied on to solve future problems. The mental models can define the identity of the family and become entrenched as the correct way to perceive, think, and feel about the family and its stakeholders.

For example, investment decision-makers may have a mental model that income beneficiaries of the family are only *consumers* of wealth and not potential *contributors* to wealth. This particular mental model can cause non-decision-makers to feel marginalized and disengaged from providing talent, knowledge, or experience to managing and growing family wealth. This assumption can cause a reinforcing negative feedback as non-decision-makers become disenfranchised from the investment process and decision-makers believe other family members are disinterested in the family's investment process (see the section on Systems Thinking: Creating and Sustaining Family Knowledge ahead).

Another example is the belief that family should only attempt to solve social or environmental problems with philanthropy, not with for-profit investing. A third mental model of a family's culture may be that investment activities are private and not shared with other family offices or outside the circle of trusted advisors. It is often challenging for controlling stakeholders to engage in a process that may challenge the status quo mental models established over many years.

A major cultural shift for many families is to accept that the Millennials of the family are ready to be engaged in investment decision making. As the Millennials mature, many want to be actively engaged in being wealth *creators* and are no longer satisfied with being wealth *consumers*. The aligned objectives of transferring knowledge to rising generations, giving back to the world, stewarding assets, and maintaining family unity provide fertile ground for the Millennials and senior generations to work together. A thoughtfully designed and diligently managed impact investing strategy can provide the practical experience the Millennials are seeking.

Systems Thinking: Creating and Sustaining Family Knowledge

"A wise woman once said to me that there are only two lasting bequests we can hope to give our children. One of these she said is roots, the other, wings."
Hodding Carter, *Where Main Street Meets the River*

Perhaps the greatest gap in developing human capital in families is not having a formalized plan on how to train the next generation. Families who desire to prepare their next-gen family members, particularly Millennials, may benefit from seeing their family as a constantly evolving system of engaged members and the knowledge that is created and transferred between the members.

Although many families built their original wealth by creating new operating companies, most family offices are not structured for ongoing entrepreneurship. A paper by the McCombie Group recommends that a direct or impact investing strategy can promote multiple generations to be "first-generation founders" and investors that can independently contribute to wealth generation.[37] Family offices that are "focused on preserving wealth have forgotten how to create wealth, which the younger generation never get to learn."[38] A 2014 study by Morgan Stanley/Campden Wealth revealed that most families do not formally support the training of next-generation family members, with 56 percent stating that their financial education is "informal" and 55 percent reporting that they are "self-taught."[39]

MIT Sloan School of Management professor Peter Senge, author of *The Fifth Discipline: The Art and Practice of the Learning Organization,* proposes that to build a learning organization it is necessary for the people to see the organization as systems thinkers see with the personal mastery to collaboratively bring to the surface and restructure the mental models of the organization.

In the parlance of Systems Thinking, families and their family office are constantly changing systems of *stocks* (engaged family members, disengaged family members, number of investments, family knowledge) and *flows* (creation of knowledge, transfer of knowledge, engagement of family members, disengagement of family members, etc.). For the family to survive and thrive, it must be continually aware of and invest in the changing stocks and flows.

Some variables, such as number of advanced college degrees, number of family gatherings, successful and unsuccessful investments, births and marriages, and so on, can increase or reinforce the stocks of *Engaged Members* and *Family Knowledge* (see circle with **R** in Figure 11.2). Other variables such as death and divorce can decrease or balance the stocks of *Engaged Members* and *Family Knowledge* (see circle with **B** in Figure 11.2). In multigenerational families there are many delays (symbolized in Figure 11.2 as '\\') such as the time between births that increase *Potential Member* and the number of graduate degrees, or lifecycle from when an investment is made to when it matures (see \\ in Figure 11.2). Senge proposes that "learning organizations" need to integrate personal mastery, evolution of mental models, building a shared vision, and team learning with the fifth discipline of Systems Thinking.[40]

Systems Thinking allows the stakeholders to view the family as a constantly changing organization with evolving or devolving dynamics of family engagement and knowledge creation. It is essential that the family resist entrenched mental models, power dynamics, and processes and embrace the natural evolution of births, maturation, and deaths of its members.

Harvard Business School professor Hirotaka Takeuchi describes "knowledge creation" as a continuous and dynamic interaction between tacit and explicit knowledge within an organization. Takeuchi describes tacit knowledge as the personal knowledge that is rooted in an individual's experience and intuition and explains that it is hard to formalize and communicate. Tacit knowledge also includes the subjective insights, ideals, and values of the individual. Explicit knowledge is described as the knowledge that can be codified and explicitly shared in documents, processes, discussions, models, and frameworks.[41]

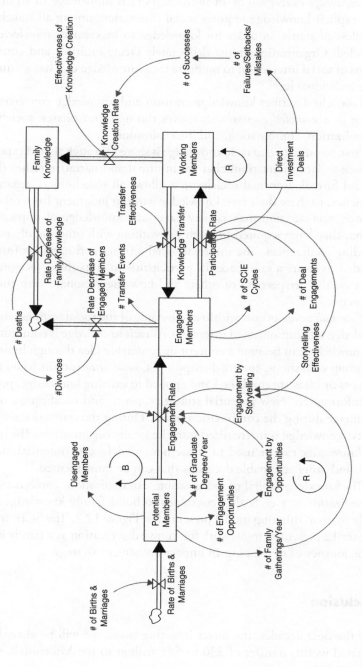

FIGURE 11.2 System Design Example of a Family's Engaged Members and Knowledge Creation Stocks

Source: SCIEFramework LLC

237

Knowledge conversion of an individual's tacit knowledge to an organization's explicit knowledge requires social interaction among all stakeholders, regardless of status, in order for knowledge to be created, transferred, and expanded. Organizations must deliberately create multiple and continuous forums of social interaction to mobilize tacit knowledge that has accumulated at the individual level.[42]

Takeuchi describes knowledge creation and knowledge conversion happening in a *knowledge spiral* that moves through four phases: socialization, externalization, combination, and internalization.

First, *socialization* of tacit knowledge is shared through shared experiences and face-to-face interactions that are informal and narrative rather than literal and formal. Informal socialization allows all stakeholders, regardless of experience, to share their tacit knowledge without judgment from others. For instance, non-decision-makers may have tacit knowledge of impact investing that they have acquired through networking with other family offices or attending conferences. The informal social settings and narrative format are intended to create a safe space for participants to empathize, recognize, and reflect on the perspectives of others and how they resonate with their own perspective.

Externalization occurs within and outside of the social settings when tacit knowledge is communicated externally. As tacit knowledge is communicated, the knowledge can become a concept or actionable idea through brainstorming, group workshops, and road-mapping. *Combination* occurs when the new concepts or ideas are combined and applied to existing knowledge, processes, and information. New potential strategies, plans, and codification of learning emerge during the combination phase. During the *internalization* phase, explicit knowledge is internalized into the family organization. The internalized knowledge can be used to create new models, experimentation, prototypes, and other actionable decisions that can be implemented.[43]

The knowledge spiral of socialization, externalization, combination, and internalization is a cycle that continues to build family knowledge per the family System Thinking model presented in Figure 12.2. The SCIE model in Chapter 12 presents a framework for knowledge creation as a family embarks on the journey of developing an impact investment strategy.

Conclusion

Over the next decades, the direct investing landscape will be altered by the estimated wealth transfer of $30 to $41 trillion to the Millennials, coupled with the Millennials' preference to invest for "profit and purpose." Many Millennials are ready to be valuable contributors to the family office direct investing decisions. Although Millennials' perspectives and processes may differ from the older generations, they share many of the same values and sense of responsibilities with regard to the family's assets. Research shows why impact investing should be considered as part of a family's long-term risk management strategy and not just an exclusive interest of Millennials. Impact investing can also provide families with valuable experiential returns, including increase of family unity and opportunities to grow family talent and knowledge. Thoughtful strategic design of the investment of assets is essential to achieve the goal of creating and transferring explicit technical and organization knowledge that will "make the family smarter." Equally important is an understanding of the family's political dynamics in order to empower and legitimize new family members by creating social networks that will "make the family stronger." The third perspective for a family to be aware of is the cultural perspective in order to identify and reflect on the mental models and values of the family to "make the family better."[44]

Notes

1. For the purpose of this chapter, we will use the World Economic Forum definition of impact investing as "an investment approach intentionally seeking to create both financial return and positive social impact that is actively measured." *From the Margins to the Mainstream Assessment of the Impact Investment Sector and Opportunities to Engage Mainstream Investors*, 2013, World Economic Forum, p. 3.
2. Pew Research Center, www.pewresearch.org/fact-tank/2015/01/16/this-year-millennials-will-overtake-baby-boomers.
3. *Millennial Innovation Survey*, Deloitte, 2013, p. 9.
4. 21/64 and Johnson Center for Philanthropy at Grand Valley Stage University, *Next Gen Donors: Respecting Legacy, Revolutionizing Philanthropy*, 2013, p. 5.
5. OppenheimerFunds/Campden Research, *Proving Worth: The Values of Affluent Millennials in North America*, 2015, p. 19.
6. Morgan Stanley Private Wealth Management/Campden Wealth, *Next Generation Wealth: Defining a New Direction*, 2014, p. 36.
7. U.S. Trust, *U.S. Trust Insights on Wealth and Worth*, 2014, p. 13.
8. Sustainable and Responsible Investing (SRI) applies negative or positive screens to a public equity and debt portfolio; for instance, screening out funds that invest in tobacco, firearms, casinos, and alcohol.

9. *Next Gen Donors: Respecting Legacy, Revolutionizing Philanthropy*, p. 7.
10. Ibid, p. 21.
11. *Proving Worth*, p. 18.
12. GrantCraft, *Next Gen Donors: Shaping the Future of Philanthropy*, 2013, p. 1.
13. Accenture, *Generation D, An Emerging and Important Investor Segment*, 2013, p. 4.
14. *U.S. Trust Insights on Wealth and Worth*, 2015, p. 5.
15. Generational labels include "GI" for members born between 1898 and 1924, "Silent" for members born between 1925 and 1945, "Baby Boomers" for those born between 1946 and 1964, and "Gen X" for those born between 1965 and 1983.
16. *Next Gen Donors: Respecting Legacy, Revolutionizing Philanthropy*, p. 21.
17. *Proving Worth*, p. 5.
18. David Shrier, MIT Sloan School of Management, *Attitudes UHNW Family Offices*, 2014.
19. Barclays, *The Value of Being Human: A Behavioural Framework for Impact Investing and Philanthropy*, 2015, p. 12.
20. *U.S. Trust Insights on Wealth and Worth*, 2015, p. 16.
21. *Proven Worth Study*, p. 4.
22. Huffington Post, "Together We Are Generation S," November 20, 2015, www.huffingtonpost.com/georg-kell/together-we-are-generatio_ b_8682700.html.
23. *The Value of Being Human*, p. 5.
24. Cambridge Associates, *Risks and Opportunities from the Changing Climate: Playbook for the Truly Long-Term Investor*, 2015, p. i.
25. www.businessdictionary.com, "Externalities are a loss or gain in the welfare of one party resulting from an activity of another party, without there being any compensation for the losing party. Externalities are an important consideration in cost-benefit analysis."
26. www.businessdictionary.com, "Soft assets are tangible (such as human resources) or intangible (such as brand, knowledge, skills) assets that (unlike the hard assets such as cash, equipment, land) are not normally included in a firm's financial statements."
27. Centers for Disease Control, *CDC Grand Rounds: Childhood Obesity in the United States*, 2011, p. 1.
28. Milken Institute, *An Unhealthy America: The Economic Burden of Chronic Disease*, 2007, p. 47.
29. www.investopedia.com, "Coined by Joseph Schumpeter in his work entitled *Capitalism, Socialism and Democracy* (1942) to denote a 'process of

industrial mutation that incessantly revolutionizes the economic structure from within, incessantly destroying the old one, incessantly creating a new one.'"

30. University of Oxford and Arabesque Partners, *From the Stockholder to the Stakeholder: How Sustainability Can Drive Financial Outperformance*, 2015, p. 9.

31. In the spirit of full disclosure, Temple Fennell, the author of this chapter, is co-founder and co-director of the education module.

32. James Gifford, Senior Fellow, Harvard; Director of Impact, TAU Investment Management.

33. Monitor Institute, *Investing for Social & Environmental Impact*, pp. 31–33.

34. TheImPact, *Impact Investing: Frameworks for Families*, 2016, p. 7.

35. Cambridge Associates and Global Impact Investing Network, *Introducing the Impact Investing Benchmark*, 2015, p. i.

36. Deborah Ancona, Thomas Kochan, Maureen Scully, John Van Maanen, and Eleanor Westney, *Three Lenses on Organizational Analysis and Action (Module 2)*, 2004, pp. 13–92.

37. McCombie Group, *Direct Investing: A Pathway to Family Stewardship*, 2012, p. 15.

38. Family Office Association, *Entrepreneurship in the Family Office*, 2010, p. 2.

39. Morgan Stanley Private Wealth Management/Campden Wealth, *Next Generation Wealth: Defining a New Direction*, 2014, p. 59.

40. Peter Senge, *The Fifth Discipline: The Art & Practice of the Learning Organization* (New York: Bantam Doubleday Dell, 1990, 2006).

41. Ikujiro Nonaka and Hirotaka Takeuchi, *The Knowledge-Creating Company* (Oxford: Oxford University Press, 1995), p. 8.

42. Ibid., pp. 6, 61.

43. Ibid., p. 5.

44. John Van Maanan, *Three Perspective on Organization, Class Presentation*, unpublished presentation, Slide 28.

CHAPTER 12

SCIE: Sustainable Cycle of Investing Engagement

Contributing Author: Temple Fennell

The SCIE framework guides a family through five steps: establishing *Family Values*, *Framing Strategy*, *Developing Strategy*, *Implementing Strategy*, and *Communication and Learning*. During each step the family develops a set of questions that result in clear objectives the family expects to achieve. The more honest and thoughtful families are in designing their questions, the more effective and sustainable the results of the process will be. Good questions lead to good strategy, and hopefully intended results.

The *Family Values* and *Framing Strategy* steps address soft issues such as what is the purpose of the new investment strategy, is there a desire to engage and train the next generation (Next Gens), and is building buy-in and engagement across the family members important to strengthen family unity. The *Developing Strategy* and *Implementing Strategy* steps address strategic issues such as what sector and assets classes to invest in, what risk the family is willing to take, and what human and financial resources the family will commit. The *Communication and Learning* step recommends practices for the family to proactively communicate and learn from the results of the new investing strategy.

The SCIE framework brings together as many family stakeholders as possible in the development of a new investment strategy. Family stakeholders include family members, nonfamily executives, and trusted family advisors. Developing an investment process that engages both knowledgeable, empowered stakeholders and less knowledgeable, less empowered stakeholders to establish and sustain an impact investing strategy is a difficult design challenge. The SCIE cycle addresses the design challenge by applying the Design Thinking methodology developed by the Institute of Design at Stanford University and the design thinking firm IDEO. The development of SCIE was also greatly informed by Harvard Business School professor Hirotaka Takeuchi's work on "knowledge creation" within an organization and MIT Sloan School of Management professor Peter Senge's work on creating a "learning organization."

Professor Takeuchi describes an organization not as a machine, but as a living organism that survives and thrives in uncertain conditions by creating and transferring new knowledge. Families are constantly evolving systems of human resources and knowledge (see Figure 11.2 of Chapter 11). The SCIE model is an adaptation for family offices of the model presented in Ikujiro Nonaka and Takeuchi's book, *The Knowledge-Creating Company*, that presents a five-phase process for knowledge creation: (1) sharing tacit knowledge; (2) creating concepts; (3) justifying concepts; (4) building an archetype; and (5) cross-leveling knowledge.[1] The SCIE framework also incorporates the three guiding principles of Senge's "Society for Organizational Learning":

Learning Is Social: People learn best from and with one another, and participation in learning communities is vital to their effectiveness, well-being, and happiness in any work setting.

Learning Communities: The capacities and accomplishments of organizations are inseparable from, and dependent on, the capacities of the learning communities which they foster.

Core Learning Capabilities: Organizations must develop individual and collective capabilities to understand complex, interdependent issues; engage in reflective, generative conversation; and nurture personal and shared aspirations.[2]

The senior generations often recognize the importance of engaging and training the Next Gens; however, they struggle with how to prepare, educate, and mentor the Next Gens. Long-term success of a family is highly dependent on the Next Gens' ability to find their role in continuing the family legacy while also stewarding and creating wealth. The SCIE cycle can provide senior generations and Next Gens a roadmap to begin developing

Next Gen investment experience. It is meant to be a cyclical process that engages and reengages stakeholders to support knowledge creation, knowledge transfer, generational succession, and expansion of a family's *circle of competence*.

The application of SCIE in this chapter specifically addresses the challenges of creating an impact investing strategy. The SCIE framework is intended to result in the following outcomes for the family office:

- Create a set of both tangible objectives (i.e., financial returns) and intangible objectives, or *experiential returns* (see Chapter 11).
- Define success and failure for the family before risking capital in a new investing strategy.
- Provide a platform to engage and train Next Gens to be valuable contributors in investment decisions.
- Implement an impact investing strategy based on communal objectives informed by the family stakeholders' needs and values.
- Provide investment opportunities across a spectrum of risk-adjusted returns from below market to above market.
- Strengthen and perpetuate family unity by engaging investment- and non-investment-minded family members in a common purpose.
- Create parity between generations by leveraging the unique talents and knowledge of the Next Gens and senior generations.

The Purpose of SCIE

The natural birth and maturation of family decision-makers is in a constant state of evolution across several macroeconomic cycles. The age, experience, economic environment, and composition of the decision-makers change dramatically in a family and can happen over short periods of time. In our family, many members of the third generation were in college or starting a family when we set up the family office and a direct investment strategy. Seven short years later, most have graduated from college, some have MBAs, and young kids are in school, freeing up the parents to participate in family investment decisions.

The source of a family's wealth, typically a business created by the first generation, also goes through a cycle of wealth creation, growth, stagnation, and decline. In order to sustain and build financial capital for future generations, families need to expand their circle of competencies into new areas of investment and value creation. Families need to constantly innovate with new investment objectives to continue to build the family knowledge, talent, and assets necessary to sustain family unity and wealth.

In addition to preserving and growing financial capital, families need to grow the nonfinancial capital of *engaged family* members and *family knowledge*. Nonfinancial capital of a family can be thought of in terms of four different assets: *human capital* is the added value to the family of knowledge, expertise, skill, commitment, and dedication of each family member; *relationship capital* is the added value that comes from the emotional connection, committed care, organization, and mutual support of family members; *social capital* is the sense of belonging and responsibility regarding the family's reputation in and contributions to the community and world; and *spiritual capital* is the added value for a group of individuals to be committed to a deeper purpose and legacy of values.[3]

Deep-rooted family structures, mental models, and decision-making processes often marginalize family members interested in the development of new investment strategies and objectives. Many organizations, including family offices, react to uncertain and changing internal and external situations retroactively rather than proactively by challenging existing knowledge systems and innovating new ways of thinking and acting. Organizations that innovate are able to "create new knowledge and information, from the inside out, in order to redefine both problems and solutions and, in the process, to recreate their environment."[4] By working collaboratively through the SCIE model, multiple stakeholders can bring individual talents and perspectives to the creation and execution of an impact investing strategy.

The purpose of SCIE is to build and maintain buy-in from stakeholders with diverse and sometimes conflicting perspectives and priorities. Introduction of change in any organization is challenging and involves stakeholders who are "allies" for change, "resistors" of change, and "fence-sitters" unsure of change. The SCIE cycle is designed to keep the discussion moving forward to actionable decisions that avoid choices that force an either/or decision. An *either/or* decision can cause decision deadlocks or analysis-paralysis versus choices that are framed as *this-and-that* decisions. The purpose is to keep the conversation moving forward with the allies and fence-sitters while acknowledging the concerns of the resistors. This-and-that choices may require allies to compromise on full-change solutions and resistors to accept more new ideas than they would prefer.

As families go through the inevitable changes of natural maturation, the family decision-making process must adapt to the changing stakeholders.

SCIE is designed to be a repeatable and sustainable decision-making model that is applied to foster knowledge creation and to provide a structure for the family to become a learning organization.

The SCIE Framework

Before the family begins the process of developing an investment strategy and identifying potential investments (i.e., *how* the family will deploy capital), it is essential to discuss and define *why* the family is willing to risk capital and *what* are the intended rewards of taking this risk (see Figure 12.1). It is essential that the family acknowledge the diverse stakeholders' views of the risks and potential consequences, both positive and negative, before committing capital to a new investment strategy.

The Soft Issues Are Often the Hardest

The first two steps of SCIE, *Family Values* and *Framing Strategy*, are first steps that are often overlooked because they are soft issues dealing with stakeholders' personal motivations, perspectives, emotions, wants, and needs. Many families focus their investment time and energy on tactical asset allocation and do not spend time on understanding the soft issues, such as what the fam-

FIGURE 12.1   SCIE Framework

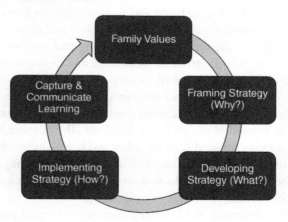

Source: SCIE Framework LLC

ily stands for, what is the purpose of staying together as a family, what sort of organization the family wants to be in 10 years, what kind of world the family wants to live in, and how to make that world a reality.

An inclusive discussion of the soft issues is often the hardest, most personal, and sometimes conflictual discussion a family office can have. The soft issues often involve highly subjective opinions and intuitions rooted in personal experience, ideals, values, and emotions.[5] Direct investment strategies, and particularly impact investing strategies, can present structural, political, and cultural challenges for many family offices, as discussed in Chapter 11. It is best to begin the process with a clear statement of family values.

Family Purpose, Values, and Mission

Creation of the family's purpose, values, and mission can be the foundation for all decisions regarding investments, operating a family business, and family legacy. The family purpose is an aspirational and immutable statement for why the family stays together and works together. Family purpose is further defined by a set of core values that are deeply held and understood by all family stakeholders and should also be resilient to change over time. Engaging in a values discovery and definition process can be a useful tool for creating family unity as well as a filtering tool for investment decisions. Establishing family values is an important first step of the SCIE model and is covered in Kirby Rosplock's first book, *The Complete Family Office Handbook*. (Hoboken: Wiley, 2014).

Family mission is the vision that the family works to realize and is made actionable by a set of goals and objectives that must be achieved for the mission to succeed. The family's mission, goals, and objectives may change over time as the members, resources, and world changes. During the early years of our family's direct investing strategy, family members engaged in a vision, mission, and values statement creation process through telling stories that captured the essence of the family over several generations. Seven years later this process continues to provide focus and clarity. The value statements inform all aspects of our family office from investments to operation of our business to establishment of governance. Our values and mission are the beginning and bedrock of the engagement of all of our stakeholders with myriad interests, experience, knowledge, and talents.

Following are our values statements available on our family office's website.[6]

Keller Enterprises: Who We Are

Keller Enterprises is a family company integrating venture investing, venture philanthropy, and venture farming. Our operating business, Inglewood Farm, is located in central Louisiana.

Our Purpose

- To build the assets of Keller Enterprises, LLC, by seeking opportunities that we can obtain more effectively working together than we can on our own.
- In so doing, to enrich the lives of our members, employees, and the communities to which we, as a family, are connected.
- To deliver long-term returns to our members by seeking ventures, partnerships, and investments that reflect our family's core values.

Our Values

INDUSTRIOUSNESS: We foster a culture that encourages members and employees to be productive and industrious.

STEWARDSHIP: We do not take for granted the opportunities afforded to us by preceding generations. With these opportunities comes responsibility, and with our history as our guide, we will be responsible stewards of the assets we manage.

RESPONSIBLE CITIZENSHIP: We endeavor to be good citizens of our communities, generous managers of our employees, and thoughtful investors of our assets; and all of these with an awareness of our responsibility and desire to protect our environment.

TRANSPARENCY: Recognizing that our family legacy is one of good faith and clarity of purpose, we will pursue opportunities that we clearly understand, and with partners who value transparency and conduct business in such a manner.

RESPECT: We will operate in a manner that encourages all members to become engaged and participate in family business affairs. We strive to create an environment characterized by mutual respect, in which every member's views are heard and valued.

COURAGE: We believe that our family's success in business is a product of thoughtful, considered risk-taking and that our future success will be as well; in the pursuit of such opportunities we should never be afraid to do what is right and stand up for the greater good.

SCIE Model Mapping to Design Thinking

The SCIE cycle is inspired by the human-centered design methodologies developed by the Institute of Design at Stanford's "An Introduction to Design Thinking Process Guide," which proposes five phases of the cycle: Empathize, Define, Ideate, Prototype, and Test (see Figure 12.2).[7] The five phases of Stanford's human-centered Design Thinking process are modified for the investment decision-making context of family offices.

Phase I: Empathize: "Understand people, within the context of your design challenge. It is your effort to understand the way they do things and why, their physical and emotional needs, how they think about the world, and what is meaningful to them."

Phase II: Define: "Bringing clarity and focus" in order "to craft a meaningful and actionable problem statement—this is what we call a point-of-view. This should be a guiding statement that focuses on insights and needs of a particular user, or composite character."

Phase III: Ideate: "A process of 'going wide' in terms of concepts and outcomes. Ideation provides both the fuel and also the source material for building prototypes and getting innovative solutions into the hands of your users."

Phase IV: Prototype: "Iterative generation of artifacts intended to answer questions that get you closer to your final solution."

Phase V: Test: "Solicit feedback, about the prototypes you have created, from your users and have another opportunity to gain empathy for the people you are designing for."

FIGURE 12.2 The Five Phases of the Design Thinking Process Guide Cycle

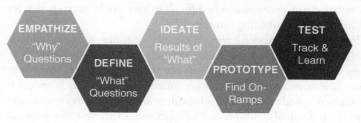

Framing Strategy

Framing Strategy starts with bringing the family stakeholders together to explore *why* the family wants to pursue a new investment strategy such as impact investing.

If the family mission is taking the family in a new direction, the family needs to agree on why the mission is important enough to risk the family's capital, reputation, time, and energy. Engage stakeholders by discussing *why* this is important for each member as well as the family overall. Have open discussion between stakeholders to understand their personal perspectives, priorities, and needs in order to understand how they think about the world and what is meaningful to them. The nonfinancial reasons why the family is willing to risk capital are called *Experiential Returns.*

The *Why* Questions

The *why* questions of the Framing Strategy step are designed to explore whether the family is ready to engage in a process that may involve a considerable amount of change to the status quo. The goal of this step is to hear all views and build empathy for the different perspectives and interests of the family stakeholders, not necessarily to arrive at consensus. The *why* process is not about expressing and negotiating positions, also known as "positional bargaining." The outcomes of the *why* process are aligned with "interest-based" negotiations in which participants strive to understand the interests of each party, as described in the book *Getting to Yes* by Roger Fisher and William L. Ury. (New York: Penquin, 1991)

Establishing the intention of the family stakeholders is the most important ex-ante buy-in that must occur in the knowledge-creation process. "The sharing of tacit knowledge among multiple individuals with different backgrounds, perspectives, and motivations becomes the critical step for organizational knowledge creation to take place. The individuals' emotions, feelings, and mental models have to be shared to build mutual trust."[8] The goal is less about creating an agreement among stakeholders than it is about all stakeholders being heard. Interest-based conversations can be difficult to have in a large group that is potentially loaded with conflicting interests.

Families may consider having these conversations with the guidance of a skilled consultant trained to manage difficult group conversations. It is often best for the consultant to work one-on-one with each stakeholder to help them express their interests privately. It is not uncommon for family members to have interests, needs, and wants that are difficult to acknowledge or express to a family group. An individual's unexpressed interests often manifest in emotional ways that can vary from silent alienation to disruptive belligerence. The consultant may work with each person to help present their interest in a way that is honest and open, yet respectful.

The process of acknowledging and empathizing with the individual interests should be conducted in an informal social setting per Senge's principle that "learning is social." For this step to be successful, stakeholders should feel free to express their beliefs, motivations, and needs, both pros and cons, for risking capital in impact investing. Individuals' reasons may be rational and objective or they may be emotional and personal. In order to empathize, it is important for the stakeholders to suspend judgment in order to *observe, engage, watch,* and *listen.*

Participants need to accept that they are to listen and reflect on the views of all participants regardless of family power dynamics. Stakeholders should resist the temptation to challenge, negotiate, or defend positions. They should come with a fresh set of eyes to understand the way others think and execute their role in the family and the world. Discussions of constraints such as available resources and risks should also not be brought into this step. The purpose of the later *what* process is to address risk tolerance and the constraints of limited resources.

This step is particularly important for families that have Next Gens, or even older generations, who feel passionately about impact investing sectors such as clean energy, education, sustainable food and agriculture, economic inclusion, affordable housing, and others. Many family offices may not have domain expertise in these areas and may categorically dismiss impact investing as too risky or philanthropic. These concerns will be addressed in the *what* process when expected outcomes are defined.

The *why* questions will be unique for each family based on the composition of family members, individual values, definition of legacy and stewardship, and other idiosyncratic elements that make up a family. Following are questions that apply specifically to impact investing; however, questions can be tailored to guide a discussion of whether the family should be involved in any type of direct investing.

Why *Questions*

- Is helping to solve problems in the world an important part of the family legacy?
- Is the family interested in using more than just philanthropy to solve these problems?
- Is impact investing a way to start to build family talent and investment experience in the Next Gen members?
- Will impact investing strengthen family unity by involving disengaged members or members who are not included in investment decisions?
- Is expanding the family's "circle of competence" into new sectors (i.e., clean energy) and new asset classes (i.e., green bonds) an objective of the family?
- Are members willing to tolerate mistakes, setbacks, and loss of capital?
- Are members willing to bear the reputational risk of not succeeding?
- Are most family members only consumers of wealth or are they interested in being potential creators of wealth? If they are only consumers of wealth, is the family willing to risk capital to change this?

- Are the Next Gen members interested in and ready to commit to participating in the growth and stewardship of family assets?
- Are the Next Gen or other members who may not be involved in investment decisions passive by choice, by design of the family structure, or by family inertia? If the Next Gens are passive, is the family willing to risk capital to change this?
- Does the family want to protect or prepare the Next Gen members for the management of the family wealth?

Other questions can be included that are more strategic based on near-term secular global issues as discussed in "Making the Case for Impact Investing" in Chapter 11.

Discussion of the *why* questions should happen in an informal open setting with whiteboards and sticky notes. It is best to have a committee draft the initial questions with input from the stakeholders and share them with participants before the gathering. An open discussion of the *why* questions can be difficult to have in a disparate group of participants with a wide variety of both formal and informal powers. It is helpful for the group to agree to a set of rules and conduct and engage a consultant to help members stick to the five *why* process rules.

The Why *Discussion Rules*

1. Members endeavor to suspend judgment in order to *observe, watch,* and *listen* to all unique perspectives of all participants.
2. Members endeavor to resist the temptation to challenge, negotiate, or defend positions.
3. Discussion of constraints due to available resources or perceived risk should be limited.
4. Maintain focus on the goal of hearing and capturing all perspectives, not on negotiating or building a consensus.
5. Resist holding a vote immediately at the gathering. Poll the participants within a week to evaluate if the family is ready to engage in the *what* process.

This *why* process lays the groundwork for the family to frame the *experiential returns* objectives that will be clarified and defined in the *what* process. The *why* process can build personal and emotional buy-in among the stakeholders to signal if it makes sense for the family to engage in a process of developing *what* objectives they intend to achieve, what resources they are willing to commit, and the risks they are willing to take. The family should decide if they are willing to risk capital to achieve the *experiential returns* of engaging the Next Gens, strengthening family unity, expanding the family's "circle of competence," and enhancing family legacy.

Developing Strategy

Developing Strategy starts with two different types of *what* questions and should only begin after there is sufficient buy-in from the stakeholders during the *why* questions process. The *what* process is broken down into two steps: defining a family point-of-view and determining what the family wants to achieve. Once the family stakeholders have reached some degree of acceptance of *why* they are willing to take some measure of risk, the first step of the *what* process is to define what objectives the family intends to achieve.

Defining a Point-of-View: Step 2

Open discussion of each stakeholder's view of the family's objectives and importance of achieving these objectives (i.e., the family point-of-view). The outcome of this step is to provide focus and framing for developing an investment strategy and criteria for investment selection.

Point-of-View *What* Questions

The second step of the SCIE cycle is having stakeholders define a point-of-view of the objectives the family wants to achieve. Many of the objectives are qualitative, such as what problems does the family want to solve, what members want to be involved, and what is the point-of-view regarding family legacy. The qualitative objectives of the *what* questions are less about financial returns and more about experiential returns. The outcome of this step should be a family point-of-view of what the stakeholders hope to achieve by committing capital to impact investing. Defining a family point-of-view can be drafted by a smaller set of stakeholders, or stakeholders' representatives, and should be an in-person gathering.

This step begins the process of bringing clarity and focus in order to craft a meaningful and actionable problem statement. During this step the subjective tacit perspectives of stakeholders begin to be externalized into clearly articulated objectives. Participants in the *why* process received new knowledge from others passively. In the *what* process, stakeholders actively collaborate to transform interests into objectives that are specific, measurable, attainable, relevant, and timebound (S.M.A.R.T.).

This step can create confusion, conflict, and chaos as certain members' interests are accepted or discarded, and new intentions and knowledge are proposed as commitments by the family.[9] It may be helpful to have a trained outside facilitator to manage the *what* process for a family, given the potential conflict and confusion that may occur. The best case is that the family can support conflict when debating the objectives to encourage different arguments and points of view to bring more knowledge, information, and energy to the discussion.

The discussions of the *what* process should be empathetic, optimistic, and creative with little consideration for constraints due to limited resources and perceptions of risk. This discussion allows stakeholders to think differently about *what* drives family's investment decisions and *why*.

The initial *what* questions should begin as broad questions based on the results of the *why* questions.

Point-of-View What *Questions*

- What challenging world problem(s) does the family want to help solve?
- What are the financial and human constraints? What family members will commit time and energy to the objectives? What amount of time will they commit?
- What domain expertise and experience does the family have internally?
- What domain expertise exists in the family's network of advisors and other families? What domain expertise does the family need to build or gather?
- What experience and training does the family want to provide Next Gens? Positions on board of directors? Active management positions? Internships or other types of engagement?
- What insights and learning (experiential returns) do the members engaged in the investment process hope to gain?
- What experiential returns do other family members not engaged in the investment process hope to gain? What members of the investment team and family will be responsible for the impact investing portfolio?
- What are the geographies the family is most interested in? Are there members on the impact investing team who can travel?
- What are the best-case results for the experiential returns regarding Next Gen learning, building the family office network, impact returns, and so on? What are acceptable results?
- What is considered success? What is considered failure?
- What are the consequences of failure? What are the consequences for not trying?
- What are the stakeholders' views of the reputational risks that may occur with advisors and others if capital is lost or impaired?

The conversation to define a family point-of-view should be open-minded, inclusive, and optimistic. Often, stakeholders with opposing interests or views may take extreme positions to defend their positions. One stakeholder may take the position that the family categorically does not have the resources to commit to impact investing. The opposing stakeholder may believe that it is the fiduciary responsibility of the investment decision-makers to address future generations by committing to impact investing. The discussion can become paralyzed once the conversation turns to committing capital and the concomitant risks. These specific viewpoints will be addressed in the Clarifying Objectives step of the *what* process.

Example of Point-of-View *Objectives*

- Invest in companies or funds that address climate change and can include clean energy, clean water, and sustainable food production.
- Expand the "circle of competency" by focusing on no more than one sector per six-month period where the family has little or no prior experience.
- Invest in an emerging manager of a fund that is focused on the family's self-selected sector and allows full co-investment rights.
- Employ investment structures in which experienced investors of the family or advisors have previous experience.
- Identify and engage an external advisor who has experience in sectors that the family has selected to build domain expertise.
- Only invest in companies that allow Next Gen family members to serve internships.
- Only invest in geographies that are close enough for the family members responsible for the investment to be able to travel to and from within a 24-hour period.
- Only invest in deals or funds that are clearly understood by both experienced and non-experienced family members.

The Point-of-View *Discussion Rules*

1. Focus on the problem(s) the family wants to solve and what external resources and expertise the family needs to engage. Draft a single statement of the family's point-of-view.
2. Develop decision-making objectives that allow a smaller set of members to develop solutions in the next step, Clarifying Objectives.
3. Clarify who will be involved in developing the strategy according to the Define objectives and have those members make specific time commitments.
4. Clarify what the family wants to learn and what level of engagement the family members want to experience (i.e., experiential returns).
5. Conclude each topic discussion with specific actions to be taken, identify advisors with relevant domain expertise, select advisors who can source and diligence impact-related funds, develop a network of family offices pursuing similar problems, research conferences and information sources regarding the problem(s).

Clarifying What the Family Wants to Achieve: Step 3

This step generates ideas to connect the *what* objectives of the family point-of-view with *what* possible investment solutions the family can consider to achieve their objectives. Constraints such as limited financial and human capital, liquidity, return expectations, and risk tolerance are introduced into this idea-generation (ideation) step. Well-designed *what* objectives are filters to focus on what strategies or investments the family will consider. The stakeholders involved in developing the strategy should inform the family of the investment thesis, source of deals, and due diligence resources.

Clarifying Objectives with *What Questions*

This step of investment idea generation should only begin once there is clear and commonly accepted family buy-in regarding the family's point-of-view of what it wants to achieve. The outcome of the previous *why* and *what* questions should have created a shared context to start developing investment ideas. The investment ideas should be selected according to the experiential return objectives developed in the *why* questions above. It can be helpful to start the inquiry by discussing each experiential return with the phrase "How might we…?": "How might we find funds that allow Next Gens to develop knowledge of a particular sector?" or "How might we find investments that generate cash flow during the expected investment period?"

This third step of the SCIE cycle moves the conversation from a general interest in impact investing sectors and asset classes to a discussion of possible investments. This step should be conducted with the impact investing team appointed to develop the impact investing strategy. It usually requires research and collaboration with advisors and other families pursuing solutions to similar problems.

During this step the family converts the broad point-of-view to S.M.A.R.T. objectives while adding in realistic constraints such as what financial capital will the family commit, human resources available, timeframe, liquidity, expected returns, and risk appetites. Entrenched bias, assumptions, and mental models can often limit this step if the impact investing team cannot bring a fresh set of eyes to developing possible solutions.

This generative process is meant to create the broadest range of investment ideas that achieve the financial and experiential returns while adding in constraints such as amount of human and financial capital available. The qualification or status of the impact investing team members should not cause ideas to be ranked. Allowing all members to contribute ideas, regardless of investment experience, can transform personal knowledge into organizational knowledge. The one taboo is "criticism without constructive suggestion." Everyone must accept the principle that "making criticism is ten times easier than coming up with a constructive alternative."[10]

The discussion should also acknowledge the potential opportunity costs of redirecting human and financial resources away from existing investment activity. For instance, if an objective is to train the Next Gens, it is important to acknowledge that mentoring Next Gens may take time away from both investment and philanthropy professionals in the family. The family will also have to commit to devoting time to listen to the Next Gens' efforts and provide feedback.

It is essential that the stakeholders engage in this process with an attitude of trying to find and nurture solutions, not eliminate possibilities based on existing mental models. Chapter 11, Table 11.1 provides an overview of asset classes, impact sectors, geographies, impact strategies, and return profiles to consider. The filtering and focusing of the investment ideas into specific investments will occur in the fourth step, *Implementing Strategy*.

Clarifying Objectives What *Questions*

- What amount of financial capital will the family commit and over what time period?
- What part of the family's current asset allocation will the capital come from?
- Will the family carve out a portion of the assets?
- What asset allocation decision criteria would a carve-out draw resources away from (e.g., capital preservation, income generation, or targeted portfolio returns)?
- What financial returns does the family expect to achieve? Risk-adjusted market returns? Below-market returns? Breakeven?
- What benchmarks will the family use to measure the financial success of the investment? Will the family use the same benchmarks as the larger portfolio?
- What weighting of risk/return perspective and priorities will be applied to the impact investing portfolio? Preservation of capital? Short-term income generation? Long-term income preservation? Long-term patient equity capital?
- What amount of capital will be devoted to illiquid investments that may be difficult to sell or transfer ownership?

At the end of this step of SCIE, the family should know the problems they want to devote capital to, what resources they have and are willing to commit, and the financial and experiential returns they expect to achieve. It is helpful to categorize proposed solutions for each sector and asset class into defined buckets (i.e., "Rational and Reasonable," "Requires Us to Stretch," "In Our Dreams"). Once the family has codified the objectives they intend to achieve, they are ready engage in the *how* process of rigorous investment evaluation and selection based on objectives of the *what* process.

Example of Clarifying Objectives

- A commitment of $6,000,000 will be committed over a three-year time period and will be funded with available cash.

- The $6,000,000 will be carved out of current family assets and its performance will not be factored into the overall performance of the family asset allocation performance.

- Investment team will only consider funds, private debt, and income generation equity investments related to climate change.

- Initial investments only in funds that will allow the family to co-invest in the fund's portfolio company. Co-investment opportunities will not be from the carve-out and will be considered by the investment committed and funded out of the family's private investment allocation.

- At least one nonexecutive family member and one executive team member will source deals, conduct due diligence, manage, and report investments.

- At least one nonexecutive family member is willing to commit at least 12 hours per quarter to manage and report the status of the investment.

- One family executive is willing to commit at least four hours per quarter to mentor the nonexecutive family member.

- Investment team will seek opportunities that provide internships for Next Gens.

- Impact investment team will not pursue investments in which the risk of complete loss of capital is significantly high due to the structure or maturity of the company or the fund's portfolio.

- At least one Next Gen will serve on the board of each investment and prepare a quarterly report describing how the businesses have succeeded, changed, or failed and what the Next Gen family member has learned.

- Next Gen family member will attend at least two conferences per year related to the business and prepare a report once a year to the family. The report will give an overview of the industry, market opportunities, and network of new business relationships.

The Clarifying Objectives Discussion Rules

1. Commit to what amount of capital over what period of time will be committed and the sources of the capital.
2. Develop financial and experiential return objectives that are specific, measurable, attainable, relevant, and time-bound (SMART).
3. Define success by clarifying what the "best case" and "acceptable case" is for each of the objectives.
4. Bring a fresh set of eyes to the process and follow the rule that "criticism without constructive suggestion" is not allowed.

5. Select the sectors, geographies, and asset classes that will be researched and match the financial and experiential return objectives.

A thoughtful and granular discussion of the *what* process is designed to create SMART objectives, clearly define the resources that the family is committing, and openly express the actual risks as perceived by each member of the impact investing team. The impact investing team should submit the objectives to the family stakeholders for feedback but not necessarily approval. The *what* process is designed to filter and focus the *how* process of investment selection.

Implementing Strategy

When you are immersed in a vision, you know what needs to be done. But you often don't know how to do it. You run an experiment because you think it's going to get you there. It doesn't work. New input. New data. You change direction and run another experiment. Everything is an experiment but there is no ambiguity at all. It's perfectly clear why you are doing it. People aren't saying, "Give me a guarantee it will work." Everybody knows there is no guarantee. But the people are committed nonetheless.

Ed Simon, CEO, Herman Miller

The family is now prepared to implement an investment strategy as a prototype investment that supports the outcomes of the *why* and *what* questions. The *how* process establishes a set of questions and simple rules that allow the impact investing team to filter a large number of opportunities.

Implementing Strategy: Step 4

This step is the investment selection process that finds appropriate investments as "on-ramps" for impact investing. The investments need to map to the *what* objectives, resource commitments, and risk exposure determined in the *what* process. The investments are prototypes in that they require fewer resources to implement and can be scaled with more capital if successful.

Find Prototype Investments as "On-Ramps"

The investments selected in this step are considered prototypes because implementation may involve a significant amount of trial and error. This step correlates to the *Knowledge-Creating Company* phase labeled Combination where the newly created knowledge of the *why* and *what* process starts to become "systemic knowledge" through the combination of both internal and external explicit knowledge. The investment team engages in a process of sorting, adding, deleting, combining, and categorizing the explicit knowledge into actionable decisions.[11] In Chapter 11, the section "How to Source Impact Investments" offers resources and methods to begin to increase the deal-sourcing capacity of the family.

Once the family declares its interest in impact investing to its network and advisors, the family may be overwhelmed with opportunities. The objectives of the *what* process not only help the investment team filter through opportunities to consider, they also provide guidance of what *not* to consider. An efficient framework to cull opportunities that the family *will not* invest in is as important as processing what the family will consider. It is particularly important to make sure the time frame and transparency of the investment are well suited to report the status of both the financial returns and the experiential returns to the family. It is essential to start with investments that have short experience cycles (i.e., real assets, project finance, product/service launch, corporate debt, growth capital) in order to have shorter reporting cycles to maintain stakeholder buy-in. The *experience cycle* is the cycle from the time a family commits capital to some measurable, objective financial outcome (e.g., interest payment, dividend payment, liquidity event, etc.). The importance of the experience cycle is discussed further in the "Capture and Communicate Learning" section ahead.

An articulation of the purpose, values, and mission of the family can also be an efficient filter. The CIO of our family office uses the Keller Vision, Mission, and Values to quickly decide what deals the family will pass on. Without a clear filtering process, many families damage their reputation and limit their access to quality deal flow by not responding expeditiously to fund and company managers. A quick "No, thank you" with reasons why it does not fit your strategy is greatly appreciated by managers.

A clear setup of *how* rules can help the investment team parse through the myriad opportunities.

The How *Questions*

- Is the company or fund trying to solve a problem the stakeholders care about?
- If the investment is successful, will it achieve both financial returns and experiential returns?
- Do the fund managers or company management provide enough transparency or family member involvement for the family to capture the experiential returns?
- Is the impact investing team clear on what has to "prove to be true" for the investment to be successful?
- Is there sufficient support from the family's peers and advisors to provide insights before and after the investment?
- Has a process and schedule been agreed upon for when and how the status of the investment will be reported to the stakeholders?

- What is the frequency of reporting of the company or fund regarding the results of the investments?

- How closely does the timeframe of reported financial returns and impact returns match the family's expected experience cycle?

- Does the impact investing team have a member that will commit to the experience cycle of the investment?

- How will the impact investing team create a peer network of private investors or engaged industry experts to provide insights before and after the investment?

- How will the impact investing team create domain expertise necessary to develop an investment thesis? How long will it take?

- Will the expected experiential returns provide valuable insights and actionable learning that will allow the family to develop domain expertise and iterate the impact investing strategy?

If the investment team is struggling with developing a decision-making framework from the *what* objectives, it may be helpful to use a framework such as the *Simple Rules* process developed by MIT's Donald Sull in collaboration with Stanford's Kathleen Eisenhardt and published in their book, *Simple Rules: How to Thrive in a Complex World.* (Boston: Houghton Mifflin Harcourt, 2015). The Simple Rules process was developed to help decision-makers execute a strategy in a complex world with multiple stakeholders and considerations that are interconnected and may shift over time.

Simple Rules can help the investment team choose what to do, what not do, what is most important to do, and what to stop doing. Such rules increase efficiency in executing routine operations, minimize preventable errors, ensure consistency, and allow leaders to establish discipline while leaving latitude to adapt as circumstances change.

Converting the *what* objectives to a thoughtfully designed set of Simple Rules can provide guidance that allows managers, boards, and committees to operate creatively using their experience, judgment, and common sense.

Decision Rules		*What* Objectives
BOUNDARY RULES	Establish what types of investments are in and out of bounds of consideration. Rules for inclusion and exclusion.	• Only companies and funds that address mitigation of climate change. • Businesses located within 24-hour round-trip time period. • Co-investment rights for the family of all deals financed by the fund.

Decision Rules		***What* Objectives**
PRIORITIZING RULES	Rank investment competing for scarce resources based on *what* objectives.	• Investments that provide at least two summer internships for family members. • Investments with high-probability of no more than 25% of capital loss. • At least two external family offices are also investors and the family has/can build a relationship with other families.
STOPPING RULES	Establish when to end the investment selection or due diligence process.	• More than 10% of family stakeholders do not understand investment. • No nonexecutive family member is willing to commit at least 12 hours per month to manage and report status of investment to the family. • Lack of transparency revealed after reviewing investor letters and speaking to existing investors.

Process Rules		***What* Objectives**
HOW-TO RULES	Establish process while giving latitude for the investment team to stay focused on objectives.	• Investment team discusses company or fund target market with at least three competitors of the fund or company. • Investment team creates a document that matches the *what* objectives with each deal in pipeline every month. • Company/fund and family have agreed on milestones and projected funding needs.

Process Rules		*What* Objectives
COORDI-NATION RULES	Action that depend on actions of others. What to do in relation to others. Collective behavior emerges.	• Due diligence discussion with at least one unaffiliated family office investor. • Investment team meets at least once per month to review deal pipeline. • Investment team creates quarterly reports and presents portfolio in-person annually.
TIMING RULES	Describe events that need to occur before taking action. Intended to synchronize investment with family members to maintain buy-in.	• Full due diligence engagement only after at least one new family office has agreed to lead. • Follow on investment only after at least two milestones have been achieved by company/fund. • Follow on investment only after all interested family members have had opportunity to be presented to by management.

An example of a family going through the SCIE cycle is a family that identified two different, but related, problems they wanted to address with for-profit investments: Provide clean, stable, low-cost water in distressed areas and increase economic well-being of communities through increased access to financing. The family had some philanthropic experience in providing clean water in Africa, but knew nothing about for-profit investments in clean water or increased access to financing. The family believed that being a leader in global clean water was important to the family legacy and could be profitable over the long term.

The family was willing to invest $20M over the next five years to expand their circle of competence; however, they wanted the investments to be relatively conservative, with a focus on fixed-income investments with low technology risk. Clean water was an issue of strong interest for the Millennial members. The family looked at the ImpactBase funds focused on water and discovered that there were very few opportunities for fixed-income, low-risk investments in water. After thoughtful consideration of their busy lives, the Millennials realized there was only one Millennial who could devote at least four hours per month to the water investment thesis. Given the limited amount, there were more opportunities in early-stage clean water investments; however, these investments may require more time than four hours per month. The Millennials acknowledged that the family did not have enough human bandwidth to source, diligence, manage, and report to the family an investment in early-stage water funds or companies.

The second interest of the family was microfinance and supporting small business enterprises. The family saw that there were several funds and companies in the ImpactBase database that were more mature and would require less time. The family chose a fixed-income fund in the small-medium-enterprise (SME) sector as an on-ramp that aligned with the financial and human resources the family could commit as well as risk-adjusted return expectations. The family then engaged a financial advisor to guide the impact investing team through the investment thesis, fund selection, and due diligence process.

Capture and Communicate Learning

The most essential component of knowledge creation and establishing a learning organization is to maintain shareholder buy-in by proactively communicating the status of the investments. This *Communication and Learning* step of the SCIE framework is also essential in the training of the Next Gens to be valuable contributors to the impact investment strategy and support a successful transfer of investment knowledge, experience, and wealth.

Establishing Communication and Learning: Step 5

Define clear processes, format, and forums to communicate the success, setbacks, and learning from the investments to interested stakeholders. The communication should be consistent and regularly scheduled, addressing the objectives established in the previous processes.

Test, Track, and Learn

Although real and significant capital may have been committed by the family, the reality is that the initial investments are a test of the logic and objectives of the family. The logic and process may be flawed, yielding results that did not deliver either the financial or the experiential returns expected. When the inevitable setbacks, pivots, or complete failures occur, it is essential to try to capture and communicate what was learned. Successes also needed to be captured and communicated; however, they are often less valuable from a learning perspective than the setbacks and failure. This step is the most essential step in creating a sustainable and repeatable investment cycle.

The benefits of the "creative chaos" of the SCIE frameworks can only be realized when the knowledge is institutionalized through reflection-in-action to induce and strengthen the commitment of the stakeholders. The continuous process of reflecting, questioning, and reconsidering the results of the investments vis-à-vis the *what* objectives fosters organizational knowledge creation. Without reflecting the learning back to the family, creative chaos may turn into destructive chaos.[12]

It is important to create formats that are consistent and easily understood by a diverse stakeholder audience with a variety of priorities, experiences, and knowledge. Communication may happen formally in family meetings or quarterly reports and informally around a dinner table, on the golf course, or watching kids by the pool. Simple narrative formats that can be understood and repeated in informal social settings are helpful to maintain stakeholder buy-in during the experience cycle and are as important as the formal reporting. The following are two narrative formats that cover elements of the investments to help create a simple, consistent, and repeatable story for each investment.

Initial Investment Narrative Format

Company founders and fund managers work hard to convince you that their strategy is superior and that they have a unique competitive advantage. Often their investor slide-decks are 30 or more slides of market data, company data, business models, intellectual property, revenue projections, and so forth. They often spend so much effort trying to convince investors how great they are that they forget to address what the family wants out of the investment. Work with the company or fund manager to distill their story down to answer five essential questions that can be easily remembered and communicated in less than three minutes:

1. What Do You Do?
   The answer needs to cover what problem the company is trying to solve and why solving this problem matters to the family. The answer should relate to the *what* objectives of the family. The answer should cause a strong, positive emotional reaction.
2. What Have You Done?
   Develop a sense of why the management team is committed to this problem and what in their history makes them ideal to solve the problem. Should also include the strategic approach to solving the problem.

3. What Makes You Special?
   This should be a simple explanation of the company or fund's proprietary, competitive advantage that supports the company or fund's ability to solve the problem.
4. What Are You Going to Do with the Family's Money?
   A clear understanding of what the family's capital will be used for and how it meaningfully contributes to solving the problem. The answer to this should also relate back to experiential returns of the *what* objectives.
5. How Are You Going to Pay the Family Back?
   Clear articulation by the managers of what events need to happen (i.e., prove to be true) in the future that will generate liquidity for the family. A surprising number of company and fund investor managers do not explain their thoughts regarding how capital will be returned.

The impact investing team may consider creating a one-page description that is sent out to all of the family stakeholders during the investment process. This helps the family remain engaged and see how the work they did in the *why* and *what* processes resulted in action. This one-pager will initiate the *Ongoing Investment Monitoring* communication that tracks and communicates the status of the investment.

Ongoing Investment Monitoring Narrative Format

Every company and fund will have different investor letter formats reporting how the company or fund is doing. If the investment is in a relatively early vintage fund or an early-stage business, there is a high probability that the strategy will shift during the life of the investment; this is also known as *strategy shift* or *pivot*. Funds may find that their initial deal-sourcing strategy or deal structure terms are no longer yielding quality deals. The fund manager may decide they need to expand their geographies, provide a different type of capital, or seek opportunities emerging in adjacent sectors. Companies may find that their initial product or service is not able to establish traction in the market and that they need to develop a new product or service.

Investment team members responsible for the investment may follow the twists and turns of the investment, but can struggle communicating this journey to a diverse group of stakeholders. Investor letters can be 10 pages or more of narrative, charts, and financials describing the journey that most stakeholders will not read.

It is often difficult for the investment team to answer fundamental questions: Did the company create actual value the past quarter? What did they spend investor capital on the past quarter that did not work? What did management and the investors learn from the successes or setbacks? To what objectives is the company or fund committing to create value in the next quarter? What are the things that keep the managers up at night? Is there anything the family can do to help?

It is difficult enough to recall the last quarterly newsletter much less what was written the last eight investor letters over a two-year period. Following is a format of no more than two pages of bullet points laid out in five sections. The format allows interested stakeholders, regardless of investment experience, to follow the shifting journey of the investment.

Top Pages of Investor Letter—Five Sections

1. Key Value Creation Objectives/Metrics

No more than seven bullet points of SMART objectives describing what management believes need to be achieved to create value. These objectives will most likely change over a two-year period. Eight quarters of a company or fund's history can be easily followed by all family stakeholders just by reading this section of bullet points. The bullet points allow the stakeholders to track over time what the managers believe will create value.

2. Value Creation Success During Last Quarter

A family stakeholder can dig deeper to see what is working vis-à-vis the five questions in the initial investment narrative, as well as the previous quarter's two-page bullet points. These bullets points should report actual results achieved, not projected results. The value created this quarter can be tracked against section 4, Value Creation Commitments from the previous quarter.

3. Value Creation Setbacks/Deferral During Last Quarter

To maintain buy-in, it may be more important to help stakeholders follow what value creation efforts *did not* work and why. The reasons why a fund or company shifted strategy can be followed by understanding what did not work. It is essential for the managers to be forthright about their disappointments and to express the lessons learned. This explicit knowledge is essential for the knowledge creation process.

4. Value Creation Commitments for This Quarter

These bullet points also need to be SMART and reported next quarter as either setbacks or successes. Make sure these bullet points match the first section of Key Value Creation Objectives/Metrics. Managers often become too focused on initiatives that are not Key Value Creation Metrics. After a strategy shift or two, the strategy the family signed off on is probably different from what was presented in the Initial Investment Narrative.

5. Three to Five Things that Keep You Up at Night

    Investment decisions are based as much on people as they are on business plans. Work to have your managers be transparent about their worries and concerns. It is worrisome if the manager is not worried that something could go wrong. These bullet points allow family stakeholders to remain personally connected to the manager and the difficulty of value creation. Family stakeholders not directly responsible for the investment may have ideas or contacts that can help.

A rule of thumb of the Stanford Design Thinking model is "Prototype as if you know you're right, but test as if you know you're wrong—testing the change to refine your solutions and make them better."[13] During the investment experience cycle it is important to solicit feedback from the stakeholders and continue to encourage them to be engaged. When speaking to the stakeholders, refer back to questions in the *why* process and the objectives of the *what* process. If the investment does not work out as expected, the family's point-of-view may need to be rethought. Investments that were considered "Rational and Reasonable" may have been actually in the "In Our Dreams" bucket.

The investment teams should resist trying to justify why an investment did not work and focus more on laying out the facts as objectively as they can. This is difficult because the investment committee members were sure they were right and devoted a lot of blood, sweat, and tears to getting the test investment right. The investment team needs to give the stakeholders the space to interpret the results of the test. The investment team needs to listen to what the stakeholders say and the questions they have.

As an investment ends its experience cycle and the lessons are captured and communicated, it is time for the family stakeholders to come together to define needs for improvement. Did the investment achieve the financial objectives? If not, why not? Did the stakeholders feel the investment generated sufficient experiential returns? If not, why not? Testing the investment against the *what* objectives informs the next iteration of the investment cycle and may require going back to the drawing board.

The SCIE framework is intended to be repeated in multiple cycles and is a process to move potential members to engaged members to increase the knowledge creation of the family (see Figure 11.2, System Design Example of a Family's Engaged Members and Knowledge Creation Stocks, in Chapter 11).

Conclusion

This chapter introduced a new framework, SCIE, designed to create a roadmap for families to engage multiple family stakeholders in an impact investment strategy development. The SCIE framework brought together ideas from three existing models: the Design Thinking process developed by the Institute of Design at Stanford University and IDEO, Ikujiro Nonaka and Hirotaka Takeuchi's knowledge-creation framework, and Peter Senge's learning organization work. The SCIE framework was created for families willing to engage family office stakeholders in iterative steps that are highly social and inclusive. The outcome of the process is intended to create buy-in from multiple stakeholders, leading the stakeholders from the early stage of developing an agreed-upon collective intention, the *why* process, through development of expected outcomes, the *what* process, to the actual selection and implementation investments, the *how* process. The chapter concludes with a discussion of the importance of capturing and communicating the learning of investment cycles in order to establish knowledge creation and the family as a learning organization. The proposed benefit of the SCIE cycle is to help establish the family as a learning organization that builds, transfers, and sustains family talent, family legacy, and family unity.

Notes

1. Ikujiro Nonaka and Hirotaka Takeuchi, *The Knowledge-Creating Company* (Oxford: Oxford University Press, 1995), p. 84.
2. Society for Organizational Learning, Principles, www.solonline.org/?page=MissionandPrinciples, 2017.
3. Dennis T. Jaffe, "Releasing the Potential of the Rising Generation: How Long-Lasting Family Enterprises Prepare Their Successors" (Wise Counsel Research, 2016), p. 186.
4. Ikujiro Nonaka and Hirotaka Takeuchi, *The Knowledge-Creating Company* (Oxford: Oxford University Press, 1995), p. 56.
5. Ibid., p. 9.
6. kellerllc.com/who-we-are/, 2012–2017.
7. Hasso Plattner, "Introduction to Design Thinking: Process," *unpublished whitepaper,* https://dschool.stanford.edu/ . . . /**design**resources/ . . . /Mode **Guide**BOOTCAMP2010L.pdf (Institute of Design at Stanford University, 2010), Stanford, p. 1.

8. Ikujiro Nonaka and Hirotaka Takeuchi, *The Knowledge-Creating Company* (Oxford: Oxford University Press, 1995), pp. 74–76.

9. Ibid., p. 71.

10. Ibid., p. 63.

11. Ibid., p. 36.

12. Ibid., pp. 78–79.

13. Hasso Plattner, "An Introduction to Design Thinking Process Guide." *The Institute of Design at Stanford: Stanford (2010)*, p. 5.

CHAPTER 13

International Direct Investing

Contributing Author: Anna Nekoranec

As an increasing number of family offices pursue direct investment programs, many have chosen to seek opportunities outside of their home countries. Some target markets with higher projected growth, others are looking for geographic diversification, while others hope to leverage existing expertise or escape political or country risk inherent within their home country. Whatever the rationale, international direct investing, while filled with opportunity, comes with a unique set of challenges.

In this chapter, we discuss why investors are increasingly seeking investments outside of their home market. We review some of the key differences between investing abroad versus investing in the United States and how to identify the most attractive markets and opportunities. Then we analyze the key components of successful international direct investing and the most common mistakes made. Finally, we discuss ways to mitigate risk. The chapter features several interviews and case studies of leading international investors and their top considerations.

Why Consider International Direct Investing?

Why invest internationally, particularly if you are a U.S.-based investment office? One answer at the top of investors' minds is *growth*. The projected low-growth environment in the United States and the lack of certainty as to what the future holds are driving an increasing number of investors to look abroad. Another reason for going abroad is *diversification*. Geographic diversification helps mitigate single-country political and economic risk. Still another rationale is *technological change*. Technological change has made the world flat and created unique investment opportunities. Finally, for families outside of the United States, a primary driver of international investment, particularly in the United States, is the search for a *safe haven* for their capital.

For Benji Griswold, the president of Blue Water Worldwide LLC, the initial reason for going abroad was growth and diversification. He provides a summary of this rationale by drawing a parallel to Germany at the turn of the last century. "If you invested in the U.S. in the 1920s or Germany in the early 1900s everything looked great. The succeeding years, though, didn't work out so well."[1]

Griswold's family has a long successful history of direct investing. His family founded Alex Brown and Sons and his father is the chairman of Brown Advisory. Both were domestic entities focused on the financial services sector. When Griswold founded Blue Water in 2008, he chose to move into other industries and to go outside of the United States—targeting investments in the U.S. aggregates industry, electrical transmission in Peru, and class A warehouses in Argentina. Since the 2008 financial downturn, he has deployed a significant amount of capital abroad. He believes that the United States will be in a low-growth environment for a considerable amount of time and feels that there are markets outside of the United States where capital has greater value. As a result, he is able to make investments at more attractive valuations than he would be able to in the United States.

Another multigenerational family, Family X, we interviewed had similar goals. Over the last ten years they have developed investment programs in a number of emerging markets, including China, Ethiopia, Georgia, and Mongolia. The rationale behind this has been a search for higher growth markets and diversification. This family felt that being diversified in solely U.S. investments exposed them to single-country risk and limited the growth prospects for their investments. By entering these emerging markets, they felt they could be a first mover in the market and have the opportunity to build a dominant player in the sectors where they focused, which encompassed food, power, and education.

Technological change has been another impetus for other investors to look beyond their borders. The changes that have taken place over the last two decades have effectively increased communication and broken down some of the barriers to entry into foreign markets. Investors can now have face-to-face communication at the touch of their fingertips via Skype and FaceTime and access portfolio company information in seconds over the Internet. A great example of an investor taking advantage of these changes is Tready Smith, the founder and CEO of Bayshore Capital Advisors LLC, an investment advisory firm formed by a family office. Smith shares Griswold's view that interesting opportunities can be found outside of the United States and feels that the technological changes of the last decade have made such opportunities more accessible. The ability to access information on investments in other geographic regions and communicate via a handheld videoconference makes investing on foreign continents much easier than even ten years ago and has compelled Smith to venture abroad. Smith notes, "Why restrict yourself to the U.S., particularly when the world is so flat?"[2]

Technological innovation has indeed made the world flat. It has also created exciting international investment opportunities that have attracted the interest of family offices. Take Africa, for example. The lack of infrastructure within the continent has led some African countries to avoid traditional deployments and embrace technological innovation, which in turn has come to the attention of family office investors. One prime example is telecommunication. With the advent of the mobile phone and its widespread usage, much of Africa has "leapfrogged" traditional landline systems, moving immediately to mobile systems. This has led to a high demand for cell towers, creating interesting investment opportunities. Wendel, a private equity firm backed by a French family office, is one group that has taken advantage of this opportunity. In 2012, the firm deployed capital in tower builder HIS as their first investment in Africa. Wendel then raised its stake in the business to $276 million in 2013.[3]

While an increasing number of U.S. family offices are seeking opportunities abroad, a similar wave of investments by international families has occurred in the United States since 2008. These families are frequently seeking not just diversification, but also a safe haven for their capital. One large Uruguayan family and another large Spanish family have relocated family members to the United States to run real estate direct investment programs. These families believe that U.S. real estate will both provide a solid return and be a safe haven for their capital for years to come. Similarly, Wendy Craft, a well-respected family office executive, describes the desire for international investors to purchase prestigious, hard assets such as major metropolitan commercial buildings in major U.S. cities. For example, buildings in cities such as New York or Chicago are desired locations for outside investors to purchase real estate, not only for their cache, but also to mitigate country risk of their own home country.

Whatever the reason, whether growth, diversification, or increased access to international investments, international direct investing by family offices appears to be here to stay. For families who have created direct investing programs or those who are in the process of considering one, each has its own rationale that is driven by its specific circumstances. Every family is different, but the trend is undeniable.

Key Differences between Investing Abroad versus Investing in the United States

As one might expect, while the types of businesses and real estate investment opportunities may share similar characteristics, investing abroad is not the same as investing in the United States. Yes, a cell tower in the United States is not markedly different from a cell tower in Africa. That said, how they are deployed, how the business is managed, what the legal environment is like, the type of governance possible, and the type of exit options available are extremely different. Some of the differences between investing in the United States versus abroad are obvious. When one ventures outside of the United States, one encounters a diverse set of legal structures, taxes, and currency issues. Other differences, like cultural norms, are more subtle. Each region has its own set of rules, those set by the country's laws (or lack thereof), and cultural norms or the often unwritten codes of conduct and business decorum.

Understanding the key dynamics of the targeted market is paramount to success, and cultural differences are frequently one of the biggest stumbling blocks. Benji Griswold believes that a great way to understand the challenges confronting the novice international investor is to turn the tables and put yourself in the shoes of an international investor coming to the United States for the first time. Consider that this investor has minimal market knowledge and significant capital. In addition, he or she has to start from ground zero in terms of becoming acquainted with the market, building a support network, accessing deal flow, and completing a transaction. As he puts it,

> Imagine that you are from Dubai and have decided that you want to invest in Naples, Florida. You get off the plane with a sack full of money and are ready to invest. Do you really think that the first people that you meet will be

the ones in the "know" who have the best deal flow and connections? Or is it more likely that you will encounter the scam artists and be "marked" as unsophisticated easy money? If you enter a market where capital is not an issue and it is fully functioning, it is most likely that you will only see the deals that the groups with strong domestic networks have passed on.[4]

Even in countries that appear to be similar, there are significant cultural differences. For example, decision-making in Sweden is very consensus oriented. People want to have the whole team on board. In contrast, German decision-making is much more hierarchical, formal, and authoritarian. In Sweden, it is not uncommon to address colleagues or new acquaintances by first name, as we do in the United States. In Germany, full titles are frequently used. These include the equivalent of *Mr.* and academic titles (e.g., Herr Doktor Ing. Schumann).

While there is a veritable laundry list of potential differences that should be addressed, cultural differences are frequently some of the most challenging to navigate. Other considerations for any investor venturing abroad include:

- Government regulation
- Rule of law
- Currency issues
- Economic stability
- Political stability
- Tax structures
- Management sophistication
- Labor training and availability
- Governance structures
- Investor protections and rights
- Exit opportunities

One way to address these issues and mitigate risk is to either take on a local partner or deploy the capital needed to have sophisticated employees on the ground. We address this later in the chapter, but it is important to note that a local network provides the boots-on-the-ground intelligence, oversight, and hands-on knowledge that are must-haves for several reasons. First, it builds trust and an authentic presence. Second, it helps demonstrate commitment and accountability. Third, it fosters the network of business relationships, particularly the management of the company that will help ensure the investment stays on track. For investors deploying capital abroad, having a local presence, either through a native partner or employees with on-the-ground expertise, is not a "nice to have"—it is a downright necessity.

How to Determine Where to Invest

Once a family office has made a decision to venture abroad, the next question is where? How does one begin to understand which country provides the best long-term investment opportunities? Should this decision be based on market knowledge? Market dynamics? In-house expertise? Or a combination thereof? The most sophisticated and successful investors have well-developed criteria that they utilize in order to determine which markets to enter. Those include projected growth in the region, valuation levels, the level of development of their personal networks, their ability to transfer skills, market dislocations, political stability, ties to the United States, and demographics.

Griswold, who made the decision to venture abroad early in his career, uses three criteria to evaluate international opportunities (see Figure 13.1). He focuses on markets with demonstrated economic growth, limited investment competition, and where capital has a higher implied discount rate. In his eyes, "Two things cure all ills—low cost and high growth."[5] The limited competition and high discount rate provide the valuation opportunity and coupled with high growth give Griswold a large margin of safety.

With this statement, Griswold brings a key element of successful investing to the forefront: If one is able to buy into an investment at a good value or low cost, and that investment experiences tremendous growth, then as long as one is able to exit, the probability of achieving a strong return scenario is very high, even if the project stumbles along the way.

Griswold believes that when a family office decides to venture outside of the United States they should start by asking themselves the following key questions:

1. What local relationships do you have?
2. What local operational advantage do you have?
3. What technical know-how or regulatory insights do you have?

Griswold, who has over ten years of experience successfully investing in some of the most challenging markets, suggests that there is a Venn diagram of

FIGURE 13.1 International Opportunity Filter

Economic Growth Potential	Limited Competition in Target Country	Capital with a Higher Implied Discount Rate

FIGURE 13.2 Opportunity Set for Direct Investing Abroad

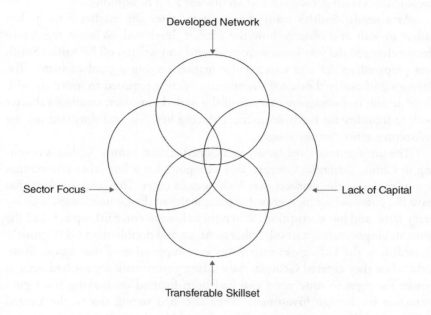

Developed Network

Sector Focus ⟶   ⟵ Lack of Capital

Transferable Skillset

the perfect opportunity (see Figure 13.2). That opportunity lies at the intersection of four circles: (1) a well-developed network, (2) focus on a sector, (3) a lack of capital in that market, and (4) a transferable skillset.

In contrast to Griswold, Tready Smith of Blue Water seeks a market dislocation that provides an attractive entry valuation in order to enter a new market. First, Smith uses a top-down approach based upon extensive market analysis to identify interesting opportunities. Then she waits for a market dislocation to provide an entry point. As she puts it, "Luck is when opportunity meets preparation."[6]

A prime example of this strategy is Smith's acquisition of an Italian non-performing loan (NPL) portfolio. Several years prior to the acquisition, she had invested with a distressed bond manager who was active in the Italian market. Smith's team leveraged this relationship to gather market intelligence and build a strong analytical understanding of the Italian loan market and its idiosyncrasies. Based upon the team's analysis, they believed that loans could be purchased at attractive values, producing above-market rates of return. However, the bank regulatory environment in Italy was impeding the rate at which these loans were processed. When Smith started looking at the market, Italy had four times the NPLs of continental Europe, which created ample deal flow; however, the Italian regulatory environment inhibited the processing of these loans, creating a logjam and an unclear path to liquidity.

As a result, Smith's team chose not to enter the market directly, but rather to wait and observe how the market developed. When a regulatory decree changed the way loans were processed and written off by banks, Smith was prepared to act and entered the market buying a pool of loans. The decree significantly shortened the amount of time required to move an NPL from default to foreclosure to a sale of the underlying asset, creating a shorter path to liquidity for her investment, reducing her risk, and thus creating the risk/return ratio that she sought.

The multigenerational family mentioned earlier, Family X, that is investing in China, Ethiopia, Georgia, and Mongolia has a few other criteria that it uses to define the markets that it chooses to enter. They seek markets that have the potential for high growth, strategic ties to the United States, high literacy rates, and low corruption. When they chose to enter Ethiopia, it had the most stable government in sub-Saharan Africa and double-digit GDP growth. In addition, the U.S. government was very supportive of the region. Similarly, when they entered Georgia, the existing government regime had been in power for eight to nine years and had been focused on making the region attractive for foreign investment. They also had strong ties to the United States, a high literacy rate, and a very educated working class.

How Population Change Can Impact Target Market Opportunities

Another seasoned investor, Sami Karam, a former portfolio manager for legendary investor George Soros, takes a unique analytical approach to determine what markets offer the most compelling investment opportunities. Karam founded a company, Populyst, which analyzes which countries provide the best investment markets. Karam focuses on demographics. As he explains it, without taking demographics into account when analyzing countries as potential investment opportunities, it is a bit like looking at a sealed environment and thinking that it won't change. And we all know that never happens.

Karam believes that demographic trends are a key component of what drives economic growth, but his analysis departs from classic demographic analytics by focusing on changes in dependency ratios. He defines dependency ratio as the number of dependents to workers. According to Karam, "A growing population and declining dependency ratio is a very positive combination for an economy in general. We have had a growing population and a low dependency ratio in the United States since the mid-1970s and it has been great. Our grandparents and parents had more children and, therefore, had less money to set aside for discretionary spending, luxuries, saving, and investing. By contrast, our generation has had fewer children and thus more money to save and invest. This was a huge boost for the economy."[7]

Karam goes on to describe how now in the more developed nations, namely the United States, Japan, Europe, and China, the dependency ratio has begun to rise for the first time in decades. This is less helpful to the economy. As a result, an increased share of the workers' funds will be dedicated to taking care of dependents rather than investment and discretionary consumption. Since the United States reached an inflection point on the dependence side in 2005 that will remain in place for the next two to three decades, reviewing investments outside the United States may be prudent.

If Karam is correct, such dynamics can have a material impact on family office direct investing results. Instead of a tailwind for investing, family offices making investments in countries that have high dependency ratios could be facing significant headwinds. It won't matter how strong the companies are if the general purchasing power of the population is declining, leading to decreased growth.

Karam's Populyst index also concentrates on two other components that are interesting for families seeking to make direct investments abroad: productivity and society/strength of institutions. Productivity encompasses things like innovation in the country, investment in education, and investment in infrastructure. All of them are factors that can positively impact economic growth. Society/strength of institutions, on the other hand, is what Karam uses to describe an environment that is friendly for business and that is characterized by low corruption, strong property rights, robust contract law, and so forth.

An evaluation of the U.S. investment environment based on these criteria provides an interesting story of what has happened here since the 2008 financial crisis and serves as an illustration of a filter that families can use to evaluate a target country's investment environment. During this period, U.S. demographics went from being positive to neutral. The population was still growing, but the dependency ratio was also increasing. The other two components were still going strong. Since 2008, innovation (at newer companies like Facebook or existing companies like Apple and Gilead Sciences) and the strength of our institutions (Federal Reserve intervention) boosted the economic environment. Without these two things, Karam believes that after 2008 we would have experienced a severe depression.

If a family office were to use Karam's template as a screen to identify countries that could offer interesting investment opportunities, the results based upon current rankings might be surprising. There are currently no countries that have a plus-6 or plus-5 rating (the highest score possible). The United States and most of Europe are plus-4 and Germany is only a plus-2 as a result of its poor demographics. That said, countries that have high dependency ratios might suggest that investment opportunities in those geographies would revolve around goods and services targeted at an aging population, such as healthcare and senior housing.

Another aspect to Karam's work that might be helpful for the family office evaluating a target geography is how these ratios will change over time based upon population growth. In terms of looking for long-term investment opportunities, Karam believes that one should focus on countries that will move from a −2 to a +2 rating. According to Karam, "In order to see this, you need to see OK demographics, a minimum of investment and infrastructure, and a place that is building institutions to lower corruption." Based upon these criteria, India appears to be an interesting opportunity over the next 10 years and sub-Saharan Africa over the next 15 (see Figure 13.3).

FIGURE 13.3   Future Population Growth

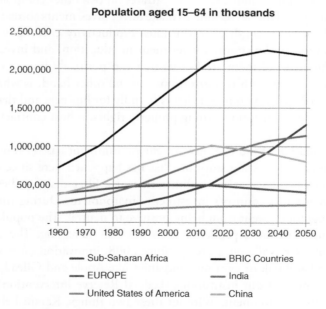

Population aged 15–64 in thousands

Legend:
— Sub-Saharan Africa   — BRIC Countries
— EUROPE   — India
— United States of America   — China

Source: Populyst, United Nations Population Division

As is evident from the story of each of these investors, identifying a market that is appropriate to enter requires a significant amount of diligence. Once a market checks the box on growth, political stability, valuation, and so on, other issues need to be reviewed. In addition to the filters described earlier, some key questions to be reviewed include:

- Have you identified interesting sectors for investment?
- Do you have geographic and cultural expertise and access to local resources and advisors?
- Is the legal system friendly, developed, and does it protect investors?
- What type of political risk, if any, exists?
- Has the country's currency been stable?
- How will you deal with currency risk?
- Can your position be hedged?
- Are sales in U.S. dollars?
- How susceptible is the company to strikes or unions?
- What are worker protection laws like?
- What are the social security obligations in the country? Can you fire people?
- Are social costs significantly higher than in the United States and as such do you have increased liability?
- Is the environment known for corruption and red tape?
- Do you need to worry about the Foreign Corrupt Practices Act?
- What remedies do you have if the investment does not go well?
- What controls do you have over exits?
- Are there viable exit opportunities?
- What is the tax impact of foreign income?
- Do you keep the money generated from these investments offshore or bring it home?
- How easy is it to get to the foreign base of operations?
- How robust is the infrastructure in the targeted market?

For the investment office seeking to invest abroad, there is a significant amount of analysis to be completed prior to entering a new market. This analysis will be costly in terms of both time and capital and will require a significant amount of attention that may pull resources away from a domestic investment program. As a result, it should not be embarked upon with limited resources or a casual eye toward investing. In the next section, we discuss the key components for success in these markets. The families that have been able to achieve above-market rates of return have consistently done their homework and viewed these investment programs as long-term commitments rather than short-term trades.

Keys to Success in International Direct Investing

What are the keys to successful international direct investing? While there is no foolproof recipe that will ensure success, the investment programs of family offices that have enjoyed above-average returns in the international markets share similar characteristics (see Figure 13.4). First and foremost, they *focus*, concentrating on one country or sector. Second, they exploit *niche industry expertise* that they have developed at home or abroad. This enables them to leverage a knowledge base and network that has already been built. Third, they choose *strong local partners* with well-developed networks. Fourth, through either good fortune or hard work, they have the foresight to *pick the right markets*. An additional benefit is the flexibility of the *family office structure*. Finally, it helps to *start small and know your partner*. While these elements do not guarantee success, they do go a long way to mitigating the risk of failure.

Blue Water exemplifies the successful international direct investing program (see Figure 13.5). Blue Water's Benji Griswold describes the elements that create a perfect storm for success. First and foremost he believes that if you are a new entrant, you need to be in a place where capital is scarce

FIGURE 13.4   Elements of Successful International Direct Investing

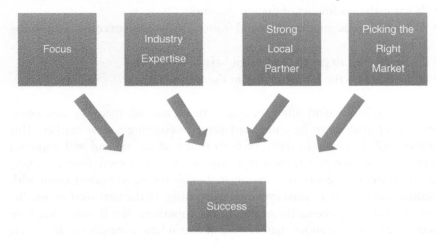

FIGURE 13.5 Perfect Storm for International Direct Investing Success

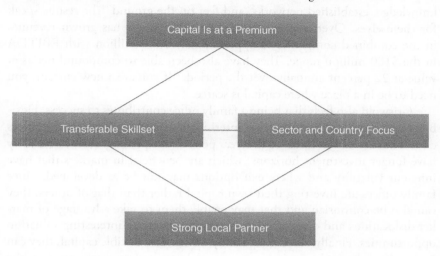

(*pick the right market*). The aggregates business and Argentina are perfect examples. When Griswold began investing, capital was leaving the sector or the country. Over the years that followed, he was able to build a reputation and network that has made him the go-to investor for deals in that space. Second, Griswold believes that it is also key for the family to have a *transferable skillset/industry experience*. In his case, his prior experience investing and turning around electrical transmission companies in South America was pivotal. His years in the industry provided him with the network, team, expertise, and deal sourcing capability that enabled him to acquire Electro Dunas in Peru at an attractive valuation and then put together a game plan to maximize operating profits and growth. Third, in his opinion, *laser-like focus* reaps significant benefits. It enables one to build networks and expertise that can be leveraged for future investments. For example, as a result of its success in warehousing in Buenos Aires and its knowledge of the Peruvian market, Blue Water is currently analyzing Class A warehouse investments in Peru. Thus, they are able to leverage their customer base and knowledge from Argentina and the team and country expertise that they have developed in Peru. Fourth and finally, choosing *a strong local partner* is paramount to success. Griswold partnered with the Baker family, who founded and built Florida Rock in his U.S. aggregates business investments, and with the Harriet family of Argentina for his warehouse investments in Buenos Aires. These strong local partners provided essential components that helped Griswold mitigate risk and maximize value, including capital, market knowledge, established networks, and feet on the ground. The results speak for themselves. Over a seven-year period, Blue Water has grown revenues in the combined companies to approximately $300 million with EBITDA in the $100 million range. They have also been able to compound net asset value at 22 percent annually over the period. "If you are a new entrant, you need to be in a place where capital is scarce."[8]

Griswold also feels that being a family office contributes to success. Flexibility is a strategic advantage when entering these markets. Since family offices do not have to exit in three- to five-year periods like private equity funds, they have longer investment horizons, which are beneficial in markets that have inherent volatility and where exit options may not be as developed. Since family offices are investing their own capital rather than that of others, they can also be contrarian and that may enable them to take advantage of market dislocations and distress. Such environments create interesting valuation opportunities. Finally, since most family offices have flexible capital, they can invest throughout the capital structure and can be less rigid regarding the amount of capital that has to be deployed.

The Role of a Partner in International Investing

One of the most successful international direct investing family offices of the last decade (we'll call them Family A) has created tens of billions of dollars by investing across geographies. While they have experienced losses in the portfolio, net-net they may have outperformed most institutions and family offices. What is most remarkable about their performance is that it has been produced through investments in a wide array of asset classes, sectors, and geographies. When asked what the recipe for their success is, they respond: Start small and know your partner.

While starting small may seem to be inefficient from a capital deployment standpoint (i.e., it takes a similar amount of time to do a small deal as it does a large deal), small investments provide two advantages. First, they enable the family to build a knowledge base and network without taking too many resources away from their core investment program. Second, they mitigate risk. If the investment doesn't work out or the investment environment changes, then the amount of resources devoted to doing a workout can be managed without fear that the core portfolio will be at risk. Betting the ranch is never a good idea when it is the first investment in a foreign country.

Similar to Benji Griswold, Family A believes a good foreign partner can be *the* determining factor to success abroad. Family A, which has

FIGURE 13.6 Elements of a Great International Partner

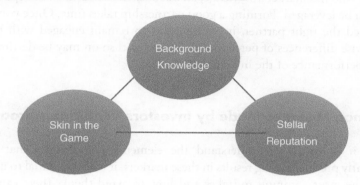

successfully invested in Europe, South America, the United States, Israel, and Russia, focuses on finding a key partner with background knowledge, skin in the game, and a stellar reputation each time they enter a new market (see Figure 13.6). Reputation is extremely important to this group. Over the years, they have found that the right partner can provide the intangibles that produce above-average returns, namely access to deal flow and credibility in the market. According to them, you need to consider that your partner's reputation will become your reputation, so choose wisely.

How does a family choose the right partner? Family A offered some insight on that topic. Due diligence is extremely important. You must confirm everything that the partner tells you. As they stated—trust, but verify.

When choosing partners some key considerations include:

- What is their reputation?
- Have they dealt with foreign investors in the past?
- Why do they want to partner now?
- Who is the competition?
- What is the expectation of the foreign partner?
- How entrepreneurial, aggressive, and forward looking are they?
- Are they technically savvy?
- Do you see eye to eye?
- Has the partner attracted good people?
- Do they have the same standards and expectations that you do?
- Do they speak the same language?

While there are differences among the various programs described earlier, a common theme emerges. It is of paramount importance to have a local partner who has market knowledge, an established network, and a reputation that can be leveraged. Forming a good partnership takes time. Once you have identified the right partner, it is important to remain engaged with them. Otherwise differences of perception, opinion, and so on may be detrimental to the performance of the investment.

Common Mistakes Made by Investors Venturing Abroad

While it is critical to understand the elements or strategies that most frequently produce strong results in these markets, it is also essential to understand the most common mistakes and how to avoid them. There can be a multitude of factors that contribute to failure in these markets (see Figure 13.7). First, entering a market when it is fully priced and functioning well can often lead to below-par returns. Frequently, markets with valuations at all-time highs leave no margin for error. Second, attempting to apply the way things are done in a home market to a foreign market usually does not translate. Laws vary across borders, as do management styles. Third, a lack of market or cultural knowledge can lead to serious pitfalls in terms of how the investments are set up or strategies are executed. Finally, foreign investments are time-consuming and resource-draining. Families should not embark on this path unless they are prepared to make the capital and time commitment necessary to properly manage these types of investments.

In some ways it may seem counterintuitive to avoid a market when it is functioning well. However, vibrant markets often mean high prices. When

FIGURE 13.7 Common Mistakes

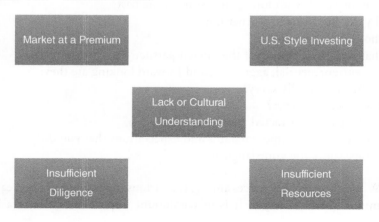

coupled with the fact that new entrants may not have access to the best opportunities, this strategy can be a recipe for disaster. Think of the current state of the U.S. real estate market. When Class A office buildings are trading at cap rates of 4 percent there is little or no margin for error and minimal prospects for capital appreciation. The case is more extreme when focusing on international markets that frequently are less liquid. Many families prefer to enter these markets when capital is at a premium and view entering a market that is performing well as a mistake. One family commented that this has been the biggest mistake made by private equity funds venturing into Latin America.

Another frequent error revolves around attempts to impose U.S. structures and practices in other countries rather than first gaining an understanding of how things work in those regions. Less sophisticated international investors often believe that U.S. conditions and cultural beliefs are transferable into other markets. This can be with regard to governance, legal systems, or simply common business practices. The results usually are not favorable.

Issues confronted by investors in the early 1990s when the Eastern Block countries opened up provide an interesting illustration. Several strategic investors and seasoned family offices entered the market in an attempt to capitalize on the seemingly low prices and the future market growth. Many were unprepared for the less-than-developed legal system. One story that senior White and Case lawyers used to illustrate the hazards of not knowing the legal market situation revolved around an elderly widow who received a large building in Prague from the enacted Restitution Law. Her family had owned the building prior to World War II and as a result the state was obligated to give it back to her. Once she had title she proceeded to sell the building to a foreign corporation that wanted to enter the market. Then she sold the same building to another foreign corporation. All three parties ended up in the court system, which was in a period of transition. The lady claimed that she had no memory of the transactions and the proceeds were nowhere to be found. In the end, she ended up with the building and proceeds and the corporations lost millions. In this example, there was an underlying assumption on the part of the corporations that the rule of law in this country was similar to that in the United States. Unfortunately, they found out the hard way that this was not the case.

As noted earlier, cultural differences can also be a sand-trap for investors. China is frequently one of the countries where some of the differences seem most pronounced. In Tim Clissold's book, *Mr. China: A Memoir* (New York: HarperBusiness, 2005). He describes how, in one of his investments, the owner/manager moved down the street and created a competing enterprise and thought that there was nothing wrong with the move. Similarly, in some parts of Eastern Europe it was common practice to pad bills and to try to trick investors. When caught, the perpetrator would move forward as if nothing were wrong and the relationship had not been damaged. For an American, such behavior is hard to understand and even more challenging to accept.

If an investor does not have a full understanding of the local market, then chances are that mistakes will be made and more capital and resources will be required in order to manage and exit the investment, driving down investment returns. One seasoned investor summed it up, "If you don't know the market and culture, the investment will own you, rather than you owning the investment."

Finally, one of the most common errors made by groups beginning to invest abroad is underestimating the amount of resources required. While it may sound appealing to make an investment in China, India, or Africa, the reality is that such investments will require a special team, significantly more time than home-based investments, and potentially more capital. For example, if the family office puts a dedicated team on the ground in the target market, it will be very costly and require a long-term commitment. Many groups are reluctant to do this and try to run foreign investments from their U.S.-based teams. While this can be an interim solution, it is certainly not a perfect one. The time required to manage these investments frequently exceeds the time required to manage home country investments because of the market and cultural learning curve involved. As a result of the time differences, communication is often challenging, with conference calls taking place in the wee hours of the morning. Finally, it often requires significant time just to travel to these locales.

For family offices investing abroad, it is important to understand and accept that the world does not function the same way as it does in their home country and that mistakes will be made. By paying attention to the most common ones, the cost of making such mistakes can be minimized.

Risk Mitigation

Once the decision has been made to enter a foreign market, as with any other investment, risk mitigation becomes mission critical. How does one mitigate risk in these markets? Every situation is different, but as a rule of thumb, some of the keys to success that were described earlier also lend themselves to risk mitigation. For example, leveraging existing skills and experience, investing in sectors that you already know, and partnering with groups that have well-developed networks and on-the-ground expertise, a family office can offer a path to navigating the turbulent waters of international investing. One of the areas that wasn't mentioned earlier was the importance of putting the *correct governance and controls* in place at the outset of a deal. This in and of itself can make or break the investment. Also, having clear milestones and *timelines for investing* can also have a tremendous impact. Finally, *active monitoring*, having a plan B if something happens to your partner, and having a clear path to profit repatriation are crucial components of risk mitigation.

Why are controls so important? As in any investment without the proper controls in place, it is nearly impossible for the investor to adequately protect his capital. Controls (see Figure 13.8) must include having the definitive say with regard to the budget and key voting issues such as the uses of capital, the sale of the business, selling equity or taking on debt, and the structure and composition of the board. In each jurisdiction, what can be achieved and how these concepts can be structured will differ. A deep understanding of the rule of law in the target market becomes critical.

Next, milestone funding that is in vogue in most venture deals can also play a role in risk mitigation in international direct investing. What is milestone funding? Conceptually, rather than invest the entire allocation at one time, one divides the investment amount and invests according to a timeline based upon the achievement of stated milestones of the management team. The advantage of this type of investing is that it minimizes the amount of capital at risk if the company is not meeting its stated goals. If the company does achieve its stated goals or milestones, then additional capital can be deployed.

Finally, another consideration in risk mitigation is how to monitor the investment. Given the time differences and the challenges involved in trying to respond quickly to any crisis that might arise, it is important to have feet

FIGURE 13.8 Key Controls and Governance Issues

Budget Control

Voting Control

Appropriate Board Structuring

on the ground. As mentioned earlier, having a local partner can be extremely important. Establishing some type of local presence also contributes to increased deal flow. That said, it is important to have a plan B if something happens to your partner. If the partner is not performing or for some reason has become less active in the investment, it will be necessary to be prepared to become more involved in order to protect the investment. Reference Chapter 9, "Investment Monitoring, Exit Strategies, and Harvesting Returns."

In summary, some of the risks involved in foreign direct investing can be mitigated by upfront planning and diligence and the creation of a backup plan if all else fails.

Foreign Families in the United States

While most of the focus of this chapter deals with U.S. families investing abroad, it is also important to note that an increasing number of foreign family offices have accelerated their investment in the United States. Drawn by U.S. attractiveness as a safe haven and the growth that the economy has experienced since 2008 as a result of innovation, the United States remains an intriguing place for foreign investment. The rationale for investing in the United States varies, but frequently centers around capital preservation, transparency, currency stability, and political stability and opportunity.

The head of a Middle Eastern family office stated that over the last ten years throughout his market there has been a renewed emphasis on board, corporate governance, and best practices. This has been driven by the downturn in 2008, which caused families to refocus their priorities. In terms of the markets that are most interesting to them, this is influenced by currency stability. Most families, he says, focus on the stronger economies with the more stable currencies. In order of priority, that is the United States, Europe, and Asia.

Another impetus for families to invest outside of their home markets is the economic upheaval and political instability present there. In some regions, such as the Middle East, these families are not just concerned about economic downturn or low growth, but are equally concerned about invasion, political upheaval, and asset destruction. When viewed through those lenses the U.S. potential low-growth environment appears attractive.

Another large Kuwaiti family has been attracted by the technological innovation and growth dynamics of the venture market here in the United States. They have taken current returns from their portfolio and very successfully deployed those in venture transactions. They believe that this market is one of the few that is able to provide such dynamic returns. Their track record has proven them correct. One of their deals alone had a 50× change in valuation within a year.

Interestingly, the advice of the foreign investors entering the United States is not dissimilar to that of the U.S. investors venturing abroad. The head of the Kuwaiti family office mentioned earlier offers this advice to those seeking to invest abroad:

- Be careful.
- Learn from mistakes.
- Find good partners.
- Hire good lawyers.
- Focus on maintaining a good reputation.

Sounds familiar, right?

Conclusion

For families considering investing abroad, it is critical to thoroughly diligence what this will entail prior to making the first investment. Assuredly, this will take time and resources away from any existing domestic investment programs, no matter how detailed the plan or how much is devoted to it in terms of resources. Once a family has made the decision to enter a foreign market as a direct investor, they need to be prepared to invest a significant amount of time and resources identifying the target market and sectors, how to enter, and, as we have stated repeatedly, picking the right partner. That partner may be a co-investor or be the head of the office in the identified region who will be the boots on the ground.

Patience is needed. Successful investment programs are dependent on well-developed networks and reputation. These are built over time with much effort. In addition, it is important to plan for both success and failure. It is assured that the path to the former will not be smooth and more than likely will not happen without a few failures. How resources and capital are managed will play a critical role in determining the long-term success and viability of an international direct investment program. Blue Water is a great example. They took the time to build the on-the-ground teams and produce results in their targeted areas. They invested over eight years building a strong platform in their identified sectors, and their efforts have paid in both financial results and attractive deal flow.

Investing abroad is not for the faint of heart, nor is it for the groups that are not prepared for the added expense. Risk can be mitigated and the probability of success increased by following a few tried-and-true rules:

1. Pick markets where capital is scarce or valued, where there is political stability and projected growth.
2. Pick a good local partner that has skin in the game, is well regarded, and has experience.
3. Go into sectors where you have skills, expertise, and networks.
4. Build a good team that has on-the-ground expertise and that can devote significant time to the market.
5. Start small.
6. Focus.

International direct investment programs should not be viewed as short-term trades, but rather as long-term investments.

Notes

1. Interview with Benji Griswold, December 2015.
2. Interview with Tready Smith, December 2015.
3. Carolyn Cohn, "With Plenty of Money and Time, Family Offices Eye Risky Markets," October 4, 2013, Private equity section. www.reuters .com.
4. Interview with Benji Griswold, December 2015.
5. Ibid.
6. Interview with Tready Smith, December 2015.
7. Interview with Sami Karam, December 2015.
8. Interview with Benji Griswold, December 2015.

Appendix A: Private Equity Strategies Summary

Appendix A.1 Private Equity Strategies Summary 1 of 3

	Venture Capital	Growth Capital	Buyouts	Mezzanine Financing	Distressed Assets	Real Estate
Category description	• Investments in innovative early-stage startups • Investing in option value • Ideal company characteristics include: 1. significant market size, 2. fast growth, 3. defensible position, 4. high gross margins, and 5. low capital intensity • Concentrated in patent dependent technology sectors and consumer Internet firms	• Expansion capital to fund growth of profitable businesses, taking them to the next level • Generally execution-oriented middle market firms; may be capital intensive	• Purchase of mature businesses, typically financed using high degrees of leverage • Targets mature companies	• Subordinated loans typically used to finance acquisitions or recapitalizations • Typically also receive small grant of warrants • Similar target companies to growth capital or buyouts—often work in conjunction	• Investments in poorly performing, neglected companies at a discount to "true value" • Involves purchasing debt claims to gain firm ownership and turn company around • Most relevant when distress is caused by internal problems (i.e., overlevered) rather than external factors	• Equity investments across varying phases of the real estate lifecycle • *Development—* Speculative construction • *Value-Add—* Pre-existing properties needing physical, financial, or operational improvements • *Core—* Pre-existing properties that yield stable cash flows
Cash flow characteristics	• Cash flow negative; often pre-revenue • Returns generated completely from exit	• Cash flow positive • Profits typically reinvested into company rather than paid out as dividends; therefore, returns generally generated from exit	• Cash flow positive, margins may have room for improvement • Demonstrated history of stability or growth & strong collateral	• Cash flow positive • Demonstrated history of stable cash flows • Returns primarily from ongoing interest + principal loan repayments	• Cash flow negative • Returns typically generated from exit	• Generally cash flow positive, with exception of development • Returns generated from both ongoing rent and capital appreciation

Risk-return profile	• Aggregate returns target +30% IRR* (no leverage used)
	• For individual deals, hurdle rate of +50% IRR
	• High degree of failure-performance distribution is typically:
	  ○ 60–70% total loss
	  ○ 20% breakeven
	  ○ 10–20% "home run" success
		• Levered returns targeting ~30% IRR
		• Unlevered returns 17–22% IRR
		• More moderate risk-return profile than venture capital given proven business model and underlying fundamental value
		• Moderate likelihood of significant losses
			• Levered returns targeting +25% IRR
			• Unlevered hurdle rates range from 12–17% IRR
			• Moderate likelihood of significant losses
				• Aggregate return of 15–20% IRR, including equity "kicker"
				• Loan interest rate of 12–15%
				• Low likelihood of significant losses
				• Seniority over equity reduces risk-return profile
					• Levered returns targeting 25–30% IRR
					• High potential for losses, given uncertainty involved in legal risk and turning around operations
						• Target rates typically increase across the developmental-to-core continuum and vary with use of leverage:
						  ○ *Development*—+20% IRR unlevered, +30% IRR levered
						  ○ *Value-Add*—8–12% IRR unlevered, 15–20% IRR levered
						  ○ *Core*—4–8% IRR unlevered, 10–14% IRR levered

Capital uses	• Capital goes into company • Used to finance product development and initial operating expenses	• Capital goes into company and/or to owners (typically a partial buyout) • Used to finance expansion	• Capital goes to business owners	• Capital goes into company or to owners as a recapitalization	• Capital goes to cash out current creditors • Used to finance "turnaround" efforts and necessary capital expenditures	• Capital goes to owners or to construction/renovation costs

*Created by David McCombie, CEO of the McCombie Group LLC, 2017.

	Venture Capital	Growth Capital	Buyouts	Mezzanine Financing	Distressed Assets	Real Estate
Leverage	• 0%, traditional term loans with stipulated interest payments rarely used	• 10–60% LTV	• 50–80% LTV	• N/A, mezzanine financing is a debt instrument	• 10–70% LTV	• 50–85% LTV, depending upon nature (lower for development & greater for stabilized properties)
Core value drivers	• Identifying disruptive ideas & competent management teams • Developing commercially viable products/services • Explosive product uptake trajectory • Coordinating IPO or sale to large incumbent	• Sourcing attractive businesses at low valuations • "Multiples arbitrage" • Expansion via organic revenue growth or bolt-on acquisitions • Professionalization to ready firm for sale to larger incumbent	• Financial engineering • Streamlining operations • Aligning management incentives with financial performance • Bolt on acquisitions	• Sourcing safe, stable borrowers with low probability of default • Minimization of fraud risks • Cost-efficient monitoring of outstanding loan portfolio • Salvaging/working out troubled credits	• Purchasing assets at significant discount to "true value" • Successfully navigating multi-party negotiations • Cost cutting • Diagnosing & mitigating company performance issues	• Choosing attractive locations at low prices • Managing build timeline & cost overruns (for development) • Maximizing occupancy of existing properties • Often sale to entities with lower cost of capital (higher valuation)
Skillset Implications	• Ability to estimate market size • Variety of "soft skills" enabling the assessment of management team quality • Cultivating human capital of portfolio companies—recruiting talent to fill gaps • Relationships with relevant potential customers, partners, & acquirers	• Corporate development skillsets • M&A experience • Business development (e.g., JV's, etc.) • Strategy • Sales and marketing capabilities to oversee expansion plans • Relationships to source proprietary deals without auctions	• Experience with levered finance (typically acquired through investment banking) • Performance improvement skills • Lean six sigma • Working capital cycle improvements	• Deal sourcing capabilities • Underwriting skills—financial sensitivity analysis • Commercial loan workout experience	• Underwriting & valuation skills of opaque assets • Corporate bankruptcy/ restructuring legal experience • "Turnaround" experience • Activity-based accounting • Headcount and capacity reduction	• For development and value add: Strong pulse on the local market to determine highest and best use; project management skills to minimize cost overruns • For core: Sales skills to fill up vacant units and property management capabilities to operate assets at the lowest possible cost

Investment size & nature					
• Size increases with each subsequent round: • Seed: <$200k • Angel: <$1mm • Series A: $1.5–$3.5mm • Series B: $4–$8mm • Series C: $8–$15mm • Minority investments: 10–25% equity received per round	• Equity capital invested ranges from $5–$100mm • Generally control investments assuming 50+% of target's equity • Minority positions sometimes occur, albeit with strong negative covenants	• Equity capital invested ranges from $20mm–$2bn depending on company size • Typically complete ownership	• Loan amounts range between $5–$500mm • Typically unsecured facility subordinated to bank financing	• Equity capital invested ranges from $10mm–$1bn depending on company size • Almost always control investments • Investment deployed by purchasing "in the money" claim	• Total equity capital ranges between $1–$200mm • Typically complete ownership

	Venture Capital	Growth Capital	Buyouts	Mezzanine Financing	Distressed Assets	Real Estate
Investment duration	• Opportunistic exit occurring 5–10 years from initial funding • Portfolio approach progressively "funds winners and kills losers"	• Opportunistic exit occurring between 3–6 years	• Opportunistic exit occurring between 3–6 years	• 5–8 years finite term loans	• Opportunistic exit occurring 3–7 years out, given high transactional and operational intensity	• Wide duration, ranging from 3 to 10 years • Typically duration increases across development-to-core continuum
Importance of geographic proximity	• High • Unstable nature of these early-stage companies requires constant close monitoring and mentoring to add value	• Medium • Professional operators are typically hired and relied upon • Assistance with strategic planning along with quarterly Board meetings typically occurring on site	• Low to medium • Professional operators are typically hired and relied upon • Quarterly Board meetings may be on site	• Low • Ongoing loan monitoring can primarily be done remotely • Annual check-in meetings with executives • No involvement in ongoing operations	• Medium • Despite professional management teams, financial distress requires significant "on the ground" involvement to address immediate challenges	• Medium to high; development and value-add is highly localized and contextual; core fairly insensitive to location
Deal structure variability	• Low to medium—most deals follow standardized templates (i.e., National Venture Capital Association)	• Medium—range of structural options	• Medium—range of structural options	• Low to medium—fairly standardized industry accepted terms and conditions	• High—highly contextual based upon company and stakeholder characteristics	• Medium—range of structural options; more diverse for development & value-add projects
Negotiation approach	• Collaborative—creation of long ongoing partnership	• Collaborative—creation of long ongoing partnership	• Transactional, with some collaborative elements (e.g., earnouts)	• Transactional	• Transactional, with room for creative deal making among creditors	• Transactional
No. of investments (fund level)	• 15–30 companies, given small deal size & need to diversify against high failure rates	• 8–12 companies; lower number than venture capital, given larger deal sizes & lower probability/magnitude of failure	• 5–10 companies, given large deal sizes	• 15–20 companies; greater capacity given less intensive due diligence and monitoring efforts	• 5–8 companies, given high transactional/operational intensity and large deal sizes	• Wide range depending on strategy • <5 for development • 5–8 for value add • +12 for core

Appendix B: Sample Due Diligence Checklist

I. ORGANIZATION
   A. Articles of Incorporation and Bylaws of the Company.
   B. List of states in which the Company is qualified to transact business and all certificates of authority.
   C. List of officers and directors of the Company, including a brief description of current duties and current compensation, and copy of any organizational chart.
   D. Minute books, including all shareholder, director, and committee minutes and written consents related to the Company.
   E. Stock transfer ledgers for the Company.
   F. Copy of any press release relating to the Company within the last five (5) years.
   G. List of any sale or grant of any option, warrant, right of first refusal, purchase plan, or other right to purchase capital stock, including copies of any agreements or documents relating thereto.
   H. Copies of all legal opinions prepared for the Company relating to its organization and/or its business within the last five (5) years.
   I. Copies of any offering or disclosure documents prepared with respect to the sale of the Company.
   J. Copies of all voting trust agreements and other voting agreements.
   K. Copies of all SEC filings, private placement memoranda, and other disclosure and investor documents.
   L. Copy of any shareholder agreements.

II. REAL PROPERTY
   A. List of all real property owned in fee and locations thereof (and mortgages and trust deeds related thereto).
   B. List of all leases and subleases of real property.

C. Copies of all deeds, mortgages, leasehold mortgages, trust deeds and indentures (and promissory notes relating thereto), and fixture filings with respect to real property.

D. Copies of all prior title insurance policies and title reports and/or opinions, including copies of exceptions which appear on such policies.

E. Copies of contracts and options to purchase or sell real property or to construct improvements thereon.

F. List of all liens or encumbrances against real property.

G. Copies of any appraisals of real property owned or leased.

H. Copies of any surveys relating to real property.

I. Copies of any assignments of lease made for security purposes or otherwise.

J. Copies of any engineering reports prepared regarding real property owned or leased.

K. Copies of certificates of occupancy.

L. Copies of any governmental permits required with respect to real property.

M. Copies of any guarantees or warranties relating to improvements on real property.

N. Copies of any outstanding notices of violation or similar notices received from any governmental authority or insurance company related to the use, operation, or maintenance of real property.

O. List of condemnation or eminent domain proceedings pending or threatened against real property.

III. PROPERTY, PLANT, AND EQUIPMENT

A. List of machinery and equipment, office furniture, fixtures, and inventory and locations where kept.

B. List of material and machinery, equipment, or inventory in possession of any third parties.

C. List of all liens, encumbrances, and security interests, and copies of UCC search reports.

D. Copies of all security agreements and financing statements.

E. Copies of all equipment and motor vehicle leases.

F. Copies of all contracts or options to purchase, sell, or lease personal property.

G. Copies of all installment contracts for the purchase of personal property, including equipment.

IV. CONTRACTS

    A. Copies of all agreements, orders, or commitments for the purchase or lease of capital equipment, components, assemblies, supplies, inventories, or finished goods in excess of $5,000.00 per any one agreement, order, or commitment.

    B. Copies of all agreements, orders, or commitments for the sale of products or assets in excess of $5,000.00 for any one agreement, order, or commitment.

    C. Copies of all other agreements, contracts, or commitments involving the payment or receipt of more than $5,000.00 in any individual case, including copies of all agreements relating to the borrowing of money or extension of credit, including those with affiliates, directors or officers, or other employees of the Company.

    D. Copies of all sales agency or representative, manufacturer representative, distributorship, and franchise agreements.

    E. Copies of all requirement, output, and supply contracts.

    F. Copies of all advertising and labeling agreements.

    G. Copies of all partnership or joint venture agreements.

    H. Copies of any industrial revenue bonds and other government sponsored loans, and all material documents related thereto.

    I. Copies of any acquisition or merger agreements, letters of intent, or similar commitments.

    J. Copies of all agreements with directors or officers or other employees of the Company.

    K. All agreements, contracts, or commitments limiting the ability of the Company to engage in any line of business or compete with any other person.

    L. All agreements, contracts, or commitments not entered into in the ordinary course of business.

V. LITIGATION

    A. List and briefly describe all pending or threatened lawsuits, claims, and assessments and non-asserted claims and assessments, including those for which an insurer has accepted liability, including authorities, nature of proceedings, date of commencement, current status, relief sought, and estimated actual costs.

    B. Copies of any correspondence or other documentation involving the return of merchandise based on a claim that such merchandise was defective.

    C. Copies of lawyers' responses to audit letters for the last five (5) years.

    D. Copies of all documents, correspondence, and filings relating to governmental/regulatory agency claims and assessments and proceedings, including any matters pending or threatening.

VI. INSURANCE

    A. Copies of insurance binders and list of all current insurance policies and commitments, including, but not limited to, personal injury, property, product liability, casualty, key man, directors'/officers' fiduciary liability, automobile, and workers' compensation.

    B. Copies of any summaries of insurance coverage.

    C. Notification of termination of coverage from insurers during the past three (3) years.

VII. PERMITS, LICENSES, GOVERNMENTAL COMPLIANCE

    A. Lists and copies of all permits, licenses, and governmental or regulatory franchises and indication of any permit, license, or franchise which is subject to suspension, revocation, cancellation, or modification, whether upon a change of control of the Company or otherwise.

    B. Copies of all correspondence during the past five (5) years with the Department of Justice, Federal Trade Commission, Environmental Protection Agency, or any other governmental, administrative, or regulatory agency, whether state or federal, or any similar documentation relative to equivalent International authorities.

    C. Brief discussion of compliance with administrative or regulatory agency standards, particularly OSHA, FDA, EPA, and state and local environmental agencies.

    D. Copies of any inspection or other reports issued by administrative or regulatory agencies.

    E. Description and documentation concerning past and present noncompliance proceedings, investigations, or inspections pending, threatened, or initiated by any administrative or regulatory agency.

    F. List of hazardous work conditions and hazardous waste disposals.

VIII. INTANGIBLE PROPERTY

    A. Copies of all registrations, assignments, and licenses of patents, trademarks, trade names, copyrights, and other industrial property rights, indicating when the registrations were filed.

    B. List of all pending applications for patents, trademarks, trade names, service marks, copyrights, and other intellectual property rights, including where and when such applications were filed.

C. List of all unregistered or common law patents, trademarks, trade names, copyrights, and other intellectual property rights, including any other technology not covered by the foregoing.

D. List of all intellectual property owned by third parties and licensed to the Company or used in connection with the business of the Company.

E. Details of all computer systems (e.g., hardware operating and application software, and software licensing agreements).

IX. EMPLOYEE BENEFITS

A. Copies of each employee benefit plan (as described in Section (3) of the Employee Retirement Income Security Act of 1974 [ERISA]).

B. Any correspondence or other documentation related to any employee benefit plan maintained by the Company for its employees.

C. Copies of Annual Reports (Form 5500 Series).

D. Copies of Summary Plan Descriptions.

E. Copies of each determination letter issued by the IRS with respect to any and all employee benefit plans.

F. Copies of any actuarial report issued by an enrolled actuary with respect to any and all employee benefit plans for the last five (5) years.

G. Describe any "Prohibited Transactions," as defined in Section 4975 of the Internal Revenue Code or Section 406 of ERISA.

H. Describe and state the amount of any "accumulated funding deficiency" (as defined in ERISA).

I. Copies of all employment agreements, independent contractor agreements, and consulting agreements.

J. List of all pending or threatened unfair labor practice charges, equal employment opportunity discrimination complaints, charges, or investigations, OSHA or other employee grievances, and charges filed with any federal, state, or local agency or court, and copies of all claims, reports, material correspondence, etc., relating thereto.

K. A list of complaints, claims, charges, or investigations, pending or threatened, before the Office of Federal Contract Compliance programs.

L. A list of all pending or threatened complaints, claims, charges, or investigations, pursuant to the Equal Pay Act, the Wage and Hour Act, or any other federal, state, or local statute or regulation dealing with employment.

    M. Copies of any Affirmative Action Plan adopted pursuant to federal, state, or local statute, rule, or regulation, including, but not limited to, Executive Order 11246 and its implementing regulations.

    N. A list of all pending or threatened complaints, claims, or charges asserted pursuant to any federal, state, or local statute, regulations, or rules with respect to unemployment compensation or workers' compensation or other employment-related benefits so required.

    O. Copies of any judgments, consent decrees, or decisions of any agencies or boards to which the Company is or may be subject.

    P. List of all employees, distributors, or dealers earning in excess of $25,000.00 per annum in salary or commissions.

X. LABOR

    A. Copies of all collective bargaining agreements which are presently in effect covering any group or unit of employees.

    B. Copies of collective bargaining agreements which have expired, with respect to which renewal negotiations with the collective bargaining group are pending, scheduled, or expected to be scheduled.

    C. Copies of all current employee handbooks.

    D. Copies of all current employee policy manuals or personnel policy manuals.

    E. Copies of all current personnel policies not a part of any manual.

    F. Copies of all employee work rules.

    G. Samples of all application forms, without limitation as to the type of employment sought by the applicant.

    H. Copies of all employee fringe benefit programs to the extent not submitted with respect to the request for employee benefit plans as described in Section 3 of ERISA.

XI. TAX

    A. Copies of federal income tax returns and state/local income, franchise, sales, property, and excise tax returns for all open years or similar documentation.

    B. Copies of any notices or proposed adjustments received from federal, state, local, or foreign authorities regarding returns, deficiency claims with regard to income, sales, property, or other taxes, including copies of any IRS 90-day letters, 30-day letters, and revenue reports or any similar authorities.

    C. Description of tax accounting methods (including changes in accounting methods) and depreciation methods.

    D. Copies of any extension of the statute of limitations for any tax years for any tax.

XII. FINANCIAL
  A. Copies of year-end financial statements for the past three (3) fiscal years, including balance sheets, income statements, and statements of changes in financial position.
  B. Copies of most recent interim unaudited financial statements.
  C. Description of accounting practices relative to inventories, fixed assets, reserve accounts, etc.
  D. Copies of all management letters and special reports from auditors (and responses thereto).
  E. Description of securities, indebtedness, investments, and other assets and liabilities other than normal day-to-day accounts.
  F. List of bank accounts and average balances.
  G. Copies of credit reports from banks and Dun & Bradstreet.
  H. Inventory schedule and valuation assumptions, statement of inventory turnover and obsolescence.
  I. Statement of unfilled orders present and past.
  J. List of offices where records relating to receivables are kept.
  K. Projected operating and financial statements.
  L. List of aged accounts receivable and description of credit and collection policies.
  M. Description of any material damage, destruction, or loss (whether or not covered by insurance) suffered since 1991.
  N. Depreciation schedule of fixed assets.
  O. Copies of feasibility studies, strategic planning documents, and financial forecasts.
  P. List of (and persons authorized to use) credit cards.
  Q. List of safety deposit boxes and locations thereof.

XIII. ENVIRONMENTAL
  A. Phase I and Phase II environmental assessments completed with respect to the Company's current and prior facilities.

Appendix C: Glossary

Acquisition The outright purchase of an independent company by another independent company whereby the acquirer ends up owning all or a portion of the assets of the acquired company.

Active Investors An investment strategy where the investor purchases investments and continuously monitors their activity to exploit profitable conditions.

Aggressive Portfolio Allocation A preference for even greater opportunity for returns and understanding there may be increased downside risk and volatility. Sample portfolio allocation would be approximately 50 percent of the portfolio dedicated to public equity, 20 percent of the portfolio dedicated to private equity, and 5 percent allocated to fixed income assets.

Alignment of Objectives The process of bringing the actions of an organization's business divisions and staff members into line with the organization's planned objectives.

Anti-Dilution Provisions A provision in an option or a convertible security, also known as an "anti-dilution clause." It protects an investor from equity dilution resulting from later issues of stock at a lower price than the investor originally paid.

Asset Classes One of several investment categories—such as bonds, real estate, and private equity—that institutional and individual investors consider when making asset allocations.

Asset Mix Refers to the overall percentage allocations of an investment portfolio into asset classes.

Barbell Approach Investing involves allocating roughly half of the portfolio to defensive, long-term, low-beta assets and the other half to very aggressive, short-term, high-beta assets while having little or no allocation to intermediate-term assets. This approach of focusing on only two asset classes (long and short) with nothing in the middle is where the metaphor of the barbell is derived.

Benchmarking The measure of the quality of an organization's policies, products, programs, strategies, etc., and their comparison with standard measurements, or similar measurements of its peers.

Buyouts The acquisition of a company or business unit, typical in a mature industry, with a considerable amount of debt. The debt is then repaid per a strict schedule.

Capital Stack Depicts the hierarchy of the total capital invested into a company and the relationship between each of these instruments to one another and the issuer.

CIO Skillsets Must have deep operating expertise and/or C-level experience in one or more companies. A qualified candidate will have a combination of business and investment skills along with an ability to communicate and assess risk factors that are unique to direct investing.

Circles of Competence Warren Buffett's belief that an investor's best strategy is to select an area where they can know significantly more than the average investor, and focus their efforts in that area.

Club Deals Investing in individual opportunities on a deal-by-deal basis in conjunction with other investors.

Co-Investment A minority investment made by investors in a company alongside a private equity fund manager or venture capital firm.

Co-Investment Structure When two or more investors come together with their unique domain expertise, power, and influence in diverse sectors, and political influence to create tremendous value.

Company Lifecycle Different stages in the company's existence. Each stage will be a different level of risk and possible return.

Confidential Information Memo (CIM) A memo containing a detailed description of the company, including financial projections.

Conservative Portfolio Allocation This approach is to mitigate downside risk and focus on wealth preservation rather than wealth accumulation. It utilizes fixed-income assets that generate regular income, reduce overall risk, and protect against volatility of a portfolio. The portfolio may be comprised of 40 percent or more of fixed income.

Correlation A statistic that measures the degree to which two securities move in relation to each other.

Deal Originators Those who find or originate deals. These may be private investors, brokers, bankers, incubators, universities, deal clubs, or online platforms that bring deals to the table.

Deal Sourcing The process of discovering, evaluating, and selecting various direct investment opportunities.

Deal Structure The agreement reached in a financing acquisition. The deal can be unleveraged, leveraged, equity, traditional debt, participating debt, participating/convertible debt, or a joint venture.

Debt Instruments   Paper or electronic obligation that enables the issuing party to raise funds by promising to repay a lender in accordance with terms of a contract.

Design Thinking Methodology   A methodology or process of conceiving governance and prioritization of investment approach. Five phases of the cycle include: Emphasize, Define, Ideate, Prototype, and Test.

Direct Deal Structure   The type of agreement reached in financing an acquisition. The deal can be unleveraged, leveraged, equity, traditional debt, participating debt, participating/convertible debt, or a joint venture.

Direct Investing   An investment by a limited partner, individual investor, or a fund of funds into an entrepreneurial or privately held company or business enterprise.

Direct Investing Network (DIN)   Families actively engaged in direct investing who want to share information, deals, and experiences with other active investors.

Direct Investing Team   A group of individuals that source, diligence, structure, and monitor potential opportunities.

Direct Investment Process   A process that includes due diligence and discovery, direct investment deployment and governance, and monitoring, oversight, and exit strategies. The process guides investors to source, select, and home in on appropriate direct investment opportunities.

Distressed Investing   A private equity investment strategy that involves purchasing discounted bonds of a financially distressed company. Distressed debt investors convert their holdings into equity and become actively involved with the management of the distressed company.

Domain Expertise   A broad-based understanding of an industry, technical area, or discipline.

Downside Protection   Shifting the risk of underperformance to other parties or assets.

Drag Along   A mechanism ensuring that if a specified percentage of shareholders agree to sell their shares, they can compel the others to sell, ensuring that a prospective purchaser can acquire 100 percent of the company.

Drag-along Rights   Rights that obligate the minority shareholders to go along with a sale on the same terms as the majority holder.

Due Diligence   The review of a business plan, finances, and assessment of a management team prior to a private equity investment.

EBITDA   Earnings Before Interest, Taxes, Depreciation, and Amortization—A measure of the company's profitability before any adjustment for interest expenses, tax obligations, or noncash charges associated with acquisitions and capital expenditures.

Enterprise Value   The measure of a company's total value.

Entrepreneurial Orientation   Refers to the family's strategic orientation, strategy-making practices, managerial philosophies, and behaviors that are entrepreneurial in nature.

Exit Strategy   A contingency plan that is executed by an investor, trader, venture capitalist, or business owner to liquidate a position in a financial asset or dispose of tangible business assets once certain predetermined criteria for either have been met or exceeded.

Exit Valuation   The proceeds if an asset or business were to be sold.

Expected Returns   The amount one would anticipate receiving on an investment that has various known or expected rates of return.

Experiential Returns   Valuable intangible benefits that are generated by engaging a broad base of family members in an impact investment development process. The nonfinancial returns that build the human assets, family unity, and the knowledge base of the family, but cannot be measured with the precision of financial asset metrics. The nonfinancial reasons why the family is willing to risk capital.

Expert Co-Investor   A co-investor with specialized knowledge, deal experience, and a proven track record to increase the likelihood for a positive outcome of the co-investment opportunity.

External Advisors   The person or company responsible for making investments on behalf of and/or providing advice to investors.

Externalities   A loss or gain in the welfare of one party resulting from an activity of another party, without there being any compensation for the losing party. Externalities are an important consideration in cost/benefit analysis.

Family Capital   The total resources of owning family members with components of human, social, and financial capital.

Family Communication   Define clear processes, format, and forums to communicate the success, setbacks, and learning from the investments to interested stakeholders. The communication should be consistent and regularly scheduled, addressing the objectives established in the previous processes.

Family Engagement   The measure of how well family members are engaged with an interest in financial or investment decisions.

Family Legacy   Values, wealth, philanthropy, intentions, and/or reputation that are passed down from past generations.

Family Office   Private wealth management advisory firms that serve ultra-high-net-worth investors.

Family Values   The moral and ethical principles traditionally upheld and transmitted within a family.

Financial Buyer   An entity that simply acquires a company and keeps it and its cost structure intact.

Foreign Families Families abroad that invest inside the United States. Reasons for their investing may include capital preservation, transparency, currency stability, growth opportunity, political stability, and risk protection.

Foreign Investment When an individual or a company in one country invests in another country in the form of establishing business operations or acquiring business assets.

Goal Setting Clear objective, plan, or strategy put into place for investing.

Governance Establishment of policies, and continuous monitoring of their proper implementation, by the members of the governing body of an organization. It includes the mechanisms required to balance the powers of the members (with the associated accountability), and their primary duty of enhancing the prosperity and viability of the organization.

Growth Capital The sale of equity in a (typically) privately held operating company, frequently one that is profitable, to raise funds to increase production capacity, supply working capital, or further develop the product. Both venture capital funds and mid-market buyout funds do growth capital investing.

I-bankers Investment bankers and business brokers. They are the source of deal flow. They are often hired to find an investor, partner, or buyer.

Impact Investing The specific interest in social and environmental challenges with market-based solutions.

Information Rights Negotiations part of a term sheet along with investment documents in order for the investor to have access to pertinent information such as financials, records, board minutes, and other company data related to the performance of the company.

Initial Public Offering (IPO) The sale of shares to public investors of a company that has not been traded on a public stock exchange. An investment bank typically underwrites these offerings.

Institutional Investor A nonbank person or organization that trades securities in large enough share quantities or dollar amounts that it qualifies for preferential treatment and lower commissions. They face fewer protective regulations because it is assumed they are more knowledgeable and better able to protect themselves.

Intellectual Property Creations of the mind (patents, processes, and the like) that have value in the market and can be legally protected.

Internal Rate of Return (IRR) The annualized effective compounded return rate that can be earned on the invested capital; the investment's yield.

Internal Vetting Memorandum Report that consolidates the deal team's findings to date, yielding enough information to make an informed investment decision and, if favorable, structure a term sheet and make an offer. Serves as the formal, written communication with the investment committee and the deal team. This document remains on file for the duration of the investment.

International Demographics   The international study of a population based on age, race, sex, among other characteristics.

International Direct Investing   An investment in a country other than the investor's country, by a limited partner or fund of funds into a business enterprise.

International Partners   An individual who is well regarded and has experience in international direct investing.

Investment Management   The buying and selling of investments within a portfolio. This can also include banking, budgeting duties, and taxes.

Investment Memorandum   Provides a detailed rationale for making the investment and provides information and analysis from the findings of the due diligence process. The decision-makers read the investment memorandum and have at their fingertips all the information required to make a final investment decision.

Investment Process   A framework utilized for deploying investment capital. There are five steps in an investment process: 1. defining an investment strategy/policy, 2. analyzing securities, 3. constructing a portfolio to minimize risk, taxes, and/or specific criteria, 4. evaluating the performance of the portfolio, and 5. revising and rebalancing the portfolio.

Investment Thesis   Refers to the statement of beliefs, criteria, and goals investors use to guide their decisions about investing in a business enterprise. This thesis helps investors decide what investments to purchase, what to sell, what other actions to take, as well as when and why they need to initiate these activities. The thesis also outlines metrics that help investors determine when and to what extent they have achieved their goals.

Joint Ventures (JV)   The creation of a partnership between two independent companies whereby each company contributes assets or equity to establish a mutual initiative.

Knowledge Creation   The continuous and dynamic interaction between tacit and explicit knowledge within an organization.

Learning Organization   Organization that acquires knowledge and innovates fast enough to survive and thrive in a rapidly changing environment.

Letter of Intent   A form of documentation or agreement that provides for the sharing of additional information and sometimes can provide a period of exclusivity between the parties. (See also: Term Sheet; Memorandum of Understanding)

Leveraged Strengths   The result of co-investing. It increases access and ability to leverage the strengths of partners, whether those strengths are financial or non-financial.

Limited Partner (LP)   An investor in a limited partnership. Limited partners can monitor the partnership's progress but cannot become involved in its day-to-day management if they are to retain limited liability.

Liquidation Preference   Determines the payout order in case of a corporate liquidation.

Memorandum of Understanding   A form of documentation or agreement that provides for the sharing of additional information and sometimes can provide a period of exclusivity between the parties. (See also: Term Sheet; Letter of Intent)

Merger   The combination of the assets and equity of two independent companies to form and operate as one single entity.

Mezzanine Finance   Either a private equity financing round shortly before an initial public offering or an investment that employs subordinated debt that has fewer privileges than bank debt but more than equity and often has attached warrants.

Minority Investor or Stakeholder   Ownership of less than 50 percent of a company's equity by an investor. A shareholder who does not exert control over a company.

Moderate Portfolio Allocation   A preference for balanced portfolio allocation. This approach is intended to generate more moderate growth and protect the investor from significant downside risk.

Monetization   Converting an asset or any object into money or legal tender. Typically used term when an investor exits an investment.

Monitoring   Supervising activities in progress to ensure they are on course and on schedule in meeting the objectives and performance targets.

Multiple of Invested Capital (MOIC)   A popular term for measuring a fund's performance; however, it does not account for opportunity cost. Commonly used to evaluate performance.

Multiples   A comparison of one number to another. It can be the returns from a fund or a company (total money returned compared to total money invested) or the consideration paid for a company (total price compared to EBITDA or revenues).

Network Facilitators   Individuals who are adept at building relationships and bringing together strategic parties. They thrive on connecting others to co-invest, but do not necessarily originate the deals.

Next-Generation Education   The preparation, education, and mentoring for the up-and-coming generation in the family business.

Non-disclosure Agreement (NDA)   A legal contract between two or more parties that signifies a confidential relationship exists between the parties involved.

Nonfinancial Capital   Four different assets such as Human Capital, Relationship Capital, Social Capital, and Spiritual Capital.

Pledge Fund   Where an investor invests in a portfolio of direct deals, choosing to opt in or out on a deal-by-deal basis.

Portfolio Allocation   An investment strategy that aims to balance risk and reward by apportioning a portfolio's assets per an individual's goals, risk tolerance, and investment horizon. The three main asset classes—equities, fixed income, and cash and equivalents—have different levels of risk and return, so each will behave differently over time.

Portfolio Company   A company or entity in which a venture capital firm or buyout firm invests.

Postmortem   A critical practice for improving the success of each investment transaction. It allows the investor to understand more granularly what most impacted the investment outcome's success or failure.

Pre-Negotiated Rights   Upfront considerations that direct investors need to negotiate early to result in their desired harvesting and exit strategy.

P/E Ratio   The ratio of the company's share price to its earnings per share (net income divided by shares outstanding).

Private Company Ownership   Investing in the ownership directly of a privately held company or illiquid asset like real estate.

Private Equity Fund   A private equity (PE) fund typically refers to a general partnership formed by PE firms, which is utilized to invest in private companies.

Private Information Memorandum (PIM)   A memo containing a detailed description of the company, including financial projections.

Quality of Earnings   "QoE" provides an analysis of the accuracy and sustainability of historical earnings. It also provides breakdown of revenue by components, analysis of historic revenue trends, determination of onetime expenses versus recurring expenses, determination of fixed versus variable costs, analysis of impact on both revenue and expenses due to management changes, and analysis of assumptions used in cash flow projections and scenario analysis.

Real Estate   Property comprised of land and the buildings on it as well as the natural resources of the land, including uncultivated flora and fauna, farmed crops and livestock, water, and minerals. Part of an investment strategy, it is also part of the most prevalent strategies that families invest in directly.

Registration Rights   These rights provide investors with the contractual right to demand that the company register its shares with the U.S. Securities and Exchange Commission, which is necessary for selling the shares publicly.

Repeatable Investment Process   A consistent and repeatable process to guide the investment lifecycle.

Results Measurement   See Benchmarking.

Return on Investment (ROI)   Measures how much you receive from the investment above the cost of the investment itself. It is calculated as follows: Expected gains from investment − Cost of investment.

Risk Management   The process of identifying, analyzing, and accepting or mitigation of uncertainty in investment decisions.

Risk Mitigation   The ability to use existing skills and experience to invest in sectors one already knows. Also by collaborating with groups that have well-developed networks and on-the-ground expertise.

Risk Tolerance   The degree of variability in investment returns that an investor is willing to withstand.

Safe Harbor Forum   A meeting hosted by family office associations that offers the opportunity for families and single-family offices to connect with their peers and listen to and meet finance thought leaders on many investing subjects.

SMART Objectives   Specific, Measurable, Attainable, Relevant, and Time Bound.

Socially Responsible Investing (SRI)   An investment that is considered socially responsible because of the nature of the business the company conducts. Any investment strategy that seeks to consider both financial return and social good to bring about a social change.

Sourcing   The process through which financiers can discover, evaluate, and potentially select various business opportunities.

Sourcing Opportunities   The result of finding investment opportunities.

Sponsor   Almost always involved in major decisions such as refinancing or dispositions. A person or organization that provides funds.

Stranded Asset   Any asset that loses value or becomes a liability before the end of the asset's expected economic life.

Strategic Advisors   Strategic advisors research and assess the performance of a business or department to determine its strengths, weaknesses, opportunities, and threats. This usually involves reading financial and production reports, interviewing key personnel, and evaluating the competition.

Strategic Alliance   A situation in which a private equity firm teams up with a major corporation that has made an investment in a developing country. Also, a collaboration between companies, one or both of which are private-equity backed.

Strategic Buyer   An entity that sees an opportunity to strengthen its core business by acquiring another company, usually in a related business line.

Strategic Planning   A systematic process of envisioning a desired future and translating this vision into broadly defined goals or objectives and a sequence of steps to achieve them.

Strategy Development   See Strategic Planning.

Strategy Execution   The successful implementation of a strategic plan.

Structuring Deal Terms   Determining the financial instruments that comprise a direct investment, merger combination, or business deal.

SWOT Analysis   In-depth review of the strengths, weaknesses, opportunities, and threats to devise an understanding of a situation, company, or individual.

Synergy   The interaction or cooperation of two or more organizations to produce a combined effect greater than the sum of their separate effects.

Systems Thinking   A management discipline that concerns an understanding of a system by examining the linkages and interactions between the components that comprise the entirety of that defined system.

Tagalong   Also, known as "co-sale rights," contractual obligations used to protect a minority shareholder, usually in a venture capital deal.

Tagalong Rights   Gives the minority investor the right to participate in a sale orchestrated by, and on the same terms as, the majority shareholder.

Tax-advantaged Structures   Employing top tax counsels in family offices to manage in a highly tax-advantaged manner relative to their overall portfolio of assets.

Term Sheet   Defines commonly used terms associated with many typical direct investments and will provide a deeper understanding of the terms that can be negotiated in any direct deal.

Time Horizon   The total length of time an individual expects to hold a security or a portfolio.

Ultra-High-Net-Worth Individuals   Individuals with investable assets of at least $30 million, excluding personal assets and property such as primary residence, collectibles, and consumer durables.

Valuation   The algorithm by which a private equity fund assigns values to the public and private companies in its portfolio.

Value Drivers   Common points evaluated by investors to see whether an investment meets their requirements.

Venture Capital   Early stage investing.

Venture Capital Funds   Investment funds that manage the money of investors who seek private equity stakes in startup and small-to-medium-sized enterprises with strong growth potential. These investments are generally characterized as high-risk/high-return opportunities.

Vetting Co-Investors   Thorough and diligent review of a prospective person or project prior to a hiring or investment decision.

Wealth Source   How an individual, family, or entity got the funds. For example, from selling a property, inheritance, etc.

About the Author

Kirby Rosplock, PhD

Founder & CEO, Tamarind Partners

Kirby is a recognized expert, researcher, innovator, advisor, and speaker in the family business and family office realms. She is the founder of Tamarind Partners Inc., a boutique family office research, advisory, and consultancy practice that helps families, family offices, advisors, and institutions connected to the family office market with strategic planning, generational transitions, leadership transitions, and organizational development. To learn more about Tamarind Partners, please visit www.TamarindPartners.com.

Kirby is a published author and speaker on topics related to family wealth and family business; she has presented research, case studies, keynotes, and papers in several different venues around the globe. She is the author of *The Complete Family Office Handbook: A Guide for Affluent Families and the Advisors Who Serve Them*, published by Wiley/Bloomberg, 2014. To learn more about her first book, please visit www.Rosplock.net.

For nearly a decade, Kirby was director of research and development at GenSpring Family Offices, based in Jupiter, Florida, a leading U.S. multi-family office. As the director of research and development in the Innovation and Learning Center at GenSpring, Kirby's responsibilities spanned the development of the firm's wealth management process, directing corporate research efforts and leading the development and delivery of various tailored learning experiences for families. Kirby is very committed to women, wealth, and family enterprise and led GenSpring's Women and Wealth Study in 2006, which involved more than 100 affluent women from across the country whose combined net worth exceeded $2 billion. Kirby has developed resources to aid families in the myriad areas related to their human and intellectual capital. Kirby created programs on communication, governance, family wealth education and strategic planning, entrepreneurship, family banks, succession, facilitation, and hosting effective family meetings. She was the editor of *A Thought Leader's Guide to Wealth* (GenSpring, 2009) and has authored numerous articles, papers, book chapters, and research reports.

Kirby grew up in an enterprising multigenerational family whose core interest was timber and diversified over generations into various closely held businesses. Dr. Rosplock has served on several boards and is a former board member of Babcock Lumber Co., her family's business, and Family Enterprise USA, a nonprofit advocacy organization for family enterprise, a co-trustee of the Harbeck Family Foundation, and a global advisor to financial institutions, families, family office executives, and multi-family office and wealth advisors.

Kirby has a BA from Middlebury College, an MBA from Marquette University, and a PhD in Organizational Systems from Saybrook University. Her dissertation, published in 2007, was entitled "Women's Interest, Attitudes and Involvement with Their Wealth." Kirby is a Fellow at the Family Firm Institute (FFI), a former board member of the FFI Practitioner, and a faculty member of the FFI GEN Course in the Family Wealth Advisory Certificate program. She is the Dean of Family Office at the Purposeful Planning Institute.

About the Chapter Authors

(Ch. 2) **Nathan Hamilton**, CFA, currently works as an investment banker within the Technology, Media, and Telecom group at Goldman Sachs. Nate was previously a co-founder and partner at FDX Capital, where he served on the investment committee responsible for deal execution and deal sourcing for the firm. Prior to that, Nate was a director within the investment bank at UBS, where he was responsible for trade idea generation and portfolio management strategy for the firm's global macro hedge fund clients. Nate graduated *cum laude* from Vanderbilt University with a degree in Economics, and received his MBA from University of Chicago Booth School of Business. He holds his Series 7, 79, and 63 securities licenses.

(Ch. 2) **Sara Hamilton** is founder and CEO of Family Office Exchange (FOX). A recognized visionary in the private wealth community, Sara provides strategic direction for FOX and leads the development of programs and services supporting wealthy individuals, family office executives, and wealth advisory firms globally. For the past three years, she has been named as one of the "Top 50 Women in Wealth Management" by *Wealth Manager*. Sara is the co-author of *Family Legacy and Leadership: Preserving True Family Wealth in Challenging Times* and serves on the executive education faculty of the University of Chicago Booth School of Business for the "Private Wealth Management" course offered twice a year in Chicago.

(Ch. 4) **David McCombie** is founder and chief executive officer of McCombie Group LLC, a collection of influential families actively seeking to invest long-term capital into established family-owned businesses. A thought leader on private equity, he has been a featured speaker at various international investment conferences and has been profiled in the *Wall Street Journal* and *Bloomberg*. David also serves as an adjunct professor at the University of Miami School of Business. Prior to forming his firm, David worked at McKinsey & Company and Citigroup. David graduated from

Harvard Law School, and also did extensive coursework in corporate finance at the Harvard Business School. He graduated Phi Beta Kappa from the University of Miami with a degree in Economics and Finance. He is also a licensed Florida attorney.

(Ch. 7) Euclid Walker is the managing partner of Parkway Investment Management LLC, an alternative investment management and advisory firm. Prior to founding Parkway, he was a founding member of a middle-market investment firm. He also founded Renascent Capital group in 2004 to provide strategic and capital-raising advice to corporate clients and family offices. Prior to forming Renascent, Mr. Walker was an executive director of Morgan Stanley, where he worked for over 10 years in various capacities, including private equity investing; managing the Johannesburg South Africa office; and serving as operations officer for Corporate Finance and Banking Departments in Europe, the Middle East, and Africa and as executive director for Midwest investment banking business. Mr. Walker is a Phi Beta Kappa graduate of Morehouse College in Atlanta, Georgia, where he currently serves as chair of the Trusteeship committee of Morehouse's Board of Trustees. He is a member of the Palm Beach County Investment Policy Committee.

(Ch. 8) Jolyne Caruso is founder and CEO of The Alberleen Group, an advisory firm servicing middle-market companies and family office investors. She has over 30 years of experience in global capital markets and asset management businesses, including as global head of Absolute Return Strategies at Lehman Brothers while serving on the Management Committee of the firm. Ms. Caruso was also a co-founder and president of Andor Capital Management, a technology-focused hedge fund. From 1992 to 2001, she was head of Equities–Americas at J.P. Morgan and was chairwoman of J.P. Morgan Securities. She began her career at Bear Stearns. Ms. Caruso holds a BA with honors from Barnard College, Columbia University, and is chair of Barnard's Board of Trustees. She is a director of Kleinfeld Inc., and The Center for Clean Air Policy (CCAP), serves on the fund advisory board of Golden Seeds, and is an advisor to Columbia University/ Entrepreneurship and Massey Quick.

(Ch. 9) Adam Goodfriend is a co-founder and chief investment officer of The Alberleen Group and serves on the management committee of the firm. He is responsible for all of Alberleen's principal merchant banking activities and for determining the overall investment strategy for the firm. Mr. Goodfriend has over 25 years of investment banking, capital markets, and asset management experience. From 1990 to 2003, he was responsible for structuring and executing public and private transactions, initially as a founding member of the high-yield bond origination group of Chase Securities (a predecessor of J.P. Morgan Chase). He was a product group head at SG Cowen, and subsequently a managing director at Bank of America Securities. In 2003, Mr. Goodfriend left banking to co-found The Airlie Group, a $1.2 billion high-yield bond and leveraged-loan hedge fund. He subsequently held senior investment positions in ultra-high-net-worth family offices. He earned his BA from Johns Hopkins University, and an MBA from the University of Pennsylvania's Wharton School. Mr. Goodfriend serves on the board of directors of Tyrogenex LLC.

(Ch. 10) Robert G. Blabey III co-founded Align Private Capital to serve the investment needs of single-family offices. Specifically, Align works with family members or their family office investment professionals to create tailored investment solutions based on their needs. Engagements have included: comprehensive portfolio analysis/construction/management, direct real estate investing, manager review/selection, distressed workouts, direct investing vetting/due-diligence/post-investment oversight/sale/disposition, family-to-family partnership execution and co-invest, and private company balance sheet management.

For the ten years prior to forming Align Private Capital, Rob worked as chief investment officer for two large single-family offices (the Collier family and the Statler family) and for a multi-family office that specialized in the alternative investment vertical. In each of these positions, he managed both public market and private investing initiatives for families with sophisticated investment requirements and diversified holdings. Before working in the single-family space, he was an investment partner at Trident Partners, a private equity and hedge fund firm. He began his career in the International High Yield Investment Banking and Capital Markets Division of Donaldson, Lufkin & Jenrette in New York and London and prior to that in the International High Yield Capital Markets Group at Chase Manhattan Bank. Rob is a graduate of Hamilton College.

(Chs. 11 and 12) Temple Fennell is an active investor and advisor in the clean energy and sustainable agriculture/food sectors. He has more than 20 years of experience in operating businesses, direct investing, corporate finance, and project finance for early-stage and growth companies. He co-founded "Impact Investing Strategy for the Next Generation" under the Initiative for Responsible Investing at the Harvard Kennedy School with the World Economic Forum, and helps lead the MIT "Visionary Investing" workshop programs for family offices. He is a member of the Clean Energy Venture Group, CREO Syndicate, MIT's Renewable Finance group, and board member of Keller Enterprises LLC, a single-family office active in clean energy, sustainable agriculture/food, and other direct investments. Temple has a BS in

Systems Engineering from the University of Virginia and an MBA as an MIT Sloan Fellow at the Massachusetts Institute of Technology.

(Ch. 13) Anna Maria Nekoranec is CEO of Align Private Capital. She co-founded Align Private Capital with Robert Blabey, the author of Chapter 10, to serve the direct investment needs of family offices. Anna has over 25 years of international experience making direct investments in operating businesses, real estate, and private equity funds. For the last decade, Anna has partnered with ultra-high-net-worth families on direct investments and assisted in the management of direct portfolios on behalf of families through LBK Capital, which she founded. Prior to LBK, Anna was a partner and managing director at Investor Growth Capital, a private investment fund with assets under management in excess of $1 billion. She has worked in the United States, Europe, and Asia and has reviewed investments in South America. Ms. Nekoranec has an MBA from The Wharton School at the University of Pennsylvania and a BA from the University of Virginia. She is also a co-author of *How to Buy a Business: Entrepreneurship through Acquisition.* (Chicago: Kaplan Publishing, 1993).

Index

Printed and bound by CPI Group (UK) Ltd, Croydon, CR0 4YY

16/04/2025

14658442-0005